KB253897

정말 지도자입니까?

(THE EVANGELICAL LEADERSHIP
OF JESUS CHRIST)

정말 지도자입니까?

(THE EVANGELICAL LEADERSHIP OF JESUS CHRIST)

서임중 지음

신교횃불

머리말

　지금까지는 무수한 Leader와 Leadership에 관한 이론이 나왔다. 21세기를 맞이하는 한국교회는, 우주적인 교회라기보다는 패쇄적이고 이기주의적인 교회로 변질 되었고, 사랑과 용서와 섬김의 교회라기보다는 반목과 갈등이 표출되고 있으며, 제도화, 형식화, 율법화, 직업화로 예수 그리스도의 복음인을 양육하는 교회라기보다는 기독교 종교인을 양성하는 기관으로 변질되고 있음을 심히 우려하지 않을 수 없다. 이는 복음의 상실이요, 에클레시아의 부재다. 따라서 필자는 이런 원인을 모든 리더십의 근본이요 본질인 예수 그리스도의 '복음적 리더십'의 부재로 진단하였다.

　따라서 필자는 예수 그리스도의 말씀과 의중(Mind)에서 가시적 또는 불가시적으로 계시하신 복음적 리더십을 모색하는데 심혈을 기울였고, 지도자 자신이 변하지 않고는 교회도 하나님의 나라도 요원함을 강조한다.

　그러므로 교회의 지도자가 예수 그리스도의 복음과 그의 에클레시아로 돌아가서 복음적 리더십에서 목회를 하고 교인을 양육한다면, 주님의 기도처럼 뜻이 하늘에서 이루어 진 것 같이 땅에서도 이루어지는 도구로서의 그 사명을 다 하게 될 것을 믿는다.

이러한 목적 하에서 볼 때 가장 중요한 것은, 하나님 나라를 위한 예수 그리스도의 복음으로써, 예수 그리스도에 대한(about) 복음보다는 예수 그리스도의(of) 복음에서 출발해야 한다고 본다. 왜냐하면, 지금까지는 예수 그리스도의 복음은 주변에 있게 되었고, 오히려 선지자들과 사도들의 복음이 중심부를 차지하였다. 그래서 예수 그리스도의 에클레시아는 물론 그의 복음적 지도력도 주변부에 있게 되었고, 율법적, 회당적, 성당적, 성전적인 또는 세상적 사회지도력이 교회의 중심을 차지하게 되므로, 교회가 구약적 교회 내지는 사도나 선지자, 또는 사회공동체적 지도자론으로 오늘에 이르렀기 때문이다.

따라서 필자는 구약의 지도자와 지도력에서부터 예수 그리스도의 복음적 지도자상과 그의 제자 양성론까지 논급하고자 한다.

바라기는 모쪼록 이 논문집이 교회는 무엇이며, 복음적인 지도자는 어떤 사람인가에 대한 질문에 작은 답이 되기를 소망하면서, 아울러 한국교회와 지도자들이 복음에 바로서서 주님의 교회를 섬기는 거룩한 사역을 하는데 보탬이 되었으면 하는 마음 간절하다.

끝으로 이 책의 출간을 위해 물심양면으로 아낌없는 후원과 사랑을 베푸신 포항중앙교회 당회와 기도로 동행하는 성도님들께 감사를 드리며, 이 책을 포항중앙교회에 헌정한다.

포항중앙교회 목양실에서

서임중 목사

차례

(THE EVANGELICAL LEADERSHIP OF JESUS CHRIST)

Chapter I

INTRODUCTION

THE PROBLEMATIC THINKING AND MOTIVATION THAT LEAD TO THE TITLE OF THE DISSERTATION

The futurologist or Alvin Toffler who is the most noteworthy futurologist in this period of history Alvin Toffler once prophesied that the future would be the knowledge information society moved by knowledge, escaping from the ideology discriminating capitalism and communism such as the past. In the future, the fast culture will conquer the slow culture as the information industry society.[1] In the center of

---

1) Alvin, Toffler, The Third Wave (New York, William Marrow, 1980).

these changes, today's churches and church leaders need the wisdom for confronting the material culture and information culture positively. However, the more fundamental and essential need is the church and church leader who proclaims and presents the Gospel of Jesus Christ being the way, life and life, becoming the real hope and eternal unchanging in the human spirit and heat over the period, frontier, race, nation, and culture against the human mental culture devastating relatively and his "Ecclesia."

So, I want to raise two critical problems. These are, First, are Korean churches full of Jesus Christ's Gospel? And, are Korean churches faithful to "Ecclesia" which Jesus Christ established when he proclaim God's Kingdom in His Word and Mind? The Gospel our Lord proclaimed was the God's Kingdom always accompanied by repentance(Mk1:15), love, forgiveness, and serving.

But, if the aspects of today's church and church leader would appear as those that hated, jealousy, struggle, and be proud apart form the Gospel, have different essence form the Gospel Jesus taught, covet the high position, and want to be served, futhermore, not to forgive and love but to condemn and be self-righteous, and govern, control and take the position by being tamed with dogmatic theology, church theology and non-gospel biblical theology, those small and general meeting continuously making the work of the religious judge by restoring the law deserted and completed by Jesus as the church law, in addition those priest fell to make their stomach full without caring the sheep 'life, we can' t expect not only Jesus Christ, His Gospel, His shepherding, or His mission but also Jesus Christ and His Gospel can' t but be bound in political, cultural and philosophic non-gospel.

In addition to, the church Jesus established is the evident "Ecclesia" .(Mt16:16, 18:17) Nonetheless, a number of church in the earth can' t be Called Out from untimely Jewish religion, temple religion and synagogue religion, rather have tendency to return to that. And that the church were considered and social community(Gemeinschaft or Gesellschaft) or Kuriade(κυριακη,Rev1:10, 1 Co11:20) is because of the distortion of "Ecclesia"s essence.[2]

Euangelion(ευαγγελιον), the Gospel of Jesus Christ is cosmic and worldwide, means the beginning and fundamental starting given from arche(αρκη). This "arche" means the new beginning Called Out after the End of the grand finale of darkness, emptiness, chaos, disorder and inanimate object.[3] Therefore, the Gospel has begun from Jesus Christ, the Concluding Revelation and become the good news to the whole world, and his "Bassileia" is become full of love, forgiveness, serving heart, and authority. So, wherever accepting this gospel, there opened new history of the heaven and earth, disappear the sin, death, disposal, darkness, and torture, and became full of overflowing delight like light, heat, and water and it can't be hidden, buried, and disappeared.

Therefore, to be a church and leader God establishing, one have to return to the Gospel Jesus Christ proclaimed and His "Ecclesia".

In the corner of the mission second century. Korean church must be asked to be full of Gospel and be

---

2) Hwangbo Kap, Ecclesia (seoul : Bridge, 1966), pp. 33, 164.
3) Ibid., pp. 159-189.

established as the leader performing the gospelic shepherding by returning "Ecclesia".

In fact it's true the Korean church has brought the unprecedented revival and development in the whole history and it's recognized by world church. Nonetheless, the world church evaluated the Korean church negatively, not positively. It's because chronic denomination confusion, the church division, the phenomenon show sensitive response to the social change in the social movement of church but short in the generalization task, the Christianity resembling myth. regional egoism, group egoism, individual egoism, mega church superiority, convenience religious life, the degrading phenomenon of christian moral the evil of wrong eschatologic theory, indiscriminate world mission, the excess spending phenomenon of church, indiscriminate believers scramble, the authoritative administration construct, wrong offering culture, etc., anyone can easily find these reality and none can deny it.

Why these phenomenon should be occured? It's because of the lack of the gospelic leader Jesus expected, although there are a number of theologians, priests, presbyterians, and religious leader.

The point of the word of Richard Wolff quoting the word of Karl Jaspers, "out generation is facing to the leader's panic. The leader's ability is degrading in every place. The more looking the man climbed to the top, the more looks as those who only push to the top." [4] and the persuading of J. Oswald Sanders,

"Each period must be confronted with the leadership problem and on the edge of severe leadership still in the many fields. The crisis is on, but today's leaders are short to find the solution and the only future is the reality which can't be ensure. The church also is within the starving phenomenon of powerful leadership." [5], were both exaggerating the poverty problem of church leaders.

The leader in church is most important. Because they are the guider of gospelic life leading God's people in this world and the spirit's salvation over the leadership of visual organization named church.

There's a saying. "If a business field, we have to employ not another employee but new director." [6]

---

4) Richard Wolff, Man at the Top., (Wheaton, Ⅲ, ; Tyndale, 1969), p. 13.
5) J. Oswald Sanders, Paul The Leader., (Chicago : Moody Press, 1984), p. 8.
6) Frank Goble, The Man at the Top., (Thornwood, N.Y. ; Caroline House Publishers, 1972)., P.1.

It says about the very importance of the leader's position. The obligation of the fact of believers' wandering without the sense of mission and the delight of salvation lies on the shoulder of church leaders.[7)]

Nowadays the world church esteems the visual growth of Korean church but don't give their positive esteem as the Jesus Ecclesia overflowing with love, forgiveness and serving heart, we can't but charge the Korean church's leaders the obligation of these comment.

Jesus is requiring the leaders having the gospel character. It's also the command to require change of the church leader's change through the Gospel. Without the change the church leaders, none can expect the change of Korean church.

Under the these critical mind and motivation, I want to make new understanding of Jesus Christ's Gospel and grope the leader's picture prophesied through Jesus' Ecclesia, lighting on the fact the most fundamental

---

7) Robert A. Raines, New Life in the Church., (N.Y.; Harper and Row, 1961)., p.15.

leader's picture is Jesus Christ. It's the fundamental
critical mind and motivation to write this treatise.

THE PURPOSE OF THE DISSERTATION

So far, there published sandlike theories about Leader and Leadership. For example, 'dictorial leadership', 'permissive leadership', 'democratic leadership', 'patriarchal leadership', 'priest leadership', 'partial leadership', 'managing-type leadership', 'specialist-type leadership', 'steward leadership', 'servant leadership', 'shepherd leadership', 'creative leadership', 'traditional leadership', 'authoritative leadership', 'reasonable leadership', 'charismatic leadership', 'symbolic leadership', 'administrating leadership', 'oppressive leadership', 'mediation-type leadership', 'problem-solving leadership', 'humanics leadership', 'object-seeking leadership', 'inciting leadership', 'education-type leadership', 'overlooking leadership', 'persuading leadership', etc.. Then it's very sorry that the Korean church facing 21 Century is Concluding rather than cosmopolitan and degraded into egoistic church, antagonism and conflict rather than love, forgiveness and serving heart, institutionalization, formalization, legalization and professionalization, the raising up the christian religious man rather than the institution of raising up the gospelic person of Jesus Christ. It's the loss of Gospel, the absence of Ecclesia. Therefore, I diagnosed it's the absence of the 'evangelical leadership' of Jesus Christ the essence and foundation of all leadership.

Therefore, the purpose of this treatise is to grope the evangelical leadership prophesied visibly in the Word and Mind of Jesus Christ and make evident that without the change of leader himself, the Kingdom of God is in remote place.

Howard Hendricks threw the challenging stone waking up the leader's space of this bok 'Teaching to Change Lives'.

"If you want, write down the answer of following question in the black space of this book. : Recently what kind of change was occurred? That is to say, last week? last month? last year? Can you answer that very concretely? Can't but give a vague answer? Right. How are you growing up? 'With every method.' You can answer like this. It's wonderful work. Listen one thing among them. As you know, the effective teaching only came out of the changed person. The more changed, the more used as the instrument changing other's lie. If you want to be an apostle, you must first be changed." [8]

Then, the important thing is not that the human nature denies the change fundamentally, but to refuse truly is 'to be changed'. [9] So, if the church leader would return to the Jesus Christ's Gospel and His Ecclesia and work with evangelical leadership and raise up the believers, he could complete his mission as the instrument in realizing God's Will in this world as it is in heaven according to the Lord's prayer.

Under the light of this purpose, the most important thing is to start with the Gospel of Jesus Christ rather than the Gospel about Jesus Christ as the Jesus Christ' Gospel for the God's Kingdom. Because, so far the Gospel of Jesus Christ has been around and the gospel of an priests and apostles has taken the center. So, as the evangelical leadership as well as the Ecclesia of Jesus Christ is around and the leader and leadership grounded on the law, synagogue, temple and church or world and society took the center of church, the church came to now

---

8) Howard Hendricks, Teaching to Change Lives (Portland; Multnomah, 1987), 32.
9) George F. Trusell, Helping Employees Cope with Change : A Manager's Guidebook (buffalo ; PAT Publishers, 1988

as the leadership theory of Old Testamental church or apostle or prophesy or community.

Therefore, I want to discuss from the old testamental leader and leadership to the evangelical idea of leadership of Jesus Christ and even discipleship training raising theory.

Research Method & Its Limitation

In this treatise, I will not restate normal leadership announced until now. Only, in case of necessity to understand this treaties, I will consider it by quotation and verification.

In drawing up treatise, the fundamental comments are to discuss how is the evangelical leadership related with shepherding, with church, with mission, and with theology.

For this, the evident understanding about Jesus Christ's gospel and His Ecclesia and Bassileia needs and the evangelical leadership of Jesus Christ should be considered as the essential fundamental comment of the other leadership mentioned by earthly scholars. On the ground of these essence, biblical, historical and theological investigation on the leader and leadership would be done and the evangelical leadership of Jesus Christ after examining the leader and leadership appeared on the Old Testament would be discussed.

But, this treaties is confined to the limited knowledge and space, and the experience on the shepherding field and reference study rather than realistic analysis and data according to the social research method. Therefore, after the completion of this treatise, I expect it to be a gate of critical mind and guideline for returning to the evangelical leadership, anticipating the active study on the evangelical leader and leadership by referring this.

Chapter II

BIBLICAL AND HISTORICAL EXAMINATION
ON THE LEADER AND LEADERSHIP

1. The meaning of Leader appeared in the Bible

1) The examination of the leader appeared in the Old Testament in the meaning of a word.

The etymology of leader in the Old Testament appears variously. Largely summarizing, it's like followings.

First, the leader as the ruler. "Baal", "Mimshall" and "Shar" in Hebrew mean the head of governing.

Second, the leader as the governor by controling. "Shelton", "Nagide", "Adir", "Roshi"and etc. in Hebrew mean to rule, to head, dignity and head.

Third, the leader as the guider by caring. "Achar"and "Pakid", in Hebrew mean to care and to be just.

2)The examination of the leader appeared in the New Testament in the meaning of a word.

The meaning of a word of leader in the New Testament mentioned variously with several types. The vocabulary meaning the leader in Latin are mentioned as "kadegedes", "prostatis", "quberinesis", "qubernetes", "kepare", "hodegos", "hegemon"and etc. and the general meaning is the guider, the leader, the carer, and the head.

2. The definition of leader and leadership

The scholar introducing the first mentioning of the word of leader is the American socialist Ralph M. Stogdill and it was used first in England about in B.C. 1300. The use of the word of Leadership is England in 1800s after 500 years had passed since the word of leader mentioned.

Like this, the vocabulary of leader and leadership were deep related with the tradition of Anglo Saxen and have same etymological origin out of same root, and though they have difference in themselves, they must be considered as having same meaning. Generally, the meaning of these words implies Chief, Head, or King, however, they must be distinguished from the meaning of a word of the evangelical leader and leadership.

1) The definition of the leader

The definition of the leader hasn't any generalized opinion. It's because the idea of leader is various and used wit idea scope according to the application, condition and viewpoint. The lexical meaning is mentioned with various aspects according to the situation and role. It's meaning is Commander, Commandant, Boss or Master, Chief of Head, Manager, Executive, Key-Man, Opinion, Elite. In addition to the opinion of present scholars are various. I mention the relation factors of the leader and leadership like followings. First, the Situational favorableness between leader and members are the most important. Second, as the degree of the tasks construction, this means the degree of how evidently the tasks assigned to each group are decided and transmitted accomplish. Third, as the position authority of the leader, it means the authority of leader recognized publicly.

2) The definition of the leadership

According to the American political scientist James M. Burns, the definition of leadership over 130. Nonetheless, the definition accepted generally not appeared yet. The generalization of the word of leadership was in England after 1800s, or the first time mentioned the word "leader" was 1300s, and the vocabulary of leadership not appeared yet in the Oxford dictionary until 1800s.

As R. M. Stogdill mentioned the definition of leadership are so many as the people tried to define, the opinions of the present scholars are various. But, the evident fact is that the leadership should be considered as the competence of the desirable purpose thorough the leader and followers.

3) The relation of the leader and the leadership in the meaning and vocabulary.

So far, there are several case of confusion the words the leader and the leadership. Generally, two vocabularies include two kinds of meaning of words. One is the action, and the other is the method of action, ability. Generally, the social scientists define the leadership as the process of organizing and gathering the people in order to accomplish the purpose of group, and the leadership as the exertion of the affect on the activity to accomplish the special purpose wanted by people. The important peculiarity in leading is the feeling of self-achievement and satisfaction of the followers. This means the leader is defined in gaining the support and cooperation from the followers through his ability and quality and simultaneously giving them somehow the feeling of satisfaction and self-achievement. Therefore, the leader and leadership and the cooperation between the individual and group can't be realized without the leader's role operation mutually with them. that is to say, the leadership become the most important factor related with organization system as well as the formation of individual action and group action.

4) Evangelical leader and leadership

Michael Youssef once mentioned the word of the leadership of Jesus Christ in his book, The leadership Style of Jesus. The evangelical leader and leadership means the very leader and the leadership rooted on the Gospel of Jesus Christ. This evangelical leader and leadership consider the Word Jesus Christ, the unique and true leader becoming the hope of human being and the Concluding Revelation of whole human being proclaimed and what were given by His life and Mind as the foundation and the essence of the all mentioned leader and leadership theory until now by all present scholars in this world. Then, who is the evangelical leader?

Fist, those who established through evangelical training, believing, following, testimoning Gospel as those who became "ιετοι", "εκιετοι", "πιοτοι" through Jesus Christ, the Gospel itself.

Second, the one must teach the Gospel. However, if the one teaches by treading in footsteps of Jewish religion or Synagogue religion, or by placing the law, dogma, belief, confess, theology, and the church law on the same level, he can't be the leader of Gospel.

Third, the one must rule with Gospel. The Gospel isn't the way of ruling but the way of serving. Normal leader displaying the leadership through governing with rule and control, but the evangelical leader must visualize the leadership with the gospel of serving.

Forth, the one practice the gospel. Jesus Christ is the Gospel itself. He was poor and became the Savior of the sinners and the friend of the tax-collector and prostitute. Therefore, the gospel of Jesus Christ must be the life itself accompanied with continuous sacrifice and service like as the village on the mountain. The one must always act with confidence before Gospel and practice the life of submission to reason not contrary to rationality according to the help of Holy Spirit and the great right way.

Fifth, the one must have the cosmic gospel. The Gospel is cosmic and worldwide. It doesn't distinguish the nation, race, frontier, and good and evil man, everybody is the object of the God's love. So, the leader of Gospel leads people into the heaven with the attitude of the understanding, embraces, generosity, and service with broad and large evangelical mind.

Sixth, the one re-examine every work with gospel. The Gospelic leader put the ultimate purpose of every work on the glory of God. Therefore, in accompanying the assigned task, he re-examine every work with the Gospel of Jesus Christ not with history, dogma, and theology.

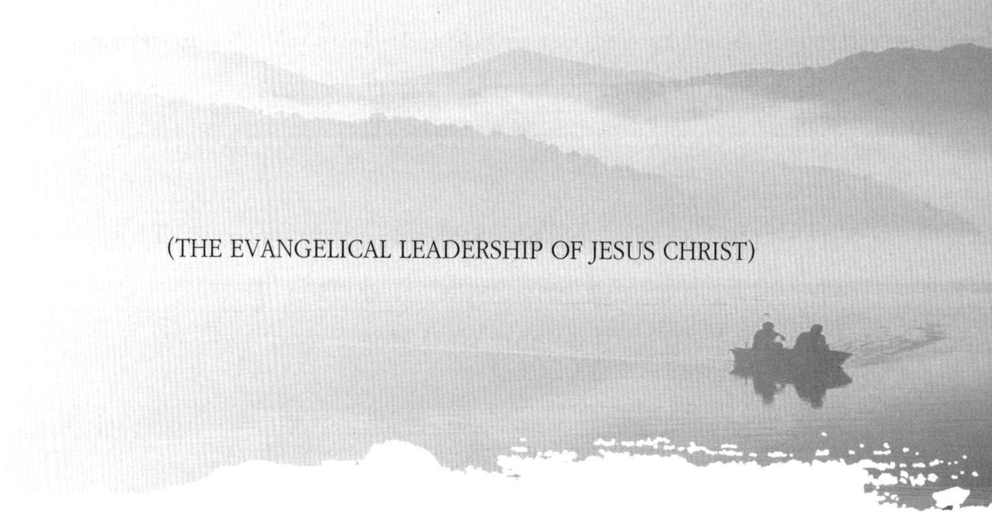

(THE EVANGELICAL LEADERSHIP OF JESUS CHRIST)

Chapter Ⅲ

THE EXAMINATION ON THE LEADER AND
THE LEADERSHIP
APPEARED IN THE OLD TESTAMENT

Before the examination of the leader and the leadership appeared in the Old Testament, the viewpoint of Bible is important. Because, there's viewpoint of looking the New Testament in the Old Testament, and looking by dividing the Old and New Testament and emphasizing the New Testament and slighting the Old Testament, and contrary, emphasizing the Old Testament and slighting the

New Testament. when I look the Old Testament in the viewpoint of Jesus Christ, He is the Gospel itself and the New Testament is the Witnesses of Gospel of Jesus Christ.

Therefore, the leader and the leadership appeared in the Old Testament is the symbolic model or revelation of the evangelical Leader and Leadership of Jesus Christ. Let's examine the leader and the leadership appeared in the Old Testament according to the history and period.

1. The Leadership of Abraham

The beginning of the leadership in the Old Testament is well considered as Abraham having the calling and choosing by God and the meaning of community. The symbolic revelation of Abraham and Jesus Christ is like followings.

Firth, Abraham was established as the symbol of Jesus Christ in the character of the cosmos and the world. Because, the name of Abraham and the whole nations on his territory means the cosmic theology.

Second, Abraham symbolizes the "Ecclesia" of Jesus Christ. Because Abraham satisfies the meaning of "κιετοι", "εκιετοι", "πιοτοι" of Jesus

Christ.

Third, The calling of Abraham is the symbol of salvation of Jesus Christ. Because Abraham is Called out of Ur of the Chaldeans, Egypt, Temple and Synagogue religion.

The leadership of Abraham was trusted from God for the kingdom of God. Second, it's the leadership as the patriarch of many nations, third, the spiritual leadership of God's kingdom, forth, the political, military, and administrating leadership.

2. The leadership of Moses

Moses was symbolized as the representative person equipped with the spiritual, personal, leading quality. He was the leader of the exodus of Hebrew governed for 430 years under Egypt and the pronoun of the Law receiving the Ten commandment in the Mt. Sinai. Especially, in the period of Moses, the so called Church-State existed. It was peculiar country national group, Theocracy and Democracy coexisting in the aspect of the pattern and structure. Moses had the excellent spiritual leadership. He was very humble(Nu12:3), the faithful leader(Heb11), the exemplary leader of prayer and word. Also he was the leader passing the gate of compromising in the center of God. In addition he established officials over thousands, hundreds, fifties and tens and trusted the tasks of administration and judgement with the leadership of the legislation and the judicature and collected the public opinion through the leaders and exhibited the leadership birthing the assembly.

3. The leadership of the Judges

The period of judges began among the undivided society not equipped with administrating system of the centralized counter after the death of Joshua. (Ju2:8). The judges charged the mission of religion and military by being called irregularly form God, in the state of without any special administrating system of King. The word of Judge is "Shopete" and has the meaning of the judge(Ex18:22), judge(Nu35:24), and judge(2 Ki23:22), however, all man called as judge wasn't the charismatic leader. The leadership of Judges oriented from the God's irregular calling and it's because the irregular attacks of the surrounding nations. Sometimes, the leadership of Judges was displayed as priest, prophesy, and warrior.

4. The Kingdom and the leadership of King

After the period of Judge, the kingdom's period came. The period of Kingdom means through the kind of Saul, David, and Solomon to the period of the dividing kingdom. The kings of this period were called as leader rather than King, and Samuel accepted that word more. In this thesis, the general survey of kingdom and the leadership of David considered as the representative leadership of Kingdom would be mentioned. The leadership of king has been understood traditionally as one of three office leader-ship of Jesus Christ. But, it's questionable the appellation, the secular king is appropriate to Jesus Christ. From this point of view, the evangelical understanding on the leadership of king is to understand Jesus Christ as the king of serving rather than a king is the more desirable.

Examining the leadership of David as the symbol of kingdom, first, the leadership as the servant of God. The concept of servant in David was confessed as the servant of God by himself in Psalms, and the phrase, my servant David, repeated 30 times from

Samuel to 1Chronicles. The leadership of David as servant was diligent and humble and the man after God's own heart.(At13:22). And, we can find the truthful humanity in 2Samuel 1:19-27, and in the scene of accepting the rebuke of the revelation Nathan and repenting, the picture as a servant of God was visualized.(2Sa12, Ps51)

Second, the leadership as the king. The leadership as a king was great. His political ability moved the capital from Hebron to Jerusalem and make it the center of politics and religion. He named Jerusalem as the castle of David and supported the symbolic power by building palace and removing the Art into there. The military leadership was exhibited by altering the territory by conquering the Philistines the old enemy of Israel. His diplomatic leadership was written in 2Samuel 5:11 "Now Hiram king of Tyre sent messengers to David, along with cedar logs and carpenters and stonemasons, and they built a palace for David." Like this, David was the promising leader in politics, military, and diplomacy, however he resulted in the deterioration in his leadership. He caused the destruction of the David dynasty and the deterioration of priest and temple religion through the compounding offering in order to keep his sovereign power. And in the case of Bathsheba, the wife of Uriah David commited the terrible sin using the sovereign power(2Sa11:1-12:25), and 2Sa 11:27 reads that the thing David had done displeased the Lord. It was the deterioration of David Leadership.

5. The leadership of the priest

The central leadership in the temple religion is very important to the priest. The priest was established to perform the task as serving man before the Lord. The leadership of the priest, firs, the leader of the offering. The offering is composed of the burnt offering, the grain offering, the fellowship offering, the sin offering, and the guilt offering. It's the leadership as managing the sacrificial offering of redemption and the fellowing of live between God and the Israelites. The special leadership of the priest is to decide the Will of the Lord. As the method of deciding the Lord's Will, he used Urim and Thummim.(Dt33:8, Ex28:15-30). Third, the leadership of the blessing and judge.

One of the unique leadership of the priest was the privilege blessing the Israelite and the trusted task. In Numbers 6:27, the blessing on Aron was done by the name of the Lord. Also, the priest displayed the leadership as the judge. In Deuteronomy 27:4, he proclaimed the laws of seasons before people. However, the deterioration of leadership as priest is caused by averted from the Lord and people, because of the compounding with violence and the ashamed part by abusing his authorities and making into the offering religion and temple religion.

6. The leadership of the elder in the synagogue-centered.

The origin of synagogue is found in the captive life of Babylon. The temple offering became to impossible to Diaspora, so they established synagogue by the unit of family and village to succeed "Tora" and offered the irregular worship. There was the elders in the synagogue and the synagogue ruler was elected as the head of synagogue. The leadership of the synagogue elders was to manage the work of synagogue and charged the combined tasks of traditional king, prophesy and priest. Especially,

They displayed leadership as the representative of the community and soon made Sanhedrin, or Gerusia, or district assembly.

As the flow of time, the leadership of the elders became to be deteriorated, Synagogue was used wrongly with hypocritical prayer and excessive mad ambition. The deteriorated Jewish Synagogue even mentioned as a synagogue of Satan.(Rev2:9)

(THE EVANGELICAL LEADERSHIP OF JESUS CHRIST)

Chapter Ⅳ

THE PRINCIPLE AND ACTUAL STATE ABOUT THE
GOSPELIC IDEA OF A LEADER AND LEADERSHIP
OF JESUS CHRIST

The human bing and Bible have produced a number of leaders until now. But, Jesus Christ is the greatest leader. Because, Jesus Christ is the Concluding Revelation.

1. The external and internal verification of the leadership of Jesus Christ

The leadership of Jesus Christ was the revelation from Heaven not form the earth. Michael Youssef mentioned seven external and internal verifications of the leadership of Jesus Christ. ①The revelation of God ②The testimony of John the Baptist ③ Self-verification of Christ ④The testimony of Holy Spirit ⑤The testimony of Bible ⑥The history of miracle ⑦ The testimony of disciples. In addition, the leadership of Jesus Christ is his essential appellation such as "Lord", "Christ", "Son of God"and "Son of Man."

2. The idea of Leader of Jesus Christ establishing "Ecclesia"and the proclamation of "Bassileia".

The idea of Leader of Jesus Christ is Leadership of "Bassileia"and as the Lord of "Ecclesia". His Leadership is the leadership of love, forgiveness, and or serving heart. It's the peculiarity beyond the comparison with earthly leadership. The Leadership of Love means the Personification itself as the completion of law and the completion of the salvation of the whole world, and the great command of Love. The leadership of the forgiveness starts from the love for human itself and present the principle the forgiven must forgive others. Therefore, the forgiveness is the prelude of the Love and the living room of the hope. In addition, the forgiveness is the essence of Gospel and means the endless love loving to the enemy.

The leadership of humility of Jesus Christ was developed as the leadership humility God' s Kingdom. Jesus Christ showed the example of serving. Teaching the principle of humility, he first mentioned the humility of God. The humility toward God is the worship, service and the life following Jesus to the end. Next, as the humility principle among mutual person, it means the Service or Serve of love, forgiveness and humility not the selfish service.

3. The idea of leader of 3 offices Jesus Christ.

What kind of leader is Jesus Christ? Even the disciples didn't have the right idea of leader about Jesus Christ. In Caesarea Philippi, at the question of "Who do people say the Son of Man is?", the answer was that some say John the Baptist; others say Elijah; and still others, Jeremiah or one of the prophets.(Mt16:14) However, Jesus Christ is the essential revealer of the symbolically revealed king, prophesy, and priest.

5) The principle and actual state about the gospelic idea of a leader and leadership of Jesus Christ

Jesus Christ raised up disciples of direct calling, establishing, and sending for "Bassileia"and "Ecclesia".

A. The principle of the leadership of Jesus Christ

The principle of the leadership of Jesus Christ mentioned in the Books of Gospel is the principle entering the Kingdom of Heaven. The principle entering the God's Kingdom is "repent and believe the Gospel"and "follow me." The reason Jesus commanded to follow Him is because of His peculiar Leadership as'good shepherd'and the head of church.

B. The principle of leader training of 12 Disciples

The principle of leader training of Jesus is the superior leadership beyond comparison with any other training principle. As the famous sculptor makes the unattractive stone mass into the gorgeous art sculpture, for a short time three years, Jesus trained mud like disciples into the cosmic evangelical missionary and he walked the final way, the way of martyrdom for the Gospel. This training principle of disciple making is only possible to Jesus Christ.

In the training principle of making disciple Jesus always planted the confidence of eternal life of God' s Kingdom and taught the love, forgiveness and serving as a good example an example.

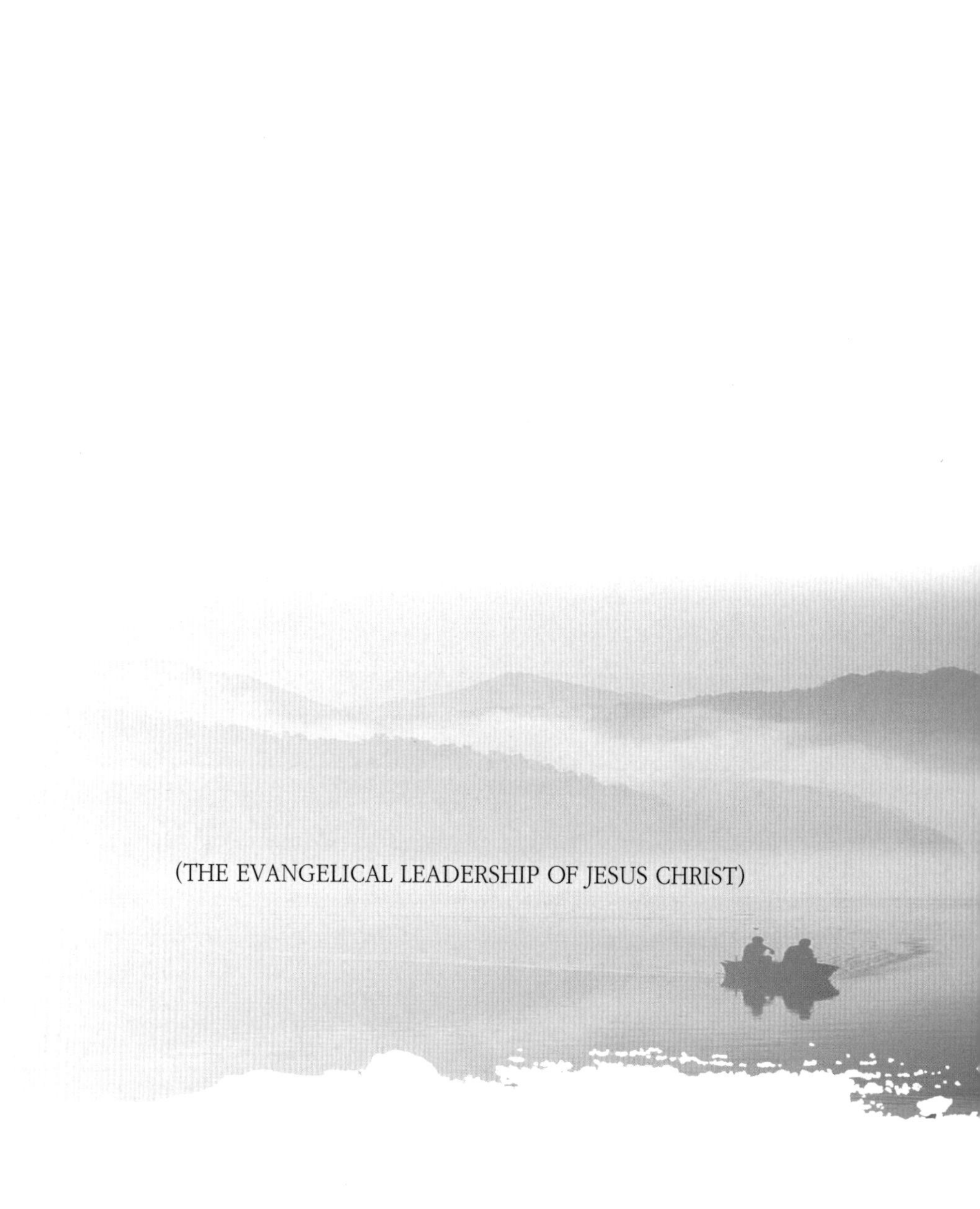

(THE EVANGELICAL LEADERSHIP OF JESUS CHRIST)

Chapter V

THE LEADERSHIP OF THE 12 CHANGED
DISCIPLES

Jesus Christ visualized his leadership by calling his disciples and establishing them as great leaders. The Gospel of Jesus Christ lied not in recognition but in change. 12 Disciples called by Jesus Christ were all different people in thought, religion, personality, and background. There were the extreme right wing, Romaist, and the realistic calculation man. However, these all man were moved by the leadership of love, forgiveness and serving of Jesus Christ and changed. They are all great missionaries and the witness of gospel ending their lifes with Gospel without exception.

The apostle Peter changed from Simon into the stone life religious leader, Peter, and his evident confession, the confidence on word, and the passion and ability of Gospel makes him display the leadership leading 3000 person to Christ in a day. Andrew was once a person of passive and conservative character, but became the great preacher by being changed with the Gospel of Jesus Christ. The apostle John was once the man of violence like his nickname, the son of thunder, narrow-minded, and full of ambition, however, he became the apostle of Love through Jesus Christ. Philip was once the man of positivism and irresolution, however, he became to learn to include God in his logical thought through Jesus Christ,. According to the transmission he was martyred in preaching in Brugia. Nathanael came from Gana and was good at the law, however, he changed and followed the Cross of Jesus Christ to the end by confessing Him as Christ, and believed Jesus as King even the moment of Jesus crucifixion after meeting Jesus Christ. Doubtful Doma was once pessimist rather than optimist and have questionable tendency rather than positive tendency and thought the wrongest rather than best. After meeting Jesus, he became to confess Jesus Christ as the way, truth and the life, and his confess after Jesus'Resurrection, "My Lord and My God" was great. In addition he was changed into courageous leader. He insisted "Let us also go, that we may die with him." (Jn11:16) The demonstrator Simon was the extreme nationalist included in Sicary, however, he was changed into the loving apostle even forgiving the enemy Matthew by being captivated by the love, forgiveness and serving of Jesus Christ. He deserted the sword born in his breast and became the witness of the love of Jesus Christ.

The tax-collector Matthew was the object of contempt and hatred, and became the wealth through extraction and impurity. However, he brought the tremendous change. He became to own the decision to departing from the desire to possess. He used his job and poverty as the instrument of God's Kingdom. He wrote down the spiritual scripture and was martyred for Gospel. Besides, a little Jacob was commonly understood as a man of humble and inferior and poor physically, but he also was martyred by being cut with saw, depending on transmission. Judah was a man of ambition and thought Jesus Christ came as King, however, he walked the way of martyr silently by holding the Cross of Jesus Christ after being changed through Jesus Christ. Lastly, the pronoun of the tragedy, Judas Iscariot was mentioned as the seller of Jesus and betrayer in Bible. He was warned three times through the meeting with Jesus Christ, but eventually he became the tragic character losing the position of eternal leader.

Chapter VI

CONCLUSION

So far, I studied the evangelical Leadership of Jesus Christ, I examined the leadership of the Old Testament characters mentioned as the essential symbol of Leadership of Jesus Christ in the aspect of history, theory, theology and Bible; the leadership of Abraham, the leadership of Moses, the leadership of Judges, the leadership of the priest in temple religion and Synagogue ruler in synagogue religion.

And, after discussing the evangelical idea of leadership of Jesus Christ, the center of this paper, and the actual state of that principle, I examined the changed leadership of 12 Disciples.

In mentioning the leadership by character in the Old Testament, Abraham visualized his leadership through God's calling and establishing. As the head of many nation, he displayed his leadership as God's love leadership, and sometimes as political, military and administrative leadership.

Moses kept the pattern of the so-called Church-State under the God's authority, made peculiar State-Nation group coexisting with Theocracy and Democracy and visualized the leadership of three authorities of legislation, judicature and administration, and spiritual leadership. Especially, he established the priest and officials over thousands, hundreds, fifties and tens, and trusted the tasks of administration and judgement, and the visualized his leadership bitrhing the office of the elder and the system of the general idea. The judges displayed their leadership as the priest, prophesy, and even the warrior.

The period of the kingdom and the leadership of kings symbolize the king, the one of traditional tree officers. However, Jesus Christ isn't the secular king in theology but the king of "Bassileia" and serving. So, the introduction of the vocabulary of king from Canaan Jebusites is certain, and there were degeneration of the religion of Lord and leadership from the period of kingdom. Especially, David appointed confusingly the succeeded Abiadal priest and Jebusites or Sadduce priest to keep his sovereign power and eventually, it brought about the degeneration and the Abiadal was driven out and made the great mistake causing the degeneration in the orthodoxy of the Lord.

The central position of the leadership in the period of temple was the priest. The origin of the priest was in Mt. Sinai and he was established as the serving man before the Lord. Especially, he displayed the leadership as the assistant helping people to live faithfully before the Lord, the mediator and the judge. So, the essential leadership of the priest was visualized as the leadership of offering, the leadership deciding the God's Will, the deliverer of the blessing and the leadership of judge. But, this priest brought about the degeneration in leadership. According to G. Fohrer, the Temple of Israel has the character as "the private worship room" of a royal family as the complex building surrounded within the Kingdom, and G. Von. Rad once stated the meaning of Arc storage is strong. Like this, in the character of the temple of Kingdom, the priest degenerated from the leadership as the priest of the Lord to the priest as the waiting woman of king.

The leadership of the synagogue ruler in the period of synagogue was the religious ceremony in the dimension of the district village unit or family unit or family unit compared to the leadership of the priest having the meaning in the dimension of the whole nation or united. In temple, the priest and the Levitis visualized their leadership, however, in Synagogue all was operated by centering the synagogue ruler. Especially, There were the elders in Synagogue, and the elders elected the Synagogue ruler as their head. The Synagogue ruler combined the office of king, prophesy, and priest. The distinctive feature of this Synagogue isn't the strictness like temple or to wear the ceremonial clothes, the preparation of the altar, and the ceremony-centering, but visualized through the district assembly, the representative institution of people, or "Gerusia" or "small Sanhedrin".

The problem was the degeneration of the elders of the Synagogue. They degenerated the temple by misconducting themselves with secular governors. According to G. Kittle, the Synagogue was degenerated as the group of the bee centering the queen bee. Jesus also quarreled with the power of

Satan in the very that Synagogue. In Revelation, the degenerated crowd of Jewish was mentioned as the Synagogue of Satan.

As we have seen, the leadership by character and by period mentioned in the Old Testament have the symbolic meaning of the leadership of Jesus Christ. Especially, the leadership in the Old Testament of the three offices of the king, the prophesy, and the priest was revealed completely through the three offices of Jesus Christ. Because Jesus Christ is the king of God's Kingdom, didn't deny to be included in the line of prophesy and the high priest fulfilling the eternal redemption by offering himself as the sacrifice on the Cross.

The proclamation of the leadership of Jesus Christ was unprecedented and blameless by Called Out from the degenerated Kingdom religion, Temple religion, Synagogue religion, Offering religion, Law religion or their religious leader through his personification.

The authority of the leadership of Jesus Christ was visualized from his essential appellation. His appellation was "the Lord", "Christ", "the Son of God", and "the Son of man". The essence of the leadership of Jesus Christ was not the ruling or condemning as the secular king, or the leadership of the secular and authoritative leadership such as religious judge or subordination, but the eternal leadership of love, forgiveness, and serving to establish "Bassileia"and "ECCLESIA". This is his Gospel. The evangelical leadership of Jesus Christ is the cosmic leadership and becoming the good news to everyone by passing over the race, class, grade, nation, frontier, thought, and religion. Therefore, to whoever believing, experiencing and following Gospel, the new change occurs through the gospelic leadership of surprising Jesus Christ.

The leadership of Jesus Christ always leads into "Bassileia". As the condition of entering "Bassileia", Jesus Christ proclaimed to repent and "follow the Gospel".

Besides, the leadership of Jesus Christ is the exemplary principle thoroughly say "follow me", and proclaimed Jesus Christ himself is the good shepherd. The apostle Paul compared Jesus Christ as the organic body and mentioned the leadership of Jesus Christ being the head of church as the

Leadership of Headership.

The training principle to make realistic leader of Jesus Christ can be seen in calling 12 Disciples, establishing, sending and trusting. The 12 Disciples of Jesus couldn't be deliquesced on the earth ideologically and environmentally. but they conformed the disciple community orienting the archetype of "Ecclesia". The 12 Disciples were changed through the evangelical leadership of Jesus Christ without exception and were martyred for the "Bassileia" and "Ecclesia" and "Gospel" of Jesus Christ. It's the leadership of raising up the greatest leader of human.

In the standpoint of looking to 21 Century, the human being and the church still remains in antagonism, conflict, jealousy, struggle, war and oppress, and degenerated into the quaracter of kingdom, earth, law, synagogue, temple and a sight spot rather than "Bassileia" and "Ecclesia" of Jesus Christ. And the plot and jealousy between priests, the conflict between the priest and elders, and the antagonism between laymen are because of the absence of gospelic Leadership of Jesus Christ with a word. The absence of evangelical Leadership of Jesus Christ have the tendency of being substituted with a number of techniques of leadership theory in administration, business, accounting and the science of district society development, and the mimic and following brought about the degeneration of Jesus "Ecclesia" and the absence of the leadership theory. Besides, the absence of evangelical Leadership of Jesus Christ causes the mistakes to mimic the compounded theology of the kingdom religion and the priest of the degenerated temple religion of the untimely Old Testament and the degenerated leadership of Synagogue of the ruler being the power by misconducted with the legalist and Satan. Besides, they were degenerated into the so-called hired shepherd using sheep thoroughly and fulfilling their own stomach by biasing on the material omnipotence of material. The evangelical Leadership of Jesus is waiting for earnestly to return to the good shepherd, the leadership of the love, forgiveness and serving of Jesus Christ'Gospel after being Called Out from the degenerated church, thought and the leadership.

Therefore, today's priest, elders and the church leaders called as the leaders of Jesus Christ must first have the new understanding about the Gospel of Jesus Christ, His "Bassileia" and "Ecclesia" and keep in mind that they were called established and sent and have the position for these.

Jesus today also, earnestly seeking for the evangelical leader of Jesus Christ testimonying the Gospel for the sake of his life by standing uprightly before the Jesus'Word after coming out from the earthly temptation and compromising and negotiating with non-gospel.

"Be faithful, even to the point of death, and I will give you the crown of life." (Rev 2:10)

(THE EVANGELICAL LEADERSHIP OF JESUS CHRIST)

제 I 장

서 론

1. 문제의 의식과 동기

미래학자 앨빈 토플러(Alvin Toffler)는 「제3의 물결(The Third Wave)」에서 미래사회는 과거와 같이 자본주의냐, 공산주의냐 하는 이데올로기에서 탈피하여 지식이 사회를 움직이는 이른바 지식 사회가 될 것으로 예견한 바 있다.[10] 미래는 정보산업사회로서 빠른 문화(fast culture)가 느린 문화(slow culture)를 정복하는 사회가 될 것이다.

이러한 변화 속에서 오늘의 교회와 교회 지도자들은 물질문화와

---

10) Alvin, Toffler, *The Third Wave* (New York: William Marrow, 1980).

정보문화에 능동적으로 대처해야하는 지혜가 요구된다. 그러나 보다 근본적이고 본질적인 요구는 교회와 교회 지도자들이 상대적으로 황폐해가는 인간의 정신문화에 대하여 시대와 국경과 인종과 민족과 문화를 넘어 온 인류의 정신과 가슴에 참 소망이 되는 영원불변의 길과 진리와 생명 되신 예수 그리스도의 복음과 그의 "에클레시아"를 분명히 선포하고 제시하는데 있다.

때문에, 필자는 감히 두 가지의 문제를 제기하고자한다. 먼저, 한국 교회는 과연 예수 그리스도의 복음이 충만한가? 그리고 예수 그리스도가 말씀과 의중(Mind) 가운데 하나님의 나라를 선포하실 때 세우신 "에클레시아(εκκλησια ; 마16:16, 18:17)"에 충실한가? 이다. 주님이 선포하신 복음은 언제나 회개가 동반된 하나님의 나라였으며(막1:15), 사랑과 용서와 섬김의 복음이었다.

그러나 오늘의 교회와 교회 지도자상의 양상을 볼 때, 예수 그리스도의 복음에서 멀어져있다. 끊임없이 미워하고 시기하며 투쟁하고 교만하며 예수가 가르치신 복음과는 본질을 달리하며 높은 자리를 탐하고 대접받기를 좋아하며 섬김 받기를 즐겨 하는 지도자들이 있다. 나아가 오늘의 교회나 노회나 총회가 용서하지 않고 사랑하지 않고 정죄하고 독선하며 교리 신학과 교회 신학과 비복음적인 성서 신학에 길들여져서 지배하며 통치하며 권세까지 차지하면서 예수로 말미암아 완성되고 폐기 처분된 율법을 교회법으로 복원하여 종교 재판을 일삼고 있지 않은가. 더욱이 하나님이 맡기신 양들의 생명은 돌보지 않고 자기 배만 부르게 하여 삯꾼으로 전락된 목회자들도 있다. 그러한 지도자라면, 그러한 교회나 노회, 총회라면, 그러한 목회자라면, 거기에는 예수 그리스도도 그의 복음도 그의 목회도 그의 선교도 기대할 수 없을 뿐 아니라, 예수 그리스도와 그의 복음은 종교적이거나 정치적이거나 문화적이거나 철학적인 비복음적인 상황들에 의하여 묻혀 있을 수밖에 없는 것이다.

뿐만 아니라, 예수께서 하나님 나라를 선포하시면서 세우신 교회는 분명 "에클레시아"이다. 그럼에도 불구하고 이 땅의 수많은 교회들은 때 아닌 유대 종교나 성전 종교나 회당 종교에서 벗어나지를 못하고 있으며 오히려 회귀(Re-Entering) 하는 경향이 있다. 또 교회를 사회공동체(Gemeinschaft or Gesellschaft)나, 큐리아케(κυριακη, 계1:10, 고전11:20)로 보는데서 "에클레시아"의 본질적 변질을 가져왔다.[11]

예수 그리스도의 복음인 유앙겔리온(ευαγγελιον)은 우주적이며 세계적이다. 알케(αρκη)로 시작된 복음은 태초요 근본적인 시작을 말한다. 이 "알케"는 창조 이전의 흑암과 공허, 혼돈과 무질서, 무생물의 세계에 대단원의 막(End)을 내리고, 분명하게 불리어 나온(Called Out) 새로운 시작을 말한다.[12] 그러므로 복음은 종결적 계시자인 예수 그리스도로부터 출발한 것이며, 온 인류의 기쁜 소식이며, 그의 "바실레이아"는 사랑과 용서와 섬김의 권능성으로 충만하다. 때문에, 이 복음을 영접한 곳마다 천지의 새 역사의 장이 열리고 죄와 죽음과 절망과 흑암과 고통이 사라지고 빛처럼, 열처럼, 물처럼 넘치는 기쁨으로 충만하게 되어 감추어지지도 묻혀지지도 사라지지도 않는다.

그러므로 하나님이 세우시는 교회와 교회지도자가 될 수 있기 위해서는 예수 그리스도가 선포한 복음과 그의 "에클레시아"로 돌

---

11) 황보 갑, 에클레시아 (서울 : 다리, 1966), p. 33, 164.
12) *Ibid*., p. 159-189.

아가야 할 것이다. 선교 2세기를 맞으면서 한국 교회는 복음이 충만하고 예수 그리스도의 "에클레시아"로 돌아가 복음목회를 수행하는 지도자로 세움받고 있는가를 질문하지 않을 수 없다. 사실 한국교회는 역사상 그 유례가 없는 부흥과 발전을 가져온 것은 세계 교회가 인정하는 사실이다. 그럼에도 불구하고 세계 교회는'한국 교회'에 대하여 긍정적인 평가보다는 부정적인 평가를 하고 있다. 고질적인 교파 난립, 교회의 분열, 사회의 변화에는 민감한 대응을 보이지만 대중화 작업에는 미흡한 현상, 무속화 되어지는 기독교, 지역, 집단, 개인 이기주의, 대형교회 우월주의, 편의주의 신앙생활, 기독교인의 윤리적 타락 현상, 잘못된 종말론의 폐해, 과도한 해외 선교, 교회의 과소비 현상, 무분별한 교인 쟁탈전, 권위주의적 교회 행정 구조, 잘못된 헌금 풍토 등 그 어느 것 하나 복음적인 내용을 찾아볼 수 없는 현실을 그 누구도 부인할 수 없기 때문일 것이다.

왜 이런 현상이 일어나야만 하는가? 신학자, 목사, 장로도 많고 종교 지도자도 많으나 주님이 세우시기로 하신 복음적 지도자의 빈곤에 있기 때문이다.

리챠드 울프(Richard Wolff)는 칼 야스퍼스(Karl Jaspers)의 말을 인용하여 지적한다. "우리 세대는 지도자의 공황에 직면하고 있다. 도처에서 지도자의 능력이 감퇴되고 있음이 나타났다. 정상에 오르는 자들을 보면 볼수록 무작정 밀고만 나가는 자처럼 보인다.[13] 오스왈드 샌더스(J. Oswald Sanders)는 "각 시대마다 리더십의 문제에 직면해야 했으며, 오늘날도 여전히 많은 영

---

13) Richard Wolff, *Man at the Top* (Wheaton, Ⅲ : Tyndale, 1969), p. 13.

역에서 격심한 리더십의 위기에 직면하고 있다. 위기가 계속되고 있으나 오늘날의 지도자들은 거의 해결책을 찾아내지 못하고 있으며, 또 미래 역시 보장할 수 없는 현실이다. 교회 역시 이러한 권위 있는 리더십의 기근 현상을 피하지 못하고 있다.[14]고 지적한다. 한 마디로 집약하면, 복음적인 지도자의 빈곤을 역설한 말이라 할 수 있다.

교회에 지도자는 참으로 중요하다. 교회라는 가시적 조직의 지도력을 넘어서 한 영혼의 구원과 이 땅의 하나님의 백성으로 하여금 복음적 삶의 안내자이기 때문이다. "어떤 사업이 실패한다면 우리는 곧 다른 근로자를 고용할 것이 아니라 새로운 지도자를 고용해야 할 것이다[15]는 지적은 지도자의 위치가 얼마나 각별한가를 깨우치는 말이다.

오늘의 교인들이 구원의 기쁨과 선교적 사명에 감각조차 잃고 방황하는 것은 교회 지도자의 책임[16]이라 할 수 있다.

오늘날 세계교회가 한국 교회를 향하여 가시적 성장을 평가하면서도 사랑과 용서와 섬김이 넘치는 주님의 에클레시아로 긍정적 평가를 할 수 없는 것은 한국 교회의 지도자에게 그 책임을 묻지 않을 수 없다.

주님은 복음다움을 지닌 지도자를 요구하고 있다. 이는 오늘의 교회 지도자가 복음으로 변화되기를 요구하는 명령이기도 하다. 교회 지도자의 변화 없이는 한국 교회의 변화를 기대할 수 없기 때

---

14) J. Oswald Sanders, *Paul The Leader* (Chicago : Moody Press, 1984), p. 8.
15) Frank Goble, *The Man at the Top* (Thornwood, N.Y. : Caroline House Publishers,1972), p.1.
16) Robert A. Raines, *New Life in the Church* (N.Y.: Harper and Row, 1961), p.15.

문이다.

본고는 이러한 문제의식과 동기 하에서 가장 근본적인 지도상은 예수 그리스도에 있음을 밝히면서 예수 그리스도의 복음의 새로운 이해와 그의 에클레시아를 통해 계시된 지도자상을 모색하고자 한다.

2. 연구의 목적

지금까지는 무수한 리더(Leader)와 리더십(Leadership)에 관한 이론이 나왔다.'독재적 리더십' '방임주의 리더십' '민주주의 리더십' '가부장적 리더십''목회 리더십' '당파적 리더십' '관리자형 리더십' '전문가형 리더십' '청지기 리더십' '종의 리더십' '목자의 리더십' '창조적 리더십' '전통적 리더십''권위주의 리더십' '합리적 리더십' '카리스마적 리더십' '상징적 리더십' '행정적 리더십' '강압적 리더십''조정가형 리더십''문제 해결형 리더십''인간주의적 리더십''목표 추구형 리더십''선동적 리더십' '교육자형 리더십''방관형 리더십''설득형 리더십'등이 있다.

21세기를 맞이하는 한국교회는 우주적 교회라기보다는 패쇄적이고 이기주의적인 교회로 변질 되었고, 사랑과 용서와 섬김의 교회라기보다는 반목과 갈등이 표출되고 있다. 제도화, 형식화, 율법화, 직업화로 예수 그리스도의 복음인을 양육하는 교회라기보다는 기독교 종교인을 양성하는 기관으로 변질되고 있음을 심히 우려하지 않을 수 없다. 이는 복음의 상실이요, 에클레시아의 부재요, 따라서 모든 리더십의 근본이며 본질인 예수 그리스도의'복음적 리더십'의 부재이다.

따라서 본고는 예수 그리스도의 말씀과 의중(Mind)에서 가시적 또는 불가시적으로 계시하신 복음적 리더십을 모색하는데 본 논문의 목적이 있으며 이를 위해 지도자 자신이 변하지 않고는 교회도 하나님의 나라도 요원함을 밝히고자 한다.

하워드 헨드릭스(Howard Hendricks)는 그의 저서 「삶의 변화를 위한 가르침(Teaching to Changes Lives)」에서 지도자의 의식을 깨우치는 도전을 던졌다.

"원한다면 다음 질문에 대해서 이 책 여백에 대답을 적어보라: 최근에 어떤 변화를 일으켰는가? 이를테면 지난주에는? 지난달에는? 지난해에는? 아주 구체적으로 말할 수 있는가? 모호하다는 대답밖에 할 수 없는가? 좋다. 어떻게 성장하고 있단 말인가?'모든 방법으로 성장하고 있다'고 여러분은 말한다. 훌륭한 일이다. 그중 한 가지만 들어보라. 잘 알다시피, 효과적인 가르침은 오직 변한 사람을 통해서만 나온다. 많이 변할수록, 다른 사람들의 삶을 변화시키는 일에 더 많이 도구로 쓰일 수 있다. 변화의 사자가 되고 싶다면 여러분 자신이 변해야 한다.'"[17]

그런데 중요한 것은 사람의 본성은 근본적으로 변화를 거부하는 것이 아니라 정말 거부하는 것은 '변한다는 것 '[18] 이다. 때문에, 교회의 지도자가 그 자신이 변화되어 예수 그리스도의 복음과 그의 에클레시아로 돌아가서 복음적 리더십에서 목회를 하고 교인을 양육한다면 주님의 기도처럼 뜻이 하늘에서 이루어 진 것 같이 땅에서도 이루어지는 도구로 그 사명을 다 할 것이다.

---

17) Howard Hendricks, *Teaching to Change Lives* (Portland: Multnomah, 1987), p.32.
18) George F. Trusell, *Helping Employees Cope with Change : A Manager's Guidebook* (Buffalo ; PAT Publishers, 1988)

이러한 목적 하에서 볼 때, 가장 중요한 것은 하나님 나라를 위한 예수 그리스도의 복음으로 예수 그리스도에 대한(about) 복음 보다 예수 그리스도의(of) 복음에서 출발하는 것이다. 왜냐하면 지금까지는 예수 그리스도의 복음은 주변에 있게 되었고, 선지자들과 사도들의 복음이 중심부를 차지하였다. 때문에, 예수 그리스도의 에클레시아는 물론 그의 복음적 지도력도 주변에 있고, 율법적 회당적 성전적 또는 세상적 사회적 지도자와 지도력이 교회의 중심을 차지하므로서 교회는 구약적 교회 내지 사도나 선지자 또는 사회공동체적 지도자론에 이끌려 오늘에 이른 것이다.

따라서 필자는 구약의 지도자와 지도력에서 예수 그리스도의 복음적 지도자상과 그의 제자 양성론까지 논급하고자 한다.

3. 연구 방법과 한계

본 논문에서는 이제까지의 연구 발표된 일반적인 리더십에 관해서는 가능한 재론하지 않으려 한다. 단, 본 논문의 주제를 이해하는데 필요하거나 도움이 될 만한 경우는 인용, 검증하면서 고찰하고자 한다.

본 논문 작성에 있어서 기본적인 내용으로는 복음적인 리더십이 목회와 어떤 관련성을 갖고 있으며, 교회와 어떤 관련성을 갖고 있으며, 선교와는 어떤 관련성을 갖고 있으며, 신학과는 어떤 관련성을 갖고 있는가를 논급하고자 한다.

이를 위해 예수 그리스도의 복음과 그의 에클레시아와 바실레이아에 관한 분명한 이해를 하고, 예수 그리스도의 복음적인 리더십을 모든 리더십의 본질적이고 근본적인 내용으로 삼고자 한다. 이러한 본질을 근본으로 하여 지도자와 지도력에 관한 성서적 역사적 신학적 고찰을 하며, 구약에 나타난 지도자와 지도력을 살펴보고 예수 그리스도의 복음적인 리더십을 논급하겠다.

그러나 본 논문은 한정된 지면 그리고 사회조사방법론에 의한 실제적 분석과 자료를 근거하지 못하고 필자의 목회 현장의 경험과 참고 문헌연구에 한정하였다. 따라서 본 논문이 완성된 이후 본 논문을 참고하여 보다 나은 복음적인 리더와 리더십에 관한 연구가 활발할 수 있기를 기대하는 마음으로 복음의 리더십으로 돌아가야 한다는 문제의식과 동기의 문이요 길잡이가 되기를 기대하는 것이다.

(THE EVANGELICAL LEADERSHIP OF JESUS CHRIST)

제 **II** 장

지도자와 지도력에 관한 성서적 역사적 고찰

1. 성서에 나타난 지도자의 어의(語意)

1) 구약에 나타난 지도자의 어의적 고찰

구약에 나타난 지도자의 어원은 다양하게 나타나고 있다. 이들
어의를 크게 종합하면 다음의 의미로 고찰할 수 있다.

① "다스리는 자"로서의 지도자

a. 바알(בָּעַל)은 "소유하다" "다스리다" "자기의 것으로 하다"의 뜻
인 동사형이다. 여기서 파생된 단어 브알(בְּעַל)이 "남편"의 뜻과 "소
유주"의 의미를 갖는데 원 어의는 하나님이 자기 백성에 대한 그의
관계를 정의하실 때 사용한 결혼 용어이다.[19] 그런데 이것이 통상적

---

19) 사54:5, 렘3:14, 31:32.

으로 가나안인들의 만신전(pantheon)에서 가장 활동적인 신의 이름이되었다. 이로 인해 이 용어는 이스라엘로 하여금 범죄케 한 제의(祭儀)가 되었고,[20] 그로 말미암아 호세아 선지자를 통하여 이스라엘은 하나님을 "그의 남편"이라 부를 것이며 "나의 바알"이라 부르지 않게 될 것임을 증언하게 된다.[21]

b. 밈샬(מִימְשַׁל), 멤샬라(ממשלה)는 "통치하다" "지배하다" "치세하다"의 뜻을 가진 마샬(מָשַׁל)에서 파생된 단어인데 '밈샬'은 지리적 영역을 지배하는 명사로 사용되기도 했지만,[22] 통치권을 가진 자의 의미로 사용되어 "다스리는 자"를 뜻했다.[23] 그리고 '멤샬라'는 "통치" "지배"의 의미를 갖고 있는데 이것이 사용된 경우에는 하나님의 통치,[24] 통치 영역,[25] 인간의 통치[26]에 대해 사용되었다.

c. 싸르(שַׂר)는 "임금" "우두머리" "지배자" "지도자" "통치자"등의 의미를 갖고 있는 이 단어는 남성 명사로서 구약에 381회 사용되었는데,[27] 이 단어는 군대장관,[28] 귀족,[29] 방백,[30] 대장,[31] 장(長),[32] 두목[33] 등으

---

20) 삿2:11, 6:25, 왕상16:31, 왕하11:18, 21:2, 23:4, 겔16:23.
21) 호2:16, 2:2, 2:7.
22) 슥9:10.
23) 단11:4.
24) 시145:13.
25) 시103:22.
26) 대하32:9. (sovereignty, government).
27) "구약 원어 신학사전 하권", (서울;요단출판사, 1986.). p.1106.
28) 창21:22, 민31:14.
29) 민22:8, 23:6.
30) 삿5:15, 삼하3:38.
31) 창37:36, 왕상9:22.
32) 창40:2, 출18:21.
33) 대상11:6, 대하8:9.

로 사용되었다.

② "통치, 지배자"로서의 지도자.

a. 쉴톤(שׁלטון)은 "권세를 가지다" "지배하다"의 뜻을 가진 〈셸레트 (שׁלט)에서 파생된〉 단어로써 관원[34] 의 의미와 함께 통치자, 지배자 의 의미를 갖고 있다.

b. 나기드(נגיד)는 "말하다" "알리다" "앞에서다" "뚜렷하게 보이다" 의 뜻을 가진 남성명사형이다. 〈나기드(נגיד)동사에서 유래한 네게 드(נגד)는 "앞에 선 것" "두드러진 것"을 말한다.〉 나기드(נגיד)는 구 약에서 약 50여회 사용된 단어로서 공간적으로는 다른 사람들 앞 에 서 있는 위치, 의미론적으로는 누구보다도 뛰어난, 두드러진 존 재를 의미한다. 이런 의미에서 나기드(נגיד)는 통치자로서의 지도 자,[35] 주권자,[36] 족장,[37] 대장,[38] 치리자,[39] 인도자,[40] 그리고 왕[41]으로 나타 나고 있다.

c. 아디르(אדיר)의 어의는 원래 형용사 개념으로 "위엄 있는" "장엄 한"이란 뜻을 갖고 있는데 이 단어가 실명사로 사용될 경우는 용사

---

34) 단3:2
35) 삼상9:16, 10:1.
36) 삼하5:2, 왕상1:35.
37) 대상12:27.
38) 대하32:21.
39) 잠28:16.
40) 사55:4.
41) 겔28:2, 단9:26.(여기에 나타난 '나기드'는 메시야를 나타내는 용어였다.)

들,[42] 통치자[43]와 대등어가 된다. 이 단어는 바벨론 포로 이후 이스라엘의 지도자로서 "백부장들과 방백"들 사이에 놓이는 단어다. 이 단어는 종말론의 입장에서는 메시야로서 이스라엘을 다스리는 분[44]으로 묘사되고 때로는 여호와 자신을 가리키는 단어이기도 하다.[45]

d. 로쉬(ראש)는 문자적으로 "사람의 몸의 머리"를 뜻한다.[46] 원래 이 단어는 사람 몸의 일부분인 "머리"를 가리키는데 사용되며,[47] 그 의미가 확대되어 집안의 어른으로서의 "가족의 우두머리"라는 뜻으로 사용되기도 했고,[48] 이스라엘 백성들을 구분할 때 그들의 "두목"의 뜻으로 사용되기도 했으며,[49] "조상, 족장"의 뜻으로도 사용되었고,[50] 지도자라는 뜻으로 사용되기도 했다.[51]

부족의 우두머리를 족장이라 한 것처럼 어떤 지역 내에서 주요 도시를 가리키는 경우에도 이 단어를 사용하였다.[52]

③ "보살피며 인도 하는 자"로서의 지도자

a. 야쏴르(ישר) 단어는 "곧다" "올바르다 "정당하다" "합법적이다"

---

42) 삿5:13.
43) 렘30:21.
44) 렘30:21.
45) 사33:21.
46) Aron Pick, Dictionary of O.T. Word. (Kregel Publications, Grand Rapids, Mich. 1982) p. 190.
47) 출12:9.
48) 출6:14.
49) 출18:25.
50) 민7:2.
51) 신1:15.
52) Lawrence O. Richards., Clyde Hoeldtke , A Theology of Church Leadership.,(Zondervan, Grand Rapid, Mich, 1981) p. 16.

의 뜻을 가진 형용사로써 문자적으로는 "올바른"이란 뜻을 갖고 있다. 이 수식 형용사가 특별히 자격을 갖춘 인간, 즉 의인[53] 및 완전한 자[54]로 사용될 때 지도자의 의미를 갖게 되는 것이다.

b. 파키드(פָּקִיד)는 "주의하다" "보살피다" "감독한다"의 뜻을 가진 명사로써 "관리" "감독자"의 의미를 갖고 있는데 RSV에서는 '지도자'를 추가하고 있다. 이 단어가 "보살피는 자"[55] "감독자",[56] "장관"[57]으로 번역되었다.

2) 신약에 나타난 지도자의 어의(語意)적 고찰

신약성서에는 지도자와 관련된 어휘가 여러 형태로 언급되어 있다. 이를 어휘별로 살펴보면 다음과 같다.

① 카데게테스(καθηγητής)는 '카타'(κατά) (to)와 '헤게오마이'(ἡγέομαι) (lead)의 합성어에서 유래된 단어로서 일반적으로 안내자(a guider), 지도자(a leader)[58] 와 교사(instructor), 선생(a teacher)[59]이란 뜻이다. 즉 지도자란 바르게 가르쳐 안내하며 지도하는 자라는 의미인 것이다.[60]

② 프로스타티스(προστάτις)는 "다스리는" "힘쓰게 하다" "지배하

---

53) 시33:1.
54) 욥1:1, 8.
55) 대하31:13.
56) 창41:34, 에2:3.
57) 삿9:28.
58) 마23:10.
59) 마23:8.
60) Harper, *The Andlytical Greek Lexicon*, (N.T.; Harper & Row) p. 352.

다"의 의미를 갖고 있는'프로이스테미'($\pi\rho o \ddot{\iota}\sigma\tau\eta\mu\iota$)에서 파생된 여성형으로서 "보호자"[61]로서의 의미를 갖고 있는 지도자의 뜻이다.

③ 쿠베르네시스($\kappa\upsilon\beta\acute{\epsilon}\rho\nu\eta\sigma\iota\varsigma$)는 "키를 잡다"(to steer)의 뜻인 '쿠베르나오'($\kappa\upsilon\beta\epsilon\rho\nu\acute{\alpha}\omega$)에서 유래된 단어로서 정치, 행정직, 관리직으로서의 다스리는 지도자를[62] 뜻한다.

④ 쿠베르네테스($\kappa\upsilon\beta\epsilon\rho\nu\acute{\eta}\tau\eta\varsigma$)는 조종사(a pilot), 선장(The captain of the ship)을 뜻하는 단어로서 이 단어가 '지도자'로 사용되는 것은 배를 질서 있게 나아가도록 결정하고 운행하는 책임적 의미로 사용되었다. [63]

⑤ 케파레($\kappa\epsilon\varphi\alpha\lambda\acute{\eta}$)는 사람의 "머리"를 뜻하는데 때로는 건축물의 머릿돌(corner stone)을 의미하기도 한다. [64] 이 단어가 예수에게 적용될 때 예수는 교회의 머리됨을 강조하고,[65] 그런 의미로 예수는 참 지도자가 되시는 것이다.

⑥ 호데고스($\acute{\alpha}\delta\eta\gamma\acute{o}\varsigma$)는 "안내하다" "인도하다"의 뜻을 가진'호데게오'($\acute{o}\delta\eta\gamma\acute{\epsilon}\omega$)에서 파생된 명사로서 "인도자" "안내자" "지도자"를 뜻한다. 그런데 이 단어는 신약 성경에서 예수를 잡고자 하는 자들의 안내자가 된 유다에게 적용되었고,[66] 소경을 인도하는 자로서 바리새

---

61) 롬16:2.
62) 고전12:28.
63) 행27:11, 계18:17.
64) Harper, op, cit., Vol. II. p.207.
65) 엡1:22, 4:15-16, 5:21:30, 골1:18, 2:10.
66) 행1:16.

인에게 사용되었으며,[67] 자신이 율법을 준행치 않으면서 다른 사람들을 인도하는 잘못된 율법 교사들을 지칭할 때 사용되었다.[68] 따라서 호데고스 (*ὁδηγός*)는 지도자의 의미로 사용되기보다는 어떤 목적, 목표에로 이끌어 가는 자를 뜻한다.

⑦ 헤게몬(*ἡγεμών*)은 "앞장서다" "길잡이가 되다" "인도하다"의 뜻을 가진'헤게오마이'(*ἡγέομαι*)에서 유래된 단어인데 "지도자" "지배자" "인도자"의 뜻을 갖고 있으며 신약에서 사용된 용례는 고을 두령,[69] 총독,[70] 관장들,[71] 방백[72] 등으로 사용되었다.

2. 지도자와 지도력의 정의

지도자(Leader)란 말이 처음으로 언급된 것을 소개한 학자는 미국의 사회학자 랄프 스토그딜(Ralph M. Stogdill)로서, 그에 의하면 지도자란 용어는 B.C 1,300년경의 영국에서 처음으로 사용되었다. 리더십(Leadership)란 말의 사용은 지도자란 말이 언급된 이후 500년이 지난 1,800년대에 영국에서 이다.

이처럼 리더나 리더십의 용어는 모두 앵글로 색슨족의 전통과 깊이 연관되어 형성되고 통용되어 온 말들로써 같은 뿌리에서 그 어원적 기원을 가지며, 자구적(字句的)인 차이는 있으나 의미적(意味的) 뜻은 동일하다고 보아야 옳을 것이다.

---

67) 마15:14.
68) 롬2:19.
69) 마2:6.
70) 마10:18, 눅20:20.
71) 막13:9, 눅21:12.
72) 벧전2:14.

일반적으로 이 말들이 지니는 어의는 우두머리(chief)나 장(head), 혹은 왕(king)이라는 말들을 함축하고 있으나, 복음적 지도자와 지도력의 어의와는 그 본질적 의미에서 구별되어야 한다.

1) 지도자에 대한 정의(The Definition of Leader)

지도자란 어의가 무엇인가? 지금까지 한마디로 일반화된 견해가 없다. 이는 지도자의 개념이 다양하고 적용과 상황과 관점에 따라 폭넓게 사용되는 말이기 때문이다. 따라서 본 항에서는 지도자에 대한 사전적 의미를 살펴보고 제 학자들이 언급한 지도자의 정의를 살펴보고 목회 지도력에 미치는 중요한 관계적 요인을 밝히고자 한다.

먼저 **LEADER**에 대한 사전적 의미를 살펴보자.
옥스퍼드사전에서는 지도자(Leader)에 관해서 "상황과 역할에 따라 다양한 관점으로 다음과 같이 구분하여 정의하고 있다."[73]
　① 지휘관 (Commander)
　② 사령관 (Commandant)
　③ 수령(首領) (Boss or Master)
　④ 장(長) (Chief of Head)
　⑤ 관리자 (Manager)
　⑥ 집행자 (Executive)
　⑦ 중심인물 (Key-Man)
　⑧ 여론 조성자 (Opinion)

---

73) *The Oxford English Dictionary*, London : Oxford Press, 1970.

⑨ 엘리트 (Elite)이다.

　황의영 박사는 LEADER에 대한 사전적 의미에 성서적 의미를 함축하면서 LEADER의 단어의 여섯 자의 스펠링을 따서 편의상 한자 한자에 지도자의 의미와 지도력 그리고 수행자의 의미[74] 로 다음과 같이 설명 분석하였다.

LEADER는 누구인가?

L (Learner) = 지도자는 배우는 사람이다.

E (Educator) = 지도자는 가르치는 사람이다.

A (Administrator) = 지도자는 다스리는 사람이다.

D (Doer) = 지도자는 실천하는 사람이다.

E (Encourager) = 지도자는 격려하는 사람이다.

R (Reviewer) = 지도자는 재검토하는 사람이다.

LEADERSHIP이란 무엇인가?

L (Listening) = 잘 들어 주는 것이다.

E (Establishing) = 조직을 구성해 이끌어 가는 것이다.

A (Achieving) = 목적을 성취하는 것이다.

D (Decision) = 의사를 결정 하는 것이다.

E (Exampling) = 본이 되는 것이다.

R (Responsibility) = 책임을 질 줄 아는 것이다.

S (Spiritual Gifts) = 성령의 은사에 속하는 것이다.

H (Humbleness) = 겸손을 통해 감화를 주는 것이다.

---

74) 황의영, 교회의 직임과 리더십, (서울 ; 생명의 말씀사, 1993.), pp. 136-174 참조.

I (Integrity) = 정직성을 보여 주는 것이다.

P (Pioneer) = 개척자가 되는 것이다.

FOLLOWER란 누구인가?

F (Fruit bearer) = 열매 맺는 사람이다.

O (Obeyer) = 순종하는 사람이다.

L (Layperson) = 평신도의 한 사람이다.

L (Loyalist) = 충성하는 사람이다.

O (Operator) = 작동하는 사람이다.

W (Worker) = 일하는 사람이다.

E (Enabler) = 촉진하는 사람이다.

R (Reproducer) = 재생산하는 사람이다.

다음으로 지도자에 대한 제 학자들이 언급한 견해는 다음과 같다.

ⓐ 리차드 울프(Richard Wolff)는 "지도자란 길을 알고 앞에 설 수 있으며 다른 사람들로 하여금 자기를 따라 오도록 할 수 있는 사람이다"[75]고 정의했다.

성경에 나타난 지도자의 공통점을 바로 여기에서 찾을 수 있다. 그것은 하나님이 이스라엘 백성들을 인도하실 때 언제나 이스라엘 민족 앞에서 낮에는 구름기둥으로 밤에는 불기둥으로 인도하심에서 그 의미를 찾을 수 있으며,[76] 여기서 "그들 앞에 행하사"라는 말씀은 하나님이 구름기둥과 불기둥으로 인도하심을 강조하는 말이다. 이것은 이스라엘의 진정한 통솔권자, 즉 지도자는 오직 여호와 하

---

75) Richard Wolff, *Man of the Top.*, (Wheaton, Ⅲ, : Tyndale, 1969), p. 13.
76) 출애굽기 13:21-22.

나님뿐이심을 선포하는 것이기도 한 것이다.

지도자는 상황에 따라 변하는 것이 아니라 항상 "그룹의 앞에서" 라는 개념이 내포되어 있다 이와 같은 사람은 그룹을 이끌어 갈 수 있는 능력 또한 소유한 자로서 그와 같은 지도자에게서 지도력이 발휘 되는 것이다.

예수께서도 진정한 지도자의 의미를 말씀하시면서 양과 목자의 관계로 비유법을 사용하면서 "목자가 앞서 갈 때 양은 뒤 따른다"[77] 고 하셨다.

ⓑ 로이드 페리(Lloyd Perry)는 "지도자는 공동체에서 선택된 자로서 그의 지위와 행동으로 공동체 전체의 행동과 활동에 강력한 영향력을 행사하는 자"로 정의 했다.[78]

물론 로이드 페리의 지도자의 정의는 복음적인 목회 지도자로서의 정의가 아닌 일반 지도자론의 정의로 이해하는 것이 보다 옳을 것이다. 왜냐하면 목회 지도자는 공동체에서 선택된 자가 아니기 때문이다. 목회 지도자는 전적으로 하나님의 선택으로 출발한다.[79]

로이드 페리의 지도자 정의는 교회 일반 항존직 선택에서 적용될 수 있는 정의로 본다. 예컨대 장로, 권사, 안수집사는 공동체에서 선택되어지고,[80] 그들의 지위와 행동은 공동체 전체의 행동과 활동에 강력한 영향력을 행사할 수 있기 때문이다.

필자는 여기에서 오늘날 교회의 지도자론에 심각한 문제성을 찾고 보다 성서적이며 복음적인 지도자론을 고찰하게 된 것이다. 그

---

77) 요한복음 10:4.
78) Lloyd Perry, *Getting the Church on Target.*, (chicago : Moody, 1977), p. 30.
79) 요한복음 15:16
80) 예장 헌법 정치 제 41조, 54조

것은 공동체 선택으로 인한 지도자가 미치는 영향이 얼마나 심각한 것인가는 이미 오늘의 교회와 목회 현장에 병적으로 곪아가고 있는 현상을 간과할 수 없기 때문이다. 공동체 선택이 복음적이지 못할 때 그 공동체가 그 지도자로 인하여 겪는 악순환이 얼마나 큰 것인가를 생각하지 않을 수 없는 것이다.

예컨데 사울왕 같은 경우는 하나님의 선택을 받은 후 공동체를 통하여 제비뽑기로 선택되어 그의 지도자로서의 직무를 수행하게 되었으나 그의 행위가 공동체 전체에 미친 영향이 너무도 중요했던 것을 성경에서 찾아볼 수 있다. 따라서 지도자의 선택은 참으로 중요한 일이 아닐 수 없는 것이다.

ⓒ 엥스트롬(Ted W. Engstrom)은 "지도자란 다른 사람의 활동을 이끌어 주고, 그러한 행동이 일어나도록 그 자신 스스로 행동하고 이룩하는 사람을 의미한다."고 정의 했다.[81]

엥스트롬의 정의는 예수 그리스도에게서도 찾을 수 있는 정의다. 예수는 언제나 제자들에게 가르칠 때마다 자신이 먼저 행동하고 제자들로 하여금 자신의 가르침대로 행하게 하셨던 것이다.

복음적인 지도자론에서 고찰하겠지만 겸손을 가르치면서 몸소 겸손을 실천하셨고, 사랑을 가르치면서 사랑을 실천하셨고, 용서를 가르치면서 용서를 실천하셨고, 긍휼을 가르치면서 긍휼을 실천하셨고, 섬김을 가르치면서 섬김을 실천하셨던 것이다. 이것이 진정한 지도자의 참 모습인 것이다.

---

81) Ted W. Engstrom, *The Making of a Christian Leader*,(Zondervan, Grand Rapid Mi, 1976), p. 24.

ⓓ 호만즈(C.C.Homans)는 "지도자란 상호작용을 일으키는 자"[82] 로 정의 했다.

ⓔ 굿윈 II세(Bennie E. Goodwin)은 "효과적인 지도자는 적합한 시기, 적합한 장소에서 적절한 사람들에게 의하여 바른 일이 성취 되도록 이끄는 사람"[83]으로 정의했다.

세례요한의 경우만 하더라도 자기를 알고, 자기의 할 일을 알고, 어려울 때 바른 결단을 내림으로써 그는 참 지도자로서의 모습을 보여 주었다. 세례요한은 예수에게 세례를 주고,[84] 많은 백성들 앞에서 자기가 해야 할 일이 예수의 오심을 증거하는 것임을 알고 그 일을 광야에서 수행하면서,[85] 자신의 제자가 예수를 따르게 되었을 때 올바른 결단을 내리면서,[86] 지도자로서의 참 모습을 보여주었던 것이다.

굿윈이 정의한 대로 자신의 개인적인 욕망이나 의지를 성취하려는 것이 아니라 바른 일이 성취되도록 따르는 자들을 이끌어 가는 지도자가 참 지도자의 모습인 것이다.

ⓕ 케틀(R. Cattel)은 "지도자는 집단의 업무를 수행하는데 있어서 가장 효과적인 변화를 만들어 내는 자"[87]로 정의 했다.

---

82) 송광택, 기독교 지도자의 Personality에 관한 연구, p. 10. 재인용.
83) Beennie E. Goodwin II, *The Effective Leader*, (I.V.P. Downers Grove, III. 1981), p.11.
84) 마가복음 1:9.
85) 마태복음 3:1-12, 마가복음 1:1-8, 누가복음3:1-14, 요한복음 1:15-28.
86) 요한복음 3:22-30.
87) R.B.Cattell, *The Dimension of Syntality in Small Group*, (Human Relations, 1953.), p.6.

ⓖ 테드(Ordway Tead)는 "지도자란 그룹에 소속된 사람들로 하여금 그룹의 목표를 성취하기 위하여 행복하게, 그리고 만족스럽게 일하는 경험을 하도록 활동하게 만드는 방법을 아는 자"[88]로 정의 했다.

ⓗ 트루만(Harry Shippe Truman) 은 "지도자란 사람들이 싫어하는 일을 할 수 있도록 시킬 수 있는 영향력을 가진 사람이다. 유능한 지도자는 저들이 싫어하던 일을 좋아하면서 일을 하도록 영향을 줄 수 있는 능력을 가진 사람이다"[89]

이상의 제 학자들의 견해를 종합하여 볼 때 지도자는 피지도자들에 대한 지도력의 발휘라고 할 수 있겠다. 물론 지도력은 개인별로 차이가 있겠지만 보편적으로 지도자에게는 지도력에 영향을 미치는 것으로 보이는 몇 가지 중요한 특성에 대하여 Keith Davis는 다음과 같이 언급하고 있다.[90]

첫째는 지능(intelligence)로서 일반적으로 지도자는 추종자들의 평균 지능보다 높은 지능을 갖고 있다는 것이다.

둘째는 사회적 성숙도와 풍부함(social maturity and breadth)인데 지도자는 감정적으로 안정되어 있으며 숙성한 편이고 풍부한 관심을 가지고 행동하는 경향이 있는 것이다.

셋째는 내적 동기부여와 성취추진력(inner motivation and achievement drives)로써 지도자는 성취에 대해서 상대적으로 강

---

88) Ordway Tead, *The Art of Leadership.*, (N. Y. : Whittlesey House, 1935), p. 7.
89) Charles R. Swindoll, *Hand Me Another Brick,* (Tran, Jonathan M. Kwon, Voice, Seoul, 1982). pp. 14-15.
90) Keith Davis, *Human Relation at Work, 4th ed.*, (McGraw-Hill, 1972), pp. 103-104.

하게 동기 부여된 추진력을 가지고 있는 것이다.

넷째는 인간관계적 태도(human relations attitude)인데 훌륭한 지도자는 추종자들의 가치와 존엄성을 인정하며 강조하는 것이다.

휘들러(F. E. Fiedler)는 지도자의 지도력 발휘는 집단 구성원과의 상호작용 유형과 상황성에 따라 결정이 된다고 보았다. 그의 연구 결과는 개인적으로 지도력에 영향을 미치는 것은 사실이겠지만 이러한 것이 지도력을 결정하는 절대적인 요인은 된다고 할 수 없을 것이다. 왜냐하면 개인적 특성이라는 것은 추상적이기 때문에 경우에 따라서 혹은 사람에 따라서 다르기 때문이다. 이처럼 유능한 지도자는 상황에 대처하는 능력을 갖고 있어야 한다. 왜냐하면 탁월한 지도자는 상황에 따라 자신의 지도력 행위를 신축성 있게 조정하기도 하고 적응하기도 하기 때문이다. 이와 같은 휘들러의 지도력의 이론과 연구는 목회 지도력에 있어서 의미 있는 연구로 보면서 지도력 분야에서 중요한 발전에 기여한 것은 의문의 여지가 없다. 그리고 휘들러의 상황 연구모델은 계속 연구가 되어야 할 것으로 본다.

필자는 휘들러의 이론에 공감하면서 목회 지도자의 지도력의 관계에 있어서 작용하는 요인은 다음과 같다.

첫째는 지도자와 구성원과의 관계(leader-member relationship)인데 이것은 지도자와 구성원과의 개별적인 관계를 말한다. 즉 상황호의성(situational favorableness)을 결정하는 가장 중요한 요인이 되는 것이다.

둘째는 과업 구조의 정도(degree of task structure)로서 이것은 각 집단에 할당된 여러 가지 과업들이 얼마나 명확하게 결정, 시달되어 있는가 하는 정도를 뜻하는 것인데 호의성결정(好意性決定)에 있어서 두 번째 중요한 요인이 된다.

셋째는 지도자의 직위 권한(leader's position power)로서 이것은 지도자의 직위에서 공적 권한으로부터 인정받는 지배력, 즉 권력을 의미한다.

2) 지도력에 대한 정의(The Definition of Leadership)

미국의 정치학자 번즈(James M. Burns)는 "리더십이란 말에 대한 정의가 130가지나 된다. 그럼에도 아직까지 보편적으로 받아들여질 수 있는 리더십에 대한 정의는 정립되지 않았다"[91] 고 언급한 바 있다.

필자 역시 전술한 바와 같이 지도자의 정의는 다양하여 한 마디로 정의하기 어려우나 지도자를 피지도자에 대한 지도력으로 포괄적으로 정의 한 바 있다.

① 리더십이란 어원과 그 유래

리더십의 어원은 앵글로 색슨어(Anglo-Saxon)의 '레단'(ledan)에서 나온 것으로 '리탄'(lithan)이 어근이다. 이것은 '간다'(to go)라는 뜻의 움직임을 나타내는 동적인 성격을 갖고 있는 용어다.[92] 따라서 지

---

91) James MacGregor Burns, *Leadership*, (New York : Harper and Row, 1978), p. 2.
92) H. Q. Dept. of the U.S.Army Military Leadership F.M. 22-100, 1961. (육군본부 군 통솔력(군야전교법) 22-100, 서울, 1964), p. 5.

도자는 무슨 일을 먼저 행하는 사람, 먼저 이루는 자를 뜻한다. 그러므로 지도자는 선두자, 안내자의 역할을 하게 되며 그룹의 앞에서 걸어간다는 의미를 갖고 있는 것이다.

지도력이란 말이 일반화된 것은 진술한 바와 같이 1800년대 이후 영국에서 이나, '리더'라는 어휘가 처음으로 언급된 것은 1,300년대로 보며, '리더십'이란 어휘는 1,800년 까지는 등장되지 않았다고 옥스퍼드 사전에서 밝히고 있다.[93]

② 리더십에 대한 연구의 약사

리더십에 관한 연구는 1900년대에 이르러 활발하게 연구되었다. 특히 리더십에 중요한 영향을 미친 대학 가운데 Iowa대학을 들 수 있다. 이 Iowa 대학은 집단 역학(Group dynamics)의 선구자인 K.Lewin의 지도 아래 1930년대 후반 P.Lippitt와 R.K.White에 의해 Iowa대학에서 선도적 연구가 있었고,[94] 이 연구는 3rd 리더십의 유형, 즉 전제적, 민주적, 자유방임적 리더십을 가정하고 있는데,[95] 이 결과로서 리더십의 개념정리를 일반화 하는 데는 실패하였다. 그 이유는 경영관리론적 입장에서 리더십의 연구로써 특히 복음적 목회적 리더십으로서는 근본적으로 그 개념을 달리할 수 있는 것이다.

---

93) R. M. Stogdill, *op.cit.* p. 7.
94) F.Luthans, *Organizational Behavior*, 3rd ed., (McGraw-Hill, 1981), p.44.
95) K.Lewin, R.Lippitt, and R.K.White, *Patterns of Aggressive Behavior in Experimentally Created* ⟨Social Climates, (Journal of Psychology, May 1939), pp.271-276.

그 후 1945년 Ohio대학에서도 리더십에 관한 연구가 있었는데 이 연구는 리더의 행동에 관한 여러 가지 차원을 분석한 것이었으며,[96] 1947년 Michigan대학에서도 리더십 연구가 있었는데 그것은 집단 생산성과 집단 구성원들의 참여로 인한 만족감에 기여하는 원칙을 규명하려는 것이 목적 이었다.[97]

이와 같은 미시간 대학의 리더십 연구는 인간관계론 자들이 그들의 이론을 설명하고자 할 때마다 인용하는 근거가 된 것은 평가할만한 것이었다.[98]

일반적으로 리더십에는 사회 정치적 개념과 경영 관리적 개념, 그리고 행동과학적 개념으로 분류가 되기도 하고, 또는 퍼스널리티의 특성(Personality Traits)에 근거하여, 리더가 발휘하는 영향력에 중점을 두고, 집단의 변화를 가져오는 집단상황(Group Situation)을 강조하는 입장에서, 그리고 추종자들의 행동방향의 공통성과 이해의 일치를 전제로하여 인간관계(Human Relations)와 이의 상호작용(Interaction)의 측면에서 리더십을 정의하려는 것으로 분류할 수 있다. 따라서 리더십은 조직체의 외부 환경의 적응, 내부조직의 안정, 그리고 조직체의 기본 성격을 형성하는 중요한 역할로 보면서 리더십의 중요 기능으로 첫째는 조직체의 사명

---

96) R.M.Stogdill, and A.E.Coons, eds., *Leader Behavior:Its Description and Measurement*, Research Monograph, No. 88, (Ohio State University, Bureau of Business Research, 1957)참조
97) Rensis Likertm, "*Foreward*," in Daniel Katz, Nathan Maccoby, and Nancy C. Morse, *Productivity, Superuision and Morale in An Office Situation*, (University of Michigan, Survey Research Center, 1950)참조.
98) F. Luthans, *Organizational Behavior, 3rd ed.*, (McGraw-Hill, 1981), pp. 417-418.

과 사회적 역할의 설정, 둘째는 조직체 목적의 제도적 구현, 셋째
는 조직체의 제도적 구현, 넷째는 조직체 내부의 갈등 조정의 기능
을 말한다.[99]

경영관리적 개념으로는 리더십을 조직체의 경영관리 각층에
서 수행하는 보편적 기능으로 본다. 일반적으로 경영관리 과
정은 기획(planning), 조직(organizing), 지휘(directing), 통제
(controlling)의 기본 기능으로 구분 되는데,[100] 그 중에서도 지휘 기
능을 리더십과 동일시하고 있음을 볼 수 있다.[101]

근자에 이르러서는 행동과학 분야에서 리더십은 어떤 조직 상황
하에서 어떠한 목적을 달성하기 위하여 집단 구성원에게 영향을
주는 과정으로 이해하는데 여기에는 다음과 같은 몇 가지 기본 요
소가 포함된다.[102]

첫째는 지도자(Leader) 둘째는 추종자, 또는 수행자(Follower),
셋째는 상황 변수(situational variables)이다.[103]

---

99) Philip Selznick, *Leadership in Administration*(New York : Harper And
Row Publishers, 1957), pp. 61-64, 135-138. 참조.
100) Harold Koontz and Cyril O'Donnell, *Principles of Management : An
Analysis of Management unctions*, 5th ed. (New York : McGraw-Hill Book
Company, 1972.), p557.
101) *Ibid.*, p. 557.
102) Ralph M. Stogdill, Definition of Leadership, *Handbook of Leadership.*
(New York :Free Press, 1974), pp. 7-16. 참조.
103) 이 같은 요소를 제시한 대표적인 학자는 다음과 같다.
　* P. Hersey / K.H.Blanchard, *Management of Organizational Behavior,*
　　(Prentice-hall, 1982, 4th) p.83.
　* R.E.Rogers / R.H McIntire, *Organization and Management Theory,* (Wiley
　　& Sons, 1983), p. 171.

이것을 아래와 같은 함수로 표현할 수 있다.

$$L = F (i.\ f.\ s)$$

$$\mathbf{L} = \text{Leadership} \qquad l = \text{leader}$$
$$f = \text{follower}$$
$$s = \text{situation}$$

리더십의 개념 정의에 있어서 행동과학적 개념이 일반적 개념과 몇 가지 차이점을 찾아볼 수 있다.

첫째는 일반 사회적 개념은 리더십을 사회나 조직체의 상위 계층에 국한하는 반면에 행동과학적 개념은 집단 구성원 모두가 발휘할 수 있는 보편적인 기능이나 역할로 보고 있다.

둘째는 경영 관리적 개념은 리더십을 주로 공식적인 직위 관점에서 보는 경향이 많고 특히 고전적 경영관리 개념에서 이러한 개념이 현저히 나타나고 있는데, [104] 이에 비하여 행동과학적 개념은 자생적인 관점에서 구성원들간의 상호관계를 중요시 하고 있는 것이다.

따라서 리더십의 개념에 관해서는 통일성 있는 정의를 내리기가 어려운 것이 사실이다. 이와 같은 일반적으로 리더십에 관하여 연구, 토의는 지금까지 많은 관심을 집중시키는 것은 물론 리더십의 중요성을 인식하면서도 그 본질적 개념과 기본적 특성에 대해서는 아직 통일적인 이해와 인식은 이루어지지 않고 있는 실정이다.

③ 리더십에 대한 정의

스토그딜(R.M.Stogdill)이 "리더십의 정의는 그 개념을 정의 하

---

104) Henri Fayol, *General and Industrial Administration* (New York: Pitman Publishing Company, (1949).

고자 시도하는 사람들의 수 만큼이나 많다[105] 고 언급한 것처럼 전술한 바와 같이 리더십에 대한 정의는 130가지나 되나 일반화된 정의는 없다 따라서 본 항에서는 제 학자들의 정의를 살펴보고 복음적 리더십에 대한 정의를 4)장에서 언급하고자 한다.

ⓐ **W.G.Bennis**는 "리더십은 타인을 자기가 바라는 방법으로 행동하도록 유도하는 과정"[106]이라고 정의 했다.

ⓑ **A.D.Szilagyi** 는 "리더십은 목표 달성을 위하여 어떤 사람이 다른 사람에게 영향을 미치려고 하는 두 사람 이상 사이의 관계에 관련된 과정이다"[107]라고 정의 했다.

ⓒ **K.Davis**는 "리더십이란 다른 사람들이 목표를 향하여 열심히 일하도록 용기를 주고 도와주는 하나의 과정이다"고 정의했다. [108]

ⓓ **R.M.Hodgetts**는 "리더십이란 어떤 특정한 목적의 달성에로 사람들의 노력을 인도(direct)하기 위해 그들에게 영향을 미치는

---

105) R.M.Stogdill, *Handbook of Leadership ; A Survey of Theory and Research.* (New York: The Free Press, 1974), p. 259.
106) Warren G. Bennis, *Leadership Theory and Administrative Behavior : The Problem of Authority*, (Administrative Science Quartery, Vol.4, 1959), pp.259-301
107) A.D.Szilagyi / M.J.Wallace, Organization Behavior and Performance, (Scott, Foresman, 1983), p. 265.
108) K.Davis / J.W.Newstrom, *Human Behavior at Work,* (McGraw-hill, 1985), p.158.

과정이다"고 했다. [109]

ⓔ **E.P.Hollander**는 "리더십이란 집단, 조직 및 사회의 목적과 같은 서로의 목적 달성을 위해 자기의 추종자(follower)들에게 영향을 미치는 과정이다"고 정의 했다. [110]

ⓕ **A.G.Jago**와 **R.B.Dunham**은 "리더십이란 하나의 과정이고 속성(property)이다. 리더십의 과정은 특정한 목적을 달성하기 위해 조직화 된 집단 구성원의 활동을 지휘하고 협조시키기 위해 사용하는 비강제적인 영향활동이다.

그리고 리더십 속성은 그 같은 영향력을 성공적으로 발휘 하는 것이라고 지각된 사람에 귀속된 일련의 특성이다"고 정의 했다. [111]

ⓖ **Engstrom**은 "리더십이란 그 정의를 내리기가 매우 힘들지만 모든 지도자들에게 한 가지 공통되는 특징은 저들에게는 '일을 만들어 가는 능력'(The Ability To make things happen)이 있다. 그것은 바로 그의 지도하에 있는 자들에게 적절한 격려와 자극을 줌으로 저들이 소유한 잠재력을 총동원하여 의미있게 헌신하도록 만드는 행동"이라고 정의 했다. [112]

---

109) R.M.Hodgetts, *Management;Theory, Process, and Practice*, (Academic Press, 1986), p.516.
110) E.P.Hollander, *Leadership Dynamics*, (Free Press, 1978) pp.1-2 및K.H. Chung, *Management*, (Allyn and Bacon, 1987), p.358.
111) A.G.Jago, *Leadership:Perspectives in Theory and Research*,(Management Science,1982)p.28. 및 R.B.Dunham, *Organizational Behavior:People and Process in Management*, (Irwin, 1984), p. 362.
112) Ted W. Engstrom, *op. cit.*, p.20.

ⓗ **Lloyd Perry**와 **swindoll**은 "리더십은 영향력이다"고 간단하게 정의했다. [113]

ⓘ **Gangel**은 "리더십이란 하나의 그룹 활동에 있어 그 그룹에 속한 다른 모든 사람들을 인도하는 책임을 수행하는 것이다."[114]

ⓙ **Kimball Young**은 "리더십이란 타인의 행동을 통제하고 지휘하며 비판하는 능력"으로 정의 했다. [115]

ⓚ **Paul Pigors**는 "리더십이란 특정한 퍼스널리티의 소유자가 공통의 문제를 추구하는데 있어서 그의 의지나 감정 및 통찰력 등으로 다른 사람을 이끌고 다스리는 특성"이라고 정의 했다. [116]

ⓜ **Paul Hersey**는 "리더십은 지도자, 부하, 상황 등과 관련되는 변수가 상호의존성을 가지면서 작용하는 과정이다"라고 했다. [117]

ⓝ **Dimock**는 "리더십이란 조직 목표의 달성을 위하여 구성원이

---

113) Lloyd Perry, *op. cit.*, p. 75. and Charles R. Swindoll, *Hand Me Another Brick*, (Tran, Jonathan M. Kwon, Voice, Seoul, 1982). pp. 14-15.
114) Kenneth O. Gangel, *Building Leaders For Church Education.* (Chicago: Moody Press,1981) p.15
115) Kimball Young, *Handbook of Social Psychology*, (New York ; Appleton Century- croffts, 1951), p. 562.
116) Paul Pigors, *Leadership of domination*, (Boston ; Houghton-Mifflin Co. 1953), p. 12.
117) Paul Hersey and Kenneth H. Blanchard, *Management of Organizational Behavior :Utilizing Human Resources*, 3rd edition (Englewood Cliffs, N. J. :Prentice-Hall, 1977),p.84.

자발적으로 적극적 행동을 하도록 동기를 부여하고 영향력을 미치며 개인과 집단의 조정을 통하여 협동저구 행동을 촉진하고 유도하는 쇄신적, 창의적인 능력과 기술을 의미한다."고 했다.[118]

◎ 동양적 관점에서 리더십에 대한 견해로 손자의 '병법'(兵法)을 들 수 있는데, 손자병법에 "將者智信仁勇嚴也"라는 말이 나오는데 이는 지도자가 갖추어야 할 다섯 가지의 자질(五德)을 말하는데 다음과 같다.[119]

첫째 지(智)는 정확한 상황 판단과 합리적인 결정을 하는데 필요한 지성이다.

둘째 신(信)은 지도자와 그 추종자들과의 상호신뢰를 말한다.

셋째 인(仁)은 지도자는 자애심(慈愛心)과 인덕(仁德)이 있어야 하는 것이다.

넷째 용(勇)은 결단력과 실행력에 필요한 용기를 말한다.

다섯째 엄(嚴)은 규율의 엄정을 말한다.

이와 같은 손자의 지도력은 윤리와 도덕을 바탕으로 하고 있음을 볼 수 있다.

이상에서 다양하게 언급된 제 학자들의 견해를 종합해 보면 리더십은 관점과 역할과 상황에 따라 다양하므로 한 마디로 일반화하기 어렵다는 것이다. 그러나 분명한 사실은 리더와 리더십에 관한 다양한 분석에 크게 기여한 점이고, 또 리더십이란 지도자와 피

---

118) Marshall E. Dimock and Gladys O. Dimock, *Public Administration*, 4th edition (New York:Holt, Rinehart and Winston, 1969), p. 296; Keith Davis, *Human Behavior at Work*, 5th ed. (New York: McGraw-Hill, 1977), p. 107.
119) 占部都美, 張韋相 역, 指導力, (서울;한국경영기술개발공사, 1970), p. 5.

지도자를 통한 바람직한 목적의 능력수행으로 볼 수 있겠다.

그러나 본 연구는 복음적 지도자상을 모색하는데 있으므로 교회와 사회라는 양면적인 특수한 상황 속에서 복음적 리더와 리더십에 관한 정의가 언급되어야 하며 이를 필자가 다음 장에서 언급하고자 한다.

3) 지도자와 지도력의 어휘적 의미적 관계

전술한 바와 같이 지도자와 지도력에 관하여 개괄적인 의미를 살펴보았다. 그러나 지금까지'지도자'와'지도력'이라는 말이 혼용되어 사용되어 왔기 때문에 그 어휘적 의미 관계를 살펴 볼 필요가 있다. 양 어휘에 대한 사전적 의미는'지도자'는 영어로 Leader 이고'지도력'은 Leadership 으로 구별하고 쓰이고 있다.

일반적으로는 두 어휘는 두 가지의 어의적 뜻이 내포된다. 하나는 행위이며 다른 하나는 행위의 방법, 능력을 의미할 수 있다. 대개 사회과학자들은 리더십을 "집단 목표를 성취하기 위해 사람들을 동원 조직하는 행동 과정"[120]으로 정의 하고, 또 "리더십은 사람들이 바라는 특별 목표를 성취하도록 행동에 영향력을 행사함을 말한다.... 지도(leading)에 있어서 중요한 특징은 지도자를 따르는 추종자들의 자기 성취감과 만족감이다."(Leadership is the activities of influencing people to cooperate some goal which they come to find desirable … the unique emphasis in the idea of leading …. is upon the satisfaction and sense of self-

---

120) Julius Gould and William L.Kolb(ed), A Dictionary *of the Social Sciences* (UNESCO : Free Press of Glencoe, 1964)

fulfilment secured by the followers of the true leader...)[121] 라고 정의한다.

이것은 지도자는 그 자신이 갖고 있는 능력과 자질을 통해서 추종자(followers)로 하여금 지지와 협력을 얻는 동시에 그들에게 얼마만큼의 만족감과 성취감을 주는가 하는데서 지도력이 정의되는 것이다. 따라서 지도나 지도력은 개인과 집단의 협조는 그들과 상호작용하는 지도자의 역할이 없이는 실현될 수 없다. 즉 "리더십은 개인행동과 집단행동의 형성은 물론 이들 행동을 조직체의 성과에 연결시키는 가장 중요한 요인이 되는 것이다"[122]

4) 복음적 리더와 리더십

필자가 언급한 복음적 리더와 리더십이란 학계에 생소한 어휘이나 이를 예수 그리스도의 리더십이란 말로 마이클 유(Michael Youssef)는 그의 저서 「The Leadership Style of Jesus」에서 사용한 바 있다.[123] 복음적 리더와 리더십이란 바로 예수 그리스도의 복음에 근간한 리더와 리더십을 말한다. 이 복음적 리더와 리더십은 온 인류의 종결적 계시자요 온 인류의 소망되신 유일무이(唯一無二)한 참 지도자이신 예수 그리스도의 선포하신 말씀과 그의 의중과 삶을 통해 주어지는 것으로 지금까지 지구상에서 제 학자들이

---

121) Paul Piger, *Leadership or Domination*, (London : George Harrap, 1935) ; Ordway Tead, *The Art of Leadership*, (New York : Whittlessey House, 1935), p. 20.

122) Jonathan E. Smith, Kenneth P. Carson, and Ralph A. Alexander, "Leadership; It Can Make a Difference." *Academy of Management Journal* (December 1984), pp. 765-776.

123) Michael Youssef, *The Leadership Style of Jesus*: Victor Books, 1980.

언급한 모든 지도자와 지도자론의 근본이며 그 본질로 삼는다. 그
럼 복음적 지도자는 어떤 사람인가?

　첫째 복음적 지도자는 복음 그 자체이신 예수 그리스도를 통해
"클레토이"와 "에클레토이"와 "피스토이"한 자들로서 복음을 믿고 복
음을 따르고 복음을 증거하며, 복음의 훈련을 통해 세워진 자들을 말
한다.
　이 복음은 정치적으로나 사회적으로 그리고 종교적으로 가정과
사회와 교회와 국가와 세계에 적용할 수 있는 원리가 곧 복음이기
때문에[124] 복음적 지도자야 말로 우리가 추구해야 할 가장 이상적
모델이다. 따라서 복음적 지도력 역시 복음에서 출발하여 종결되
어지는 것이다.

　둘째 복음적인 지도자는 복음을 가르쳐야 한다.
　복음적 지도자는 복음만을 가르쳐야 한다. 만약 유대종교나 회
당종교의 가르침을 답습하거나 율법과 교리와 신조와 신학과 교회
법과 동일하게 두고 가르친다면 복음적 지도자가 될 수 없다. 예수
그리스도의 복음은 율법의 완성이요 모든 교리나 교회법이나 각종
신조나 신학의 근본이며 완성자이기 때문이다. 특히 예수 그리스
도의 복음은 예수 그리스도에 대한(about) 복음이 아니라 예수 그
리스도의(of) 복음을 말한다.[125]
　예수 그리스도의 복음의 본질은 무엇인가? 예수 그리스도의 복
음은 사랑과 용서와 섬김이다. 예수 그리스도의 사랑은 에로스

---

124) 손병호, 복음신학 원리, (서울; 도서출판 그리인, 1992.), p.41.
125) *Ibid.*, p.16.

(ἔρος), 필리아(φιλία), 스톨루게(στοργή),가 아닌 아가페(ἀγάπη)로서 하나님 사랑(love to God)과 하나님 안에서의 자기사랑(love to self in God)과 원수사랑(love your enemies)을 포함한 이웃사랑(love to neighbor)으로 예수님은 새 계명으로 명령하셨다.[126]

셋째 복음적인 지도자는 복음으로 다스리는 것이다.

복음은 지배의 도가 아닌 섬김의 도이다. 섬김이란 말은 디아코노스(διακονος)로서 영어권에서는 Servant, Minister, Serve로 봉사와 나눔의 의미를 지닌다. 예수 그리스도의 삶 자체가 바로 섬김의 도였다. 예수 그리스도는 이 땅에 성육신 하신 목적을 섬김에 있음을 선포하였다. "인자가 온 것은 섬김을 받으려 함이 아니라 도리어 섬기려 하고"(막10:45)라고 선언하였기 때문이다.그러므로 복음적 지도자와 일반적인 지도자와는 전혀 다른 리더십이 있다. 가령 일반적 지도자는 지배와 통치로 다스리면서 지도력을 발휘하지만 복음적인 지도자는 섬김의 복음으로 지도력을 나타낸다. 또 일반적인 지도자에게서는 다스림의 원리와 도구와 방법이 창과 칼, 가해와 지배, 정복과 군림과 처단이다. 또 율법적 지도자는 정죄와 출교를 이단시하는 것이다. 그러나 복음적 지도자는 사랑과 용서와 섬김의 안내자이기 때문이다. 뿐만 아니라 복음적인 지도자는 종교 사업이나 왕국적이거나 제국적인 선교를 통하여 군림하는 이른 바 로마 카톨릭적 지도자 상에 있지 아니하고, 오직 뜻이 하늘에서 이루어진 것같이 땅에서도 이루어지게 하는데 그 사명으로 행하는 지도자를 말한다.

---

126) 황보갑, *op.cit.*,p. 175.

넷째 복음적인 지도자는 복음을 실천하는 사람이다.

예수 그리스도는 행위의 복음 그 자체였다. 세상에서 가난하고 세리와 창기의 친구가 되셨으며 죄인의 구주가 되셨다. 그러므로 예수 그리스도의 복음은 산 위에 있는 동네와 같이 언제나 희생과 봉사가 동반된 삶 그 자체로 가시화 되었다. 이 같은 복음으로 세우심을 받은 복음적 지도자는 삶 그 자체가 복음적 삶이여야 한다.

언제나 복음 앞에서 소신 있게 행동하며, 대도(大道)와 정도(正道)와 성령의 도우심에 따라 역리가 아닌 순리(順理)적 삶을 살아야 한다. 복음적인 지도자에게는 결코 변질되지 않으며, 지조와 절개와 의지를 굽히지 아니하며 타협과 협상을 하지 않고 십자가를 지고 그리스도의 삶을 실천하는 자이다.

다섯째 복음적인 지도자는 우주적 복음을 지닌 자이다.

복음은 우주적이며, 세계적이다. 민족과 인종과 국경을 초월하며, 선인과 악인을 구분하지 않으며, 누구나 하나님의 사랑의 대상이다. 그러므로 누구든지 주를 믿는 자는 구원을 주시며(요3:16) 수고하고 무거운 짐 진 자들을 부르시고 쉼을 주신다(마11:28). 하나님이 그 해를 악인과 선인에게 비춰시듯[127] 복음도 악인과 선인을 구별하지 않고 빛과 같이 모든 생명을 나게 하고 자라게 하며 꽃을 피우게 하고 양식이 되게 한다. 그래서 빛은 그리스도이며,[128] 그리스도는 생명이며,[129] 생명은 그리스도 안에 있는 것이다.[130] 사랑하

---

127) 마태복음5:45.
128) 요한복음8:12.
129) 요한복음14:6.
130) 요한복음8:12.

는 사람이 빛 가운데 거하는 자이며,[131] 이것을 먼저 체득(體得)하는 것이 복음적인 지도자이다.

반면 일반적 지도자는 악인과 선인을 구별하고 강한 자와 약한 자를 구별하고 있는 자와 없는 자를 구별하여 필요와 조건에 따라 지배하고 약탈하고 정죄하고 심판하고 종속하고 다스린다.

그러나 복음적인 지도자는 자신이 체득한 그리스도의 복음으로 모든 사람을 격려한다. 때문에 복음적인 지도자는 넓고 큰 복음의 마음으로 모든 사람을 이해와 포용과 관용과 섬김의 자세로 사람들을 천국으로 안내하는 자이다.

여섯째 복음적인 지도자는 모든 일을 복음으로 재검토하는 자이다.

복음적인 지도자는 모든 일의 궁극적인 목적을 하나님의 영광에 둔다. 때문에 성서에 나타난 하나님의 복음을 모든 교회법이나 신학위에 두므로 신학적인 양식 비평(Form Criticism), 자료 비평(Source Criticism), 편집 비평(Redaction Criticism)을 학문적으로는 가능하다고 인정하지만, 복음을 믿고 따르고 행하는 것을 그 본질적 사명으로 삼는다. 따라서 주어진 과업을 이행함에 있어 역사적으로 교리적으로 제도적으로 신학적으로 검토하는 것이 아니라 예수그리스도의 복음으로 모든 일을 검토한다.

복음에는 비판이 해당되지 아니할 뿐 아니라 "원수를 사랑하라"는 역설이 이해되어지는 것도 그리스도의 말씀이 곧 복음이기에 그대로 믿고 따르면서 행하는 것이다.

다음으로 복음적 지도자에 대한 성서적 신학적 원리를 살펴보면

---

131) 요한1서2:10.

다음과 같다.

첫째, 선택된 사람

복음적 지도자의 세움의 원리는 먼저 하나님께 선택된 자이며 다음으로는 그룹에서도 선택된 자이다. 특히 기독교 지도자는 전적으로 하나님의 선택에서 출발되며 거룩하신 뜻을 이루는데 목표를 두는 것이다.[132]

복음적인 지도자는 선택의 성경적 원리에 따르면 그룹에서 우선적으로 선택된 자가 아니다. 전적으로 하나님의 선택에서 출발되어진다. 이에 관해서는 다음에서 복음적인 지도자에 관해 보다 구체적으로 고찰하고자 한다.

구약의 모든 지도자들이 하나님의 선택을 받았다. 아브라함을 선택하셨을 때는 그 마음이 주 앞에서 충성됨을 보셨기 때문이며,[133] 야곱의 선택,[134] 레위인의 선택,[135] 아론의 선택,[136] 다윗의 선택,[137] 예레미야의 선택[138] 등은 전적 하나님의 택하심에서 지도자로서 출발된 것을 볼 수 있다.

이들의 택정함은 자신의 결단과 의지에 기인된 것은 아니었다. 전적으로 하나님의 뜻과 계획에 의해서 이루어진 것임을 볼 수 있다. 아모스의 경우도 자신은 전혀 예언자로 나설 계획이 없었지만

---

132) 요한복음 15:16-17.
133) 느헤미야 9:7-8.
134) 창세기 25:23.
135) 신명기 18:5, 21:5, 역대상 15:2.
136) 시105:26.
137) 사무엘상 10;34, 16:8-10, 사무엘하 6:21, 시편 78:70.
138) 예레미야 1:5.

하나님의 택하심에 따라 이스라엘의 지도자로 앞장 설 수 있게 되었던 것이었다.[139]

그리고 하나님의 선택을 받고서도 다음으로 제비뽑기를 통한 그룹의 선택을 받은 지도자도 있었다. 이스라엘의 왕 사울이 하나님의 택하심을 입고[140] 사무엘을 통하여 기름부음을 받은 후 이스라엘 백성들 중에서 제비뽑기를 통하여[141] 그룹에서 선택함을 받게 되고[142] 왕으로 즉위하게 되었다.

지도자는 하나님의 선택과 그룹의 택함을 받은 자이다.

둘째, 그룹의 지도자

지도자란 혼자서 될 수 있는 것이 아니라 수행자, 혹은 추종자(follower)를 전제로 한다는 것이다. 그러므로 지도자는 수행자 앞에 있는 자로 정의할 수 있는 것이다. 이것은 그룹의 우두머리(chief)를 뜻하기도 하지만 보스(boss)[143] 와는 구별된다.

'근대세계정치백과사전'에서는 정치적으로 보스를 정의하기를 비도의적 중수회적(非道義的 贈收賄的) 방법으로 권력을 장악하고 정략기관(政略機關)을 이용함으로써 사회와 정권을 장악하기에 이르며... 보스 정치는 그 본질상 부패적인 것이다"[144]라고 했다. 그러므로 여기서 지도자란 보스와는 구별되고 있음을 이해할 수

---

139) 아모스 7:14-15.
140) 사무엘상 9:16, 10:24.
141) 제비뽑기는 하나님의 뜻을 알기 위한 방법이었다.(수7:15참조)
142) 사무엘상 10:20-21.
143) boss는 어원상 네덜란드어의 baas에서 전용(轉用)된 말로서 네덜란드의 이민노동자가 뉴욕의 노동청부(勞動請負)의 두목을 호칭하는 말이었다.
144) W. Theimer, *An Encyclopedia of Modern World Politics*, (1950), p. 516.

있다.

지도자가 어떤 사람인가는 예수께서 말씀하신 "문지기는 그를 위하여 문을 열고 양은 그의 음성을 듣나니 그가 자기 양의 이름을 각각 불러 인도하여 내느니라. 자기 양을 다 내놓은 후에 앞서 가면 양들이 그의 음성을 아는 고로 따라오되 타인의 음성은 알지 못하는 고로 타인을 따르지 아니하고 도리어 도망 하느니라"[145] 라는 말씀에서 정의될 수 있다.

그룹 앞에서 나가면서 대중과 떨어지지 않는, 그러면서 추종자들에게 영향을 미쳐서 공동 목표를 향해 나아 갈 수 있게 하는 것이 지도자의 참 모습이다.이 모습의 참 모델이 곧 예수 그리스도이시다. 지도자로서, 구세주로서, 우리 신앙의 개척자로서, 생명의 주관자로서 제자들과 함께 하시면서 항상 앞서서 행보 하셨던 예수의 모습에서 진정한 지도자의 상황을 알 수 있다.[146] 지도자는 항상 그룹의 앞에 선 사람이다.

셋째, 리더십

지도자는 그룹의 목표를 달성하기 위하여 기획(Plan)과 시행(Do)과 검토(See)와 피드백(Feedback)을 이행하는 사람이다.

세상에는 세 가지 형태의 사람이 있는데 첫째는 무슨 일이 일어나고 있는지 전혀 모르는 사람, 둘째는 무슨 일이 일어나고 있음을 지켜보는 사람, 셋째는 무슨 일을 만드는 사람(make things

---

145) 요한복음 10:3-5.
146) 행 3:15, 5:31, 히 2:10, 12:2.

happen)이 있는데[147] 지도자는 일을 만드는 사람이다. 물론 일을 만드는데 있어서 자기 개인주의적, 이기적 일을 만드는 것이 아니라 공동체의 유익을 위한 수행자, 혹은 추종자(follower) 모두를 위한 발전적인 일을 만드는 사람인 것은 말할 나위없다.

이와 같은 지도자에게는 추진력이 있고, 그룹의 공동 목표를 향한 꿈이 있고, 그 꿈을 성취하고자 하는 믿음이 있고, 공동체를 위한 이해와 애정이 있고, 그룹을 이끌어 나아갈 수 있는 잠재력을 발휘하여 추종자들을 각각의 개인적 능력을 발휘하도록 유도하며 솔선수범하는 사람이다.

규모 없이 행하여 일을 하지 않고 일을 만드는 자가 있는가 하면,[148] 그리스도 안에서 종용히 자기양식을 먹으면서,[149] 하나님의 택하심을 깨달아 성령의 거룩하게 하심과 진리를 믿음으로 구원을 받은자는 자기의 몫을 감당하는 사람이 복음으로 부름 받은 사람이다. 오직 목적이 예수 그리스도의 영광을 얻게 하는 것이며 이와 같은 사람이 진정한 일을 만드는 자로서 지도자의 모습인 것이다.[150]

규모 없이 일을 만드는 사람은 무질서하다. 자기 본분을 깨달아 그룹을 합력하여 선을 이루게 이끌어 가는 사람은 질서 가운데서 일을 만드는 자로서 이와 같은 사람이 진정한 지도자로서의 자세인 것이다.

복음적인 지도자는 정치적, 사회적 지도자와는 그 개념을 달리

---

147) Ted W. Engstrom, *op. cit.*, p. 20. (There are Three kinds of people in the world those who don't know what's happening, those who watch what's happening, and those who make things happen.)
148) 데살로니가후서 3:11.
149) 데살로니가후서 3:12.
150) 데살로니가후서 2:13-14.

한다.

정치적 지도자는 종종 대중의 무지, 수동성(受動性), 비합리성을 이용하여 자기의 목적 내지 야심을 실현하기도 하는데 이러한 의미에서 지도자와 추종자의 이해(利害)가 대립되는 경우도 있다.

오늘날 교회 안에서 이와 같은 복음적인 지도자의 부재로 인하여 목회 지도자와 교인들간의 이해(利害)관계로 인하여 분열과 분쟁이 끊어지지 않고 있음을 볼 수 있는데 그것은 복음적인 지도자의 부재와 더불어 지도력이 결여되는데서 이루어지는 현상이라고 볼 수 있다. 진정한 지도자는 그룹의 목표를 달성하기 위하여 추진력을 가지고 일을 만들어 가는 사람이다.

넷째, 본(本)의 지도력

지도력의 가장 위대한 힘은 명령에서 보다 지도자의 본에서 발휘된다. 예수님은 언제나 본으로 그의 지도력을 발휘하셨다. 가령 섬김의 지도력은 제자의 발을 씻어 줌으로서 사랑의 본을 계시한 것이다. 구약에서‘본’에 해당되는 단어는 כ(크)라는 전치사인데 이 말은 “…처럼, …대로”라는 의미를 갖고 있으며 “너희 열조를 본받지 말라”[151] 의‘본’에 전치사 כ(크)가 적용 되었다. 이 말은 어떤 사람이나 사물의 태도나 행동, 성격, 외모에 반영된 유사함을 나타낼 때 사용된 단어이다. 신약에서는‘본’이 여러 단어로 사용되고 있다.

①‘ὑπογραμμός’(휘포그람모스)는 “글씨를 배우는 어린이들을 위하여 선을 그리다”를 의미하는데 여기서 “보여주다” “묘사하다” “그리다” “요구하다”가 파생되었다.

---

151) 스가랴 1:4.

② ‘ὑπόδειγμα’(휘포데이그마)로서 "문서" "증거"의 뜻도 함께 갖고 있으며 70인 역에서는 이 용어를 "모델" "모사품"의 의미로 사용 하였다. 이 단어의 사용은 "예언자들의 모범"[152]과 "예수님의 제자들의 발 씻기는 상호적 섬김의 모범"[153]에 사용 되었으며, 나쁜 모범에 대한 경고도 있다.[154]

③ ‘τύπος’(튀포스)는‘표‘유형’의 의미를 갖고 있는데 예수의 손에 난 못 자국을 가리킬 때 이 단어가 사용되었으며,[155] 바울이 자신이 교회에 대하여 본이 된다는 고백을 했을 때,[156] 데살로니가 교회가 다른 교회에 본이 되었을 때,[157] 사용되었다.

이처럼 지도자에게 있어서 본은 지도력에 절대적이라 할 수 있겠다. 오늘날 이 나라에 기독교인이 1,200만이라고 하나 정치적으로 경제적으로 사회적으로 종교적으로 어둠이 걷혀지지 않고 말라기 선지자 이후 400여년의 긴 역사의 혼란의 때와 마찬가지로 어둠이 짙어있음은 본의 지도력의 상실로 진단 할 수 있다. 잎만 무성한 바리새인과 서기관과 랍비들의 지도력에서 열매로 가득한 예수 그리스도의 본의 지도력으로 돌아가야 할 것이다.

끝으로, 지도자의 육성

지도자는 태어나기도 하고 길러지기도 한다. 그래서 미국의 교

---

152) 야고보서 5:10.
153) 요한복음 13:15.
154) 벧후 2:6, 히 4:11.
155) 요한복음 20:25.
156) 빌립보서 3:17, 데살로니가후서 3:9.
157) 데살로니가전서 1:7.

육학자'베니 굿윈'은 "소질 있는 지도자들은 탄생하는 것이고, 효율적인 지도자들은 만들어지는 것이다"[158]고 했다.

세익스피어도 그의 시에서 "위대한 것을 두려워 말아라. 어떤 사람들은 위대하게 태어나지만 어떤 이들은 위대함을 성취하고 어떤 사람들은 위대함이 그냥 그들을 찾아오기도 한다."[159]고 했다.

오스왈드 샌더즈는 지도자 개념에 관하여 기독교적인 입장에서 정의하기를 "타고난 것과 영적인 것의 조화"[160]라고 했는데 이는 하나님이 주신 은사와 자재적인 지도력을 모두 발전시켜야 하는 것이다.

오늘의 교회 목회는 한마디로 비복음적인 요소가 너무 목회 현장에 깊이 파고들어 모든 것이 병들대로 병들어 버린 현상이라는 사실을 쉽게 부인할 수 없는 안타까움이 있다.

목회자 자신이 정신적, 육체적, 정서적, 그리고 영적인 지도자로서 하나님이 맡기신 백성들을 정말 푸른 초장 같은 삶으로 인도해야 하는데 지도자 자신이 먼저 그와 같은 상황의 부조화로 인하여 질서가 파괴되고 지도력의 상실은 물론 어느 것 하나도 복음적이지 못한 현상에 시달리고 있음을 간과할 수 없는 것이다.

필자는 일찍이 통전적 목회를 강조해 왔다. 예배, 교육, 선교, 봉사의 어느 한 부분만을 고집하는 목회가 아니라 성서적이며 복음

---

158) Bennie E. Goodwin II, *The Effective Leader, a Basic Guide to Christian Leadership* (Inter - Varsity Press, Illinois, 1971), p. 8.
159) William Shakespeare, *Twelfth Night*, II. iv. 158.
160) J. Oswald Sanders, *Spiritual Leadership* (Mashall, Morgan & Scott, 1976 ; Lakelanded, 1981), p.20.

적인 목회를 강조해 왔다. 그것은 교회정치나 목회 경영이나 교회 행정에 포함된 치유, 인간관계, 영성개발 등의 목회 영역은 날로 세분화 되고 있는데 선견자, 또는 선지자적 통찰력을 갖지 못한 지도자가 어떻게 이 엄청난 목회 사역을 제대로 감당할 수 있는가는 어제 오늘의 문제만은 아니었다. 따라서 이와 같은 문제를 해결하고 바람직한 목회 사역을 통한 하나님의 나라를 건설하는데는 복음적인 지도자와 지도력이 강조되지 않을 수 없는 것이다.

그것이 곧 목회 원리이며, 그와 같은 효율적이고 실체성있는 목회 지도력을 통하여 교회가 성장하고 그리스도 예수가 원하시는 '에클레시아'가 세워질 수 있는 것이라 확신하는 것이다.

이제까지 지도자가 없어서 오늘의 목회 현장이 이렇게 황량한 사막같이 되고 있는 것은 아니다.

신학적 이론과 다양한 재능과 특별한 훈련을 통하여 보다 유익하고 바람직한 목회영역을 다듬어 가지만, 본질적이고 복음적인 지도자의 지도력이 역동하지 않는 한 통전적인 목회는 기대할 수 없다는 것이 필자의 평소의 견해인 것이었다.

본 논문 작성의 의미를 거기서 찾으면서 복음적인 지도자와 지도력을 이론적으로 제시하고 그에 상응하는 목회 지도력이 이루어질 때 오늘의 목회 현장은 그리스도의 에클레시아와 바실레이아가 이루어질 것을 확신한다.

그러기 위해서 복음적인 지도자와 지도력이 요구되는 것이다.

제 III 장

구약에 나타난 지도자와 지도력의 고찰

구약에 나타난 지도자와 지도력의 고찰에 앞서서 성서적으로 보는 관점이 중요하다. 지금까지 성서의 신약과 구약의 관계를 어떤 시각에서 볼 것인가에 대하여 여전히 통일된 견해가 없다. 특히 필자가 논하고자 하는 복음적 지도자와 지도력의 초점은 예수 그리스도의 복음에서 출발하기 때문에 복음을 성서에서 어떤 시각으로 볼 것인가가 매우 중요하다.

신약과 구약의 관계를 비통일성 내지 비연속성(Disunity and Discontinuity)의 입장에서 신약을 강조하고 구약을 경시하는 입장(Adolf Harna Bultmann)이 있고, 또 구약을 강조하고 신약을 경시하는 입장(A. Von Ruler, W. Visher)도 있으며, 구약과 신약을 통일내지 연속성(Unity and Continuity)의 입장(G. Von Rad, J. Bright,

C.Westermann)이 있다. [161] 필자는 신구약성서를 통전적으로 보되 예수 그리스도를 정점으로 구약과 신약을 보는 입장이다. "예수 그리스도 없는 구약은 출구 없는 미로 속에서 헤매는 방랑자와 같을 것이고, 무너진 성터 위에 서서 저무는 저녁 노을을 바라보면서 동트는 새 아침의 메시아이신 그리스도를 바라 볼 수밖에 없다. 따라서 예수 그리스도가 없는 신약은 원인 없는 결과의 모순 덩어리로 전락할 것이다. 따라서 예수 그리스도는 신구약의 정점이며 열쇠이며 근본이요 결과이다."[162]

따라서 구약은 예수 그리스도의 표상적 계시로서 복음의 요소들(Elements of Gospel)이라 보며, 예수 그리스도는 종결적 계시자로서 복음(Gospel) 그 자체이며, 예수 이후의 신약성서는 복음의 증거들(Witnesses of Gospel)로 보는 입장에서 복음적 리더와 리더십을 논급하겠다. [163]

그러므로 구약성서에 나타난 지도자와 지도력은 예수 그리스도의 복음적 지도자와 지도력의 표상적 모형론(Typology) 내지 표상적 계시(Revelation)이다. 그 시대와 상황에 따라 하나님이 "클레토이" "에클레토이" "피스토이"한 그의 백성들[164]을 위하여 세우심을 받은 한시적인 지도자와 지도력이다.

본 논문에서는 구약에 나타나는 지도자와 지도력을 역사적 시대적 신학적 성서적 입장에서 통전적으로 살펴보고자 한다.

---

161) 황보갑, *op. cit.*, p.35.
162) *Ibid.*, p.35.
163) *Ibid*,. pp.35-36.
164) 계17:14, κλητοι(called), εκλεκτοι(chosen), πιστοι(faithful followers, NIV)를 말함

1. 아브라함의 지도력

구약성서의 지도력을 언급함에 있어 아브라함에서 출발하는 것은 첫째로 아브라함은 예수 그리스도의 복음의 우주성과 세계성 그리고 예수 그리스도의 "에클레시아"를 표상하는 인물로 세우심을 받았기 때문이다.

가령 J문서에 나타나고 있는 그의 이름에서 본명은 아브람(고귀한 아버지)이였으나 하나님께서 아브라함으로 개명케 하심은 그 뜻을 "열국의 아비"(father of many nations)로 우주성과 세계성의 복음적 의미를 계시하고 있기 때문이다. 또 J문서에서 큰 민족 즉 "가돌 고이"(a great nation)로서 단수적 의미를 지니며, 또 땅위의 모든 족속(all families of the earth) 역시 우주적 신학적 의미를 내포하고 있다. 또 E문서에서 육적 할례로서 유대인들에게 한정된 것이 영적 할례의 보편주의를 계시한 점도 복음의 우주성의 의미를 계시하고 있기 때문이다.

둘째로 아브라함에서 예수 그리스도의 "에클레시아"를 표상하고 있는 점이다. 예수 그리스도의 "에클레시아"는 "에클레토이" "클레토이"와 "피스토이"로서 그 의미를 충족하고 있는 때는 아브라함으로 봄이 타당하기 때문이다. 가령 "피스토이"($\pi\iota\sigma\tau o\iota$)는 "피스티스"($\pi\iota\sigma\tau\iota\varsigma$)의 복수형으로 "신실한 자들"이란 의미로서 교회의 공동체성의 모임을 지향하고 있기 때문이다.

셋째로 예수 그리스도의 구원론적 표상으로 족장사에서 출발하여 모세의 출애굽 그리고 가나안의 정착의 사사시대와 왕정시대 및 성전시대와 바벨론의 포로를 통해 형성된 이른 바 회당종교에까지 역사적 시대별로 언급하고 예수 그리스도의 성전과 회당으로부터 나온(called) "에클레시아"와의 연계성과 단절(End)과 새로움의 의미를 계시하고 있기 때문이다.

아브라함의 지도력 출처는 족장전승에 의존 할 수밖에 없다. 게오르그 포레(Georg Fohrer)에 의하면 족장사를 과학적으로 증명하기 힘들고 다만 족장전승과 설화의 재료를 의존 할 수밖에 없다고 언급한 바 있다.

히브리 전승에 의하면 하란 근처에서 아브라함의 조상의 이름과 일치하는 지역명이 있어(가령, 세룩, 사루기, 데라등) 이러한 명칭으로 미루어 보아 메소포타미아에서 그의 조상이 거주하였다는 사실을 추정해 볼 수 있다.[165] 뿐만 아니라 아브라함의 족속은 유프라테스강 건너편에 살면서 신(God)이 아닌 신들(gods, 月神등)인 우상을 섬기면서 살아왔다.[166] 이처럼 우상을 섬기며 살아온 아브라함은 처음부터 족속을 이끌만한 지도자로 세움 받을 만한 위인도 인물도 되지 못했다. 그러나 하나님이 현현하여 아브라함을 우상과 혈육과 본토로부터 부르시고(Calling Out) 너(thou)를 지명하여 민족의 지도자로 지도력을 발휘케 한 것은 전적인 은총의 복음에서 비롯된 것이다. 이것이 예수 그리스도의 복음의 계시인 것이다. 주님의 부르심은 "누구든지"또는 "수고하고 무거운 짐 진 자들을 부르시고"만민에게 구원을 주시는 우주적인 만민의 복음인 것이다.

아브라함의 지도력은 다음 몇 가지로 살펴 볼 수 있다.

① 아브라함의 지도력은 하나님의 부르심과 세우심과 하나님 나라의 과업을 위탁받음에서 시작되었다.

---

165) Georg Fohrer, *Geschichte Israels*, 방석종 역, 이스라엘 역사(서울: 성광문화사, 1986), pp.32-33.
166) 수24:2.

창세기 12장 1절에서 "여호와께서 아브람에게 이르시되 너는 너의 본토 친척 아비 집을 떠나 내가 네게 지시할 땅으로 가라"로 기록하고 있다. 본문에서 하나님이 아브라함의 지도자로 "부르심"(Κυριος τω Αβραμ, the Lord Said to Abram)이 있고, 또 너(σου)로 세우시고, 또 맡기신 과업 즉 "네게 지시할 땅"(της συγγενειας σου) 영원한 가나안을 표상하며, 이는 예수 그리스도가 선포하신 하나님 나라의 과업을 제자들에게 위탁한 것과 다름이 없다.[167]

그러므로 아브라함의 지도력은 하나님이 아브라함을 지도자로 세우심으로 영적으로나 육적으로 독특한 지도력의 권위가 있다.

② 열국의 족장으로서의 리더십

아브라함은 이스라엘의 족장사 즉 아브라함, 이삭, 야곱으로 이어지는 족장의 우두머리는 물론 다윗과 그리스도의 육적 조상으로서 각별한 위치에 있다.[168] 아브라함이 열국의 조상으로서의 리더십은 유대인들의 조상일 뿐만 아니라 이슬람의 종교 경전인 코란 제 14장에는 아브라함의 장이 있고, 무함메드에게 내린 성전(聖典)으로 고백하여 신앙이 되고 있다.[169] 기독교에서는 믿음의 조상으로 아브라함을 보고 있으며, 특히 바울은 예수 그리스도의 구원의 표상으로 증거하였다.

로마서 4장 11절에서 "저가 할례의 표를 받은 것은 무할례시에 믿음으로 된 의를 인친 것이니 이는 무할례자로서 믿는 모든 자의

---

167) 마28:19-20., Harry Wendt, 박종구 역, 크로스웨이 성경연구(서울: 신망애출판사, 1985),p.51.
168) 마1:1., 눅3:23-38.
169) 김용선, 코란의 이해(서울 : 민음사, 1990),pp.307-311.

조상이 되어"라고 기록하고 있고, 또 "내가 너를 많은 민족의 조상으로 세웠다 하심과 같으니 그의 믿은바 하나님은 죽은 자를 살리시며, 없는 것을 있는 것 같이 부르시는 이시니라"(롬4:17).

이처럼 아브라함을 지도자로 세우신 하나님(수24:2-18)은 오늘날에도 수많은 교회의 지도자를 세우시고(딤전1:12), 그 세우심에 합당한 하나님 나라의 일을 위임하시며 그의 지도력을 발휘토록 도우심과 그의 상을 예비하고 있음을 명심 하여야 할 것이다.[170]

③ 하나님 사랑의 영적 리더십

아브라함의 리더십이 4천년의 긴 역사의 흐름 속에서 열국의 조상으로서의 존재하고 있는 것은 리더십의 근원인 하나님을 세상 어느 것보다 더 사랑하였기 때문이다. 창세기 12장 1-3절에 하나님이 아브라함을 그의 본토(The Country) 친척(The Kindrey) 아비집(The father's house)을 떠나라고 명했을 때, 그가 혈육과 삶의 터전 보다 하나님의 언약의 복음을 따른 것은 바로 하나님을 사랑하는 증표인 것이다. 뿐만 아니라 창세기 22장에서 독자 이삭을 번제물로 바친 결단은 자식 보다 하나님을 더 사랑한 아브라함의 영적 리더십이다. 이 같은 하나님 사랑의 가시적 표증은 바로 순종의 삶 그 자체였으며, 그 순종의 결과는 아브라함으로 하여금 최상의 지도력인 여호와 이레 즉 준비하시는 하나님의 능력을 가시화 하는 결과를 가져왔다.

그러므로 복음적 리더십은 바로 세상의 어느 것 보다도 하나님

---

170) 계2:10, 눅16:10.

을 얼마나 사랑하느냐에 따라 그 지도력이 비례할 것이다. 오늘의 교회와 교회 영적 지도자들은 자기에게 부여한 하나님 나라의 과업을 위해 묵묵히 십자가를 사랑하는 헌신이 요구된다.[171]

아브라함이 하나님을 사랑한 것은 예수님께서 명하신 대 계명(마22:34-40)을 실천한 영적 지도력의 본이기도 하다. 예수님이 그의 제자 베드로에게 요구한 질문 역시 "네가 나를 사랑하느냐?" 의 질문이었다. 그 사랑의 물음에 응답한 베드로를 향해 새로운 지도자의 사명이 부여 되었다. 바로 "내 양을 먹이라. 내 양을 치라. 나를 따르라"이다.[172]

존 스토트(John R. W. Stott)는 복음서의 대 명령(마28:19-20)과 대 계명(마22:34-40)의 우선순위를 평행(Parallelism)으로 보았으나, 레오나르도 샌더슨(Leonard Sanderson)은 사랑의 대 계명이 먼저이고 선교의 대 명령을 2차로 보았다.[173]

필자는 샌더슨의 견해에 동의하면서 복음적 최고의 지도력은 바로 하나님 사랑에 있음을 밝힌다.

④ 정치적 군사적 경영적 리더십

아브라함은 하나님의 세우심을 받고 갈대아 우르를 떠나는 순간부터 그는 한 부족을 이끄는 족장이 된다. 자신의 부모 데라를 비롯하여 손자 롯과 그의 자부를 비롯한 그 가족 군단이었다.[174] 창 세

---

171) 마10:37-39, 삼상15:11.
172) 요21:15-19.
173) Leonard Sanderson & Ron Johnson, *Evangelism for All God's People* (Nashville :Broadman Press, 1990),p.22.
174) 창11:31.

기 14장 14-15절에서 아브라함의 가족군대가 318명이나 됨을 미루어 보아 적어도 1000여명 이상의 부족이 아닌가 싶다.[175]

이 같은 부족을 이끄는데는 남다른 지도력이 있어야 했다. 아브라함에게는 정치적 리더십이 있었다. 그것은 그와 최대의 라이벌 세력인 롯과의 관계에서 정치적 리더십을 발휘하여 포용과 양보와 평화를 이끌어 내었다. 이는 롯과는 더 이상 함께 거할 수 없는 거대한 가족 군단이었기 때문에 아브라함은 땅을 차지하는 모든 선택권을 먼저 조카 롯에게 부여한 것이다(창13:9). 뿐만 아니라 이웃과 동맹을 맺으면서 평화를 심어가면서 내적인 힘을 길렀던 것이다.[176]

다음으로 군사적 리더십이 있다. 족장의 순례 길에는 외부로부터 끝없는 도전으로부터 부족을 보호할 책임이 있기 때문이다. 요르단과 소돔 고모라에서 5개국이 동맹하여 조카 롯을 공격하여 롯이 잡혀가고 재산도 노략 당했다.[177] 이 같은 멸절의 비보(悲報)를 접하고 아브라함은 평소 신앙으로 훈련된 318명의 가족군대를 투입하여 5동맹국을 패망시키고 조카 롯과 그의 재산까지 도로 찾는 전과를 이룩하게 되었다.

이는 아브라함의 유비무환(有備無患)의 준비하는 정신으로 그의 부족을 지키는 군사적 지도력으로 평가 하여야 할 것이다.

끝으로 경영의 지도력이다. 그의 부족 다스리는 경영의 지도이념은 바로 여호와 하나님의 말씀에 두고 있다. 당시 가족을 위한

---

175) Pulpit, *op.cit*.,p.537.
176) 우희영, 더 많은 사람을 얻으라(서울 : 심언출판사, 1990),p.340.
177) 창14:1, 2, 10-12.

가족 공동묘지를 소유하는 것은 대단히 중요한 일이었다. 특히 공동묘지가 한국처럼 땅에 시체를 묻는 개념이 아니라 동굴 속에 시체를 넣어서 장사하기 때문에 가족공동묘지인 동굴을 확보하는 것이 그리 쉬운 일이 아니었다. 창세기 15장 12-15절, 그는 여호와 하나님과 언약의 체결에서 그의 자손은 400년 동안 이방의 객이 될 것이며, 그러나 그는 장수하다가 평안히 조상에게로 돌아가 장사될 것이라는 언약의 말씀을 간직하여 그의 경영적 리더십을 발휘하였다. 바로 그 언약의 말씀이 400년 후에 반드시 성취될 것을 믿고 막벨라 굴을 당시의 가격 400세겔을 주고 사서 소유하였다(창23:15). 그 후 하나님의 약속의 말씀이 성취되어 그 굴에 사라와 아브라함(창23:19, 25:9), 이삭과 리브가(창49:31, 35:28), 레아와 야곱(창49:31, 50:13)등 족장들의 가족묘가 되어졌다.

아브라함의 경영의 리더십은 그의 금전의 거래가 분명하고 깨끗한 지도력이었다.

아브라함이 헤브론에 거주할 때 헷족속의 추장이었던 에브론과 상당한 친분의 관계가 있어 대가 없이 막벨라 굴에 장사지내도록 배려하였음에도 불구하고 그의 분명한 금전거래는 경영의 리더십의 지도력으로 충분한 것이다. 또 조카 롯과의 관계 역시 비옥한 땅을 차지하는 것은 바로 재산과 직결되는 것이나 재산보다 평화와 관계를 중시하는 지도력을 발휘하였다. 뿐만 아니라 아브라함이 조카 롯을 구출하고 그돌라오멜을 격파한 후 수많은 전리품을 치부할 수 있었으나 그는 "천지의 주재시오 지극히 높으신 하나님 여호와께 내가 손을 들어 맹세하노니 네 말이 내가 아브라함으로 치부할까하여 네게 속한 것은 무론 한 실이나 신들메라도 취하지 아니하리라"(창14:22-23).

오늘날 교회와 교회의 지도자들의 금전관계가 불투명하고 하나
님의 이름을 빌려서 고귀한 헌금을 낭비하므로서 지도자의 지도력
상실을 초래하고 있는 점을 간과해서는 안될 것이다.

이상을 통하여 아브라함의 위대한 지도력을 살펴보았다. 그러나
아브라함에게도 지도력의 약화를 가져온 실패의 자리도 있었다.
그는 갈대아 우르를 떠날 때 친척과 아비의 집을 떠나라는 말씀에
온전한 순종이 되지 못했다. 바로 혈육의 정이었다. 그 결과 그의
부친 데라가 하란에 머물기로 고집하므로 그의 행진을 중단하는
결과를 가져왔다(창11:31-32). 다음으로 그의 실패는 인간적 두려
움이 그의 지도력을 약화시켰다. 아브라함이 애굽으로 우거할 때
그 아내 사래가 아리따우므로 자신의 보호를 위해 아내를 누이라
칭하는 불명예와 아내의 고통을 치루는 거짓과 속임수가 아브라함
의 지도력을 약화시킨 결과를 가져왔다. 그리고 하나님의 언약을
끝까지 믿고 인내하지 못하므로 엄청난 두 갈래의 종파를 분열시
키는 실수를 가져오게 되었다. 창 15장에 "네 몸에서 날 자가 네 후
사가 되리라"(창15:4)는 언약을 인내하지 못한 아브라함은 몸종 하
갈을 통해 이스마엘을 낳게 됨으로서, 이스마엘에게서 이슬람의
종파가 기원하게 되었다. [178]

---

178) 창16:15.

2. 모세의 지도력

모세는 구약성서에서 영적, 인격적, 지도자적 지도력을 갖춘 대표적인 인물로 상징되었다. 그는 에집트(Egypt)의 파라오(Pharahoh)의 통치 밑에서 430년간(출12:40) 200만 이상의 거대한 집단 히브리 민족을 우상과 고통과 고역으로부터 출애굽(Exodus)시켜 구원의 표상인 가나안 땅으로 인도한 지도력의 대명사요,[179] 시나이 산으로부터 하나님의 십계명을 받은 율법의 대명사요,[180] 출생에서부터 죽음에 이르기까지 때로는 민족의 영웅으로 왕궁의 왕자의 위치에서 살인자로 때로는 광야의 목동에서 그야말로 인생의 희비를 경험한 살아있는 지도력을 엿볼 수 있다.

특히 아브라함의 시대는 우주적인 구원과 하나님의 가족교회를 표상한 반면에 모세 때에는 소위 국가교회(Church-State)로 그 형태와 구조면에서 신정(Theocracy)과 민정(Democracy)이 함께 공존하는 이른 바 독특한 국가 민족의 집단이었다.

모세의 지도력은 최고의 지도력인 하나님의 권위 아래서 추종자들의 힘과 상황을 반영하는 탁월한 지도력을 발휘하였다.

① 영적 지도력

지위이론에 의하면 모세는 궁중에서 학문과 위치 그 자체만으로도 충분한 리더십(Leadership)을 발휘할 수 있는 조건을 갖추었으나, 보다 근본적인 리더십은 하나님으로부터 부르심과 세우심에

---

179) Leonwood, A *Survey of Isreal's History*, Grand Rapids: Zondervan, 1970, p.131.
180) 출19장-20장.

서 출발하여야 한다. 이를 필자는 "모세의 영적 리더십"이라 부르
고자 한다. 모세는 지위이론으로 볼 때 정치 사회적으로 왕자와 같
은 신분이었으며, 당시 최고의 학문을 배운 자로서 스데반은 "모세
가 애굽 사람의 학술을 다 배워 그 말과 행사가 능하더라."(행7:22)
고 증언하고 있다. 역사가 요세푸스(Josephus)는 모세는 학자로서
애굽의 과학과 지혜에 통달했으며, 정치가로는 독특한 웅변능력을
가졌으며, 군인으로서는 그가 위대한 업적을 남겼다고 언급한 바
있다.[181] 그러나 사회적 지위이론에 의한 모세의 리더십은 그의 민
족을 구원하는데 실패했으며 살인자로 전락하고 말았다.[182]

그러므로 모세를 위대한 영적 지도자로 리더십을 발휘케 한 것
은 하나님과의 만남에서 비롯되었다. 모세는 호렙산에서 떨기나
무 불꽃 가운데 임재하신 하나님의 부르심에 응답하므로 영적 지
도자로 세움을 받았다(출3:4).

모세의 영적 지도력은 바로 사회적 지위이론에서는 상상할 수
없는 영적 통찰력이 있으며, 이를 히브리 기자는 다음과 같이 증언
하고 있다. "믿음으로 모세는 장성하여 바로 공주의 아들이라 칭
함을 거절하고 도리어 하나님의 백성과 함께 고난 받기를 잠시 죄
악의 낙을 누리는 것보다 더 좋아하고 그리스도를 위하여 받는 능
욕을 애굽의 모든 보화보다 더 큰 재물로 여겼으니 이는 상 주심
을 바라봄이라"(히11:24). 그의 위대한 고려(Esteeming)와 선택
(Choosing)과 거절(Refusing)과 포기(Forsaking)는 바로 하나님의
영적인 지도력에 기인된 것이다.[183] 뿐만 아니라 그의 영적 지도력

---

181) J. Oswald Sanders, *Men From God's School*, 김용호 역(서울: 종합선교 나
침판사,1985),p. 77.
182) 출2:11-15.
183) 히11:24-28.

은 그가 하나님의 종으로서 탁월한 리더십을 발휘하였다.

그의 리더십을 정리해보면 다음과 같다.

첫째, 그의 "온유함"(민12:3)이다.

민수기 12장3절에는 "이 사람 모세는 온유함이 지면의 모든 사람보다 승하더라."라고 기록하고 있다. 모세는 홍해 앞에서 그토록 절박한 소용돌이 속에서도 기도하는 온유함이 있었으며(출14:13), 시내산에서 하나님의 언약을 파기하고 우상을 섬기는 이스라엘 백성들에게 자신의 야망을 버리고 하나님의 백성을 사랑하는 온유함이 그의 간구에서 나타나고 있다. 출애굽기 32장에서 "그런즉 나대로 하게 하라 내가 그들에게 진노하여 그들을 진멸하고 너로 큰 나라가 되게 하리라. 모세가 그 하나님 여호와께 구하여 가로되 여호와여 어찌하여 그 큰 권능과 강한 손으로 애굽 땅에서 인도하여 내신 주의 백성에게 진노하시나이까."[184] 또한 모세의 온유함은 시기와 질투를 초월한 지도력 이었다. 민수기 11장28절에는 모세를 보좌한 엘닷과 메닷이 예언함을 여호수아가 보고했을 때 모세가 그에게 이르되 "네가 나를 위하여 시기하느냐 여호와께서 그 신을 그 모든 백성에게 주사 다 선지자 되게 하시기를 원하노라"(민11:29).

둘째로 그의 "믿음"이었다. Ted W. Engstrom은 히브리서11장의 분석을 통해 영적 믿음에 기초한 모세의 지도력을 분석한 바 있는데 모세의 지도력의 요소를 믿음(Faith, 히11:24), 성실(Integrity, 히11:25), 비전(Vision, 히11:26), 결단력(Decisiveness, 히11:27), 순종(Obedience, 히11:28), 책임감(Respohsibility, 히11:29)이다.[185]

---

184) 출32:10-11.
185) Ted W. Engstrom, *The Making of a Christion Leacter*, Grand Rapids,

셋째로 그는 기도, 말씀, 본의 영적 지도자였다. Leroy Eims는 모세의 영적 지도력을 다음과 같이 언급한 바 있다. 모세는 우선적으로 백성들을 위하여 기도한 지도자였으며, 또 하나님의 말씀을 가르쳤으며, 백성들 앞에서 본을 보인 지도자였다.[186]

넷째, 하나님 중심에서 타협의 관문을 통과한 지도력이다. 모세의 영적 지도력을 약화시키려는 하나의 동인(動因)이 바로 인본주의적인 타협이었다. 바로는 모세를 향한 끈질긴 회유와 타협을 제시했다. "너희는 하나님께 희생을 드려라 그러나 애굽을 떠나지 말라"(출8:25)라고 회유했고, 또 "너희는 희생을 드리기 위해 애굽에서 나갈 것이나 너무 멀리가지 말라"(출8:28)라고 회유했고, 정에 대한 회유가 있었으니 "너희 남정만 가서 여호와를 섬기라"(출10:10-11)이다. 그러나 모세는 하나님 중심의 영적 지도력으로 바로를 제압했으며 궁극적으로 이스라엘 백성을 애굽에서 나오게 하는 위대한 지도력을 발휘하였다.

② 입법 사법 행정의 지도력

모세가 하나님의 부르심을 받고 지도자로 세우심을 받아 그에게 부여한 히브리민족의 구원의 사명은 참으로 엄청난 지도력을 요하는 각별한 위치임에 틀림이 없다. 무려 200만의 거대한 민족집단이 안정된 국토나 정권이나 주권적인 의무를 이행하는 국민도 아니면서 오직 모세만을 바라보고 따랐다. 의식주의 보장이 없는 광

---

v Pvblishing House, 1977, p.30.
186) 우희영, 목회지도자학 (서울:심언, 1993),p. 103..

야라는 특수한 지역과 40년의 긴 세월과 일인 장기 집권적 리더십으로 그의 사명을 수행한 것은 아마 인류 역사상 모세 외에는 그 유래를 찾을 수 없는 리더십이다.

J.E. Adams에 의하면 모세는 적절한 계급제도를 통해서 그의 지도력을 발휘했다. 백성 중에서 재덕이 있는 자를 선정하여 자기를 도우게 하였으며, 또 자신이 선정한 천부장 백부장 오십부장의 직위를 적절히 배치하여 효과적인 통솔을 감당케 하였으며, 가장 어려운 일은 자신이 담당하고 나머지는 다른 지도자에게 맡기는 지도력을 발휘하였다고 보았다.[187]

모세의 구체적인 조직적 지도력에는 신정(神政 ; Theocracy)의 대행제도(代行制度)와 민정(民政 ; Democracy)의 대의제도(代議制度)가 공존하는 지도력을 발휘하였다.

첫째, 신정의 위임과 대행인 제사장직, 행정직과 사법직

모세는 그의 지도력의 발휘를 위해서 독특한 위임과 대행체제를 구축하였다. 이것이 제사장직과 행정직과 사법직이다.

ⓐ 제사장직

제사장직의 기원은 족장사에 언급된 적이 있고(창14:18), 이방세계에도 이미 존재하였다[188] 그러나 야웨를 통해 가시화 된 것은 모

---

187) J.E. Adams, 정상지 역, 성공적인 목회지도(서울 : 예수 문서선교회, 1981),P.45.
188) 황보갑, *op.cit.*,p.82

세에서 시작되었다고 봄이 타당하다. 모세는 광야의 여정에서 하나님께서 명하는 데로 아론과 그의 네 아들에게 제사장직을 주어서 회막과 성막에서 종교적 행위를 하도록 하는 지도력을 발휘했다. 출애굽기28장에 보면 야웨께서 아론과 그의 네 아들을 제사장으로 세우고, 의복과 위임의 절차까지 상세히 기록하고 있다.

모세에 있어서 제사장직의 특징은 모세가 입법 사법 행정을 다 이행할 수 없는 상황에서 도입된 것으로 보여진다. 따라서 제사장직은 야웨의 위임으로, 야웨의 입법인 신정과 70인 의회인 민정의 중개자로, 때로는 판단자로, 때로는 야웨와 백성간에 생명의 고리인 제의를 담당케하는 지도력을 발휘하였다.[189]

이 제사장직은 회당시대까지 존속하였고 특히 예루살렘 산헤드린의 대표적 구성원이 되기도 하였다.

ⓑ 행적직과 사법직

모세가 이스라엘 백성을 출애굽한 이후 시나이 산에 도착했을 때 하나님은 모세에게 십계명을 계시하셨다(출19장-20장). 이 십계명이 행정직과 사법직의 근본이 되어서 두 직의 태동을 가져왔다. 그러므로 모세는 율법의 대명사로 상징되어 왔다.

미국의 최고 재판소의 배석 판사인 브류어(Hon. D.J.Brewer)는 "모세는 인류의 가장 위대한 입법자 옆에 나란히 둔다 해도 부족함이 없다. 그는 시내산 꼭대기에서 여호와의 손으로부터 어떤 면에서 인류 역사상 가장 독특한 민족의 법전이 되어온 법체계를 만드

---

189) *Ibid.*

는 능력을 부여받았다. 이 법전은 오늘날 놀랄 만한 문명사회에서
도 강력한 힘을 발휘하고 있기 때문이다"[190] 라고 언급한 바 있다.

모세의 지도력은 바로 여기에 있다. 아무리 자신이 입법의 대행
자라 할지라도 그 수많은 소송사건[191] 과 백성을 다스림에는 혼자서
는 불가능하다. 그는 장인 이드로의 건의를 받아들여 백성 중에서
하나님을 두려워하며, 진실하며, 재덕(才德)이 있고, 불의한 이(利)
를 탐하지 않는 청렴결백한 자를 뽑아 천부장, 백부장, 오십부장,
십부장과 패장을 삼고 사법직과 행정직의 직무를 위임 처리케 하는
지도력을 발휘하였다.[192]

둘째 민정(民政)의 대의제도인 장로직과 대의제도의 태동

모세의 지도력은 하나님의 직접적 개입을 통해 이루어지는 신정
과 동시에 이스라엘 백성들의 대표자를 세워서 그의 업무를 위임
처리케 하는 민정의 대의제도를 시행하였다는 점이다. 당시 제사
장들은 늘 성전에 있었고 또 선지자들이 늘 나타나는 것도 아니다.
따라서 백성들의 민의를 가까운 곳에서 수렴할 수 있는 장로들로
또는 대의원으로서 마을지도자를 부각시켰다.[193] 이들의 세움은 출
애굽의 여정에서 모세를 도울 대표자들이었다. 이들이 장로직이요
대의제도의 구성이었다.

---

190) *Ibid.*
191) 출18:13-27; 신1:13-18.
192) 신1:10-15.
193) Robert P. Kerr, *Presbyterianism for the People*, (Philadelphia, 1926), p. 17.

ⓐ 장로직

장로직의 기원은 족장시대까지 거슬려 올라가서 아브라함이 그의 늙은 종에게 소유를 맡김에서 비롯된다.

장로란 말은 히브리어로 "자켄(וקֵזּ)"이란 말로 그 뜻은 턱수염, 늙은, 장로, 연장자란 뜻을 가지고 있다. 이 같은 장로의 기원을 족장시대에서 볼 수 있으나 그 제도적 기원은 모세에서 비롯되었다. 왜냐하면 장로제도는 의회제도의 태동의 모체이기 때문이다. [194]

이처럼 장로직의 세움은 모세를 도와 민의를 수렴 보고하는 일을 담당하였으며 대개 마을의 연장자나 대표적 기능을 담당하였다.

ⓑ 의회제도

장로직의 태동은 의회를 조직하는 계기가 되었다. 이 의회제도의 조직은 모세가 주도하였으나 그것은 하나님에 의하여 시작되었다. 출애굽기 3장16절에 보면 하나님이 이스라엘 백성들을 출애굽하기에 앞서서 "너는 가서 이스라엘 장로들을 모우고"라고 말씀하셨기 때문이다. 여기서 이스라엘의 장로들은 단순한 늙은 자들을 말함이 아니고, 각 가문의 어른들로서(출6:14, 25) 당시 정치체제를 갖추지 못한 시대에 백성들의 대표자라는 의미가 주어졌기 때문이다.

아무튼 모세는 의회를 조직하여 71인의 의회원을 구성하였는데 모세가 당연직으로 의장이 되고 대제사장과 제사장 그리고 장로와 서기관으로 구성하여 모세의 출애굽의 여정을 돕도록 하는 지도력을 발휘하였다. 그 후 의회조직은 후일 이스라엘 조직의 기본적 틀

---

194) 황보갑, *op.cit.*,p.79.

이 되었으며, 영속적인 정치체제가 되었다.

③ 비극에서 영광으로

모세의 지도력은 위대하고 대단했다. 그러나 모세에게도 비극적인 실패가 있었다. 민수기 20장 5절에 의하면 가데스에서 이스라엘 백성의 불평은 대단했다. "너희가 어찌하여 우리를 애굽에서 나오게 하며, 이 악한 곳으로 인도하였느냐 이곳에는 파종할 곳이 없고, 무화과도 없고, 포도도 없고, 석류도 없고, 마실 물도 없도다." 이에 "모세와 이론이 총회를 그 반석 앞에 모으고 모세가 그들에게 이르되 패역한 너희여 들으라 우리가 너희를 위하여 이 반석에서 물을 내랴 하고 그 손을 들어 그 지팡이로 반석을 두 번 치매 물이 많이 솟아나오므로 회중과 그들의 짐승이 마시니라"[195]

이 같은 모세의 분노는 지도자로서의 지도력을 상실하는 비극으로 나타났다. 외형적으로는 이스라엘 백성들로 하여금 그들의 원성을 잠재우고 또 모세의 가시적 지도력을 과시하는 계기가 되었을지 모르나, 지도력의 근원이신 하나님으로부터 불신앙을 가지므로 그의 지도력의 상실을 가져온 비극의 소치였다. 민수기 20장12절에는 "여호와께서 모세와 아론에게 이르시되 너희가 나를 믿지 아니하고 이스라엘 목전에서 나의 거룩함을 나타내지 아니한 고로 너희는 이 총회를 내가 그들에게 준 땅으로 인도하여 들이지 못하리라 하시니라"라고 말씀하셨다.

시편 106편 33절에는 "이는 저희가 그 심령을 거역함을 인하여 모

---

195) 민20:10-11.

세가 그 입술로 망령되이 말하였음이로다."그 후 모세는 그의 불신앙을 뉘우치고 그의 지도력의 회복을 요청하였으나 하나님은 "그 일로 내게 다시 말하지 말라"(신3:25-26)고 하셨다. 지도자에게 지도력의 상실은 비극이다. 영적 지도자는 어떤 일이 있어도 하나님에 대한 불신앙을 가졌어는 안 된다는 깊은 교훈을 준다. 그러나 사랑의 하나님은 모세가 비록 가나안까지 그 백성을 인도하는 지도력을 상실했고 또 자신도 가나안을 바라보는 것으로 그의 지도력을 마무리 하였으나 변화산상에서 예수님과 함께 나타나신 엘리야와 모세의 모습에서 영적인 가나안 땅으로 들어간 영광의 모습을 보여 주었다.

하나님이 그가 세우신 지도자는 비록 비극적 사건에서 그 지도력의 상실을 가져왔으나 궁극적인 영광의 면류관을 세우신 지도자에게 수여하심은 오늘의 교회 지도자들에게 위로의 기쁨이 아닐 수 없다.

3. 사사들의 지도력

사사시대는 여호수아 사후(삿2:8) 중앙국가의 행정체제를 갖추지 못한 미분화 사회 속에서 사사시대를 맞이하게 된다. 그러나 이스라엘의 민족은 모세전승이 동인(動因)이 되어 지파동맹(Amphictyony)을 형성하였다. 이 지파동맹은 중앙 성소(세겜, 벧엘, 실로)[196]를 중심으로 종교적 정치적 행위를 하는 장으로서 모이고 흩어지는 "에클레시아"의 표상을 계시하였다.

---

196) 세겜(수24장), 벧엘(삿20:26), 실로(삿20:31).

이 지파동맹을 통해 이스라엘 민족은 모세전승을 유지하면서 지방신 특히 가나안의 바알 신 또는 아스다롯 신을 금지하였다. 그러나 지리적으로 여전히 정복되지 않은 지방의 가나안 인들은 여전히 지배적 위치에 있었기 때문에 가나안 인과 이스라엘 간의 점진적인 상호동화(a reciprocal assimilation)를 가져왔다. 이는 모세전승의 위기였으며, 종교적 혼합을 가져왔다. 뿐만 아니라 새로운 역사의 지평을 여는 축복의 땅에서 한편으로 끊임없는 배교와 불순종의 역사로 점철되어 갔다.

이러한 명암(明暗)이 교차되는 소용돌이 속에서 하나님께서는 불연속적으로 카리스마적 지도자를 세워서 종교적 동화에 제동을 걸면서 군사적 위협을 감소시키는 지도력을 가시화 하였다. 사사란 말은 "쇼파트(שׁפט)"란 말로 재판자(출18:22, 왕상3:9), 판단자(민35:24, 왕상3:28), 다스린 자(왕상23:22, 삼상8:5)의 뜻을 지니고 있으나 당시 사사라고 해서 모두 카리스마적 지도자는 아니었다. 또 모두 종교영역의 사람도 아니고 단순히 추장 정도에 거치는 인물도 있었다.[197] 이들의 출신 성분도 다양함을 볼 수 있는데 웃니엘은 추장이었고, 에훗, 바락, 기드온은 비천한 가문의 출신이었고, 야일, 입산, 압돈은 부유한 가문이며, 입다는 창기의 아들이었다(삿11:1,2). 또 엘리는 제사장이었고, 사무엘은 예언자이었으며, 삼손은 전설적인 인물이었다.[198]

그러나 구약에서는 사사들을 이스라엘의 하나님의 이름으로 특

---

197) E.L.에리히, *An Outline of Old testament History*, 배제민 역, 요점 이스라엘 역사(서울 : 기독교문사, 1978),p.41.
198) *Ibid.*

별한 일을 하도록 부름 받은 사람으로 설명하고 있다.[199] 특히 사사들이 지파 내에서 민중의 수령이나 지도자의 지위를 얻을 수 있었던 것은 바로 전쟁에서의 영웅이 되므로 추앙받게 되었다. 이 같은 사사들은 한 시대에 하나님의 부르심으로 그들의 지도력을 발휘하게 된 것이다.

① 야웨의 불연속적인 부르심에 기인된 지도력

구약에 나타나는 모든 하나님의 지도자들이 그러하듯이 사사들 역시 하나님의 부르심으로 카리스마적 지도력을 가시화 하게 되었다. 야웨가 사사들을 불연속적으로 부르신 것은 사사시대의 특징을 반영하고 있다. 그 대표적인 특징은 주변의 민족들이 이스라엘 지파를 불연속적인 무력으로 공격한 일에 기인된 것이다. 따라서 야웨는 카리스마적 지도자를 불연속적으로 세워 그의 나라를 이루어 나갔다.

가령 모압의 침입이 있을 때 하나님은 사사 에훗을 등장시켜 그들의 침입을 제지시켰다(삿3:12-30). 뿐만 아니라 에훗은 에브라임 지파와 자기 지파인 베냐민 지파의 도움을 받아 모압 왕 에글론으로부터 여리고를 재탈환하는데 성공함으로써 전쟁의 영웅으로 사사라는 지도자의 칭호에 어울리는 지도력을 점하게 되었다.

또 입다는 암몬인과의 전쟁에서 승리함으로써 자기지파의 사사 지위를 획득하였고(삿12:7), 카리스마를 받으므로 탁월한 존재로 묘사되어 있다(삿11:29).

삼손은 단지파의 위협을 말해주고 있다(삿13-16장). 강력했던

---

199) *Ibid.*

삼손의 몰락은 자신이 속해있는 지파는 물론 블레셋에 저항할 만한 위치에 있지 못한 이스라엘 전 지파의 위험이었다. 이처럼 사사들이 가져온 전쟁에서의 승리는 이스라엘 백성들로 하여금 하나님의 은총의 선물로 고백하게 함과 동시에 사사를 하나님이 보내신 자로 따르는 계기가 되었다.

또 종교적 측면에서 이스라엘 백성들이 종교적 혼합의 위기에 이르게 되었을 때 야웨는 사사를 세워 그것들과 대항하게 하였다.

가령 기드온 사사는 야웨를 위하여 바알과 대항해서 싸웠다. 당시 바알종교와의 관계는 매우 복잡한 관계임을 볼 수 있는데, 그 증거로 기드온 자신도 타고 날 때부터 여룹바알이라 이름이 불렸고, 그는 세겜 출신의 가나안 여인을 첩으로 삼았다(삿8:31). 특히 사무엘 사사는 종교적 영역에서 활발하게 활동하였는데 그의 지도력의 발휘는 여호와 신앙을 옹호하는데 있었음을 의심할 여지가 없다.

결과적으로 사사들의 출신 성분을 볼 때 그토록 지도자나 지도력을 발휘할 위인이 될 수 없었다. 이들 사사들의 지도력은 전적으로 야웨에 의해 기인됨을 알 수 있다. 오늘날 교회의 지도자 역시 그의 지도력이 언제나 하나님에 의해 기인됨을 명심하고 하나님을 떠난 삼손처럼 지도력이 상실되었을 때 모습을 상기할 필요가 있을 것이다.

② 제사장, 예언자, 용장으로서의 지도력

사사에 대한 야웨의 불연속적인 부르심은 예수 그리스도의 3직

즉 예언자, 왕, 제사장의 유형을 표상하는 지도력으로 볼 수 있다. 선지자 내지 예언자로서 대표되는 사사는 사무엘 사사이다. 그의 지도력은 유일신의 신앙을 강조하는데 있었으며, 이를 통해 허약한 이스라엘 지파들로 하여금 정치적 군사적으로 단결하는 데 큰 역할을 담당하였다. 사무엘은 두 아들에게 사사의 지위를 물려주려고 하였으나 두 아들의 부패로 사사직 승계에 실패하였다. 다음으로 사사의 제사장적 유형으로는 엘리 제사장을 들 수 있다. 엘리 역시 제사장으로서의 그의 지도력을 발휘하였으나 말년에 두 아들 홉니와 비느하스의 부패로 블레셋에 법궤를 빼앗기고 두 아들마저 죽게 되며 자신도 비참한 말로로 마감하였다.

마지막 용장으로서의 사사는 이스라엘 사사의 지도력의 대부분을 차지한다. 기드온, 입다, 삼손, 에훗, 특히 여자 사사 드보라(삿4:4)는 용기 있는 군사적 용장이었다. 이들의 군사적 지도력은 그들 지파의 촌장으로서의 충분한 지위를 얻게 되었다.

4, 왕국과 왕들의 지도력

사사시대를 지나 이스라엘은 왕국시대를 맞이한다. 이스라엘의 왕국탄생 과정은 삼상11장에서 볼 수 있다. 왕국탄생의 과정도 사사의 출현과 비슷하다. 가령 야베스(Jabesh)라는 도시에 거주하는 이스라엘 거민들이 암몬 족속으로 위협을 받게 되자 베냐민지파의 출신 사울이 등장하여 사울의 지도력 아래 야베스를 구해낸다(삼상11:7). 그 후 이스라엘 백성들은 강력한 리더십을 필요로 했다. 그들은 언제나 외세의 침입 하에 있는 이스라엘 백성들은 나라가 조직화 되고, 확장되기를 원했으며, 외세의 침입 아래 있는 상황에서는 왕권의 도입이 필연적이었다. 그 후 그들은 당시 전쟁의 영웅 사울을 길갈에서 사무엘로부터 기름부음을 받으므로 이스라엘의 왕국시대가 시작되었고, 사울이 초대 왕이 된다.

이처럼 이스라엘의 왕국제도는 사사시대와 마찬가지로 외부로부터 침입을 막아내는데 절실했기 때문이다. 이스라엘의 왕국은 사울과 다윗과 솔로몬과 분열왕국시대 까지를 말하며, 사울과 다윗은 왕의 직위를 받은 후에도 왕으로 불리는 것보다도 오히려 지도자라 불렸고, 사무엘은 그 말을 더 수용했다.[200] 본고에서는 왕국의 개괄적인 지도력을 언급하고 대표적 지도력의 상징인 다윗을 중심으로 살펴보고자 한다.

① 왕의 리더십에 대한 복음적 이해

왕의 리더십은 전통적인 예수 그리스도의 3직 리더십의 하나로 상징되어 왔다. 그러나 예수 그리스도가 과연 세속적인 왕이란 어휘로 호칭되는 것이 바람직 한 것인가에 대한 의문을 제기할 수밖에 없다. 왜냐하면 예수는 섬기는 종으로서의 리더십이지 지배나 다스림이나 정복이나 종속의 개념인 왕의 이미지가 결코 아니기 때문이다. 따라서 예수 그리스도를 왕의 리더십으로 사용에는 반드시 복음적 신학적 이해가 필요하다.

개혁성경에 왕에 대한 히브리 명사의 번역은 약 7개가 된다.[201] 그 중에서 왕이란 말의 대표적 어휘는 히브리어 말크(Malk)로서 약

200) 김희, 선지자질과 제사장직의 구약 신학적 고찰 및 그 현대적 의의 (신학지남, 제44권 3집, 1977, 9), p.11.
201) 이성호, 성구대사전(서울: 혜문사,1981), pp. 1061-1063.

2522회가 나온다.[202] 이 "말크"는 바알(Baal)이나 엘(El)처럼 명칭(name)을 말하는 것이 아니고 칭호(titel)적 의미이다.

　야웨가 언제부터 칭해졌는가에 대하여도 계속적으로 논구중이다(L.Rost). 그러나 한 가지 분명한 사실은 이 칭호가 이스라엘 왕국 제도와 같이 외래적이라는 것(H.W.Wolff)이라는 점과 예루살렘 제의와 결부되어 있고, 또 다신론적 신화를 전제하고 있다는 점, 또 다른 한편으로는 군국주의를 뒷받침하는 고대 중동의 제왕 이념에 근거하고 있다는 점이다.[203] 따라서 이는 모세전승에서 보다 가나안 여부스 족속에서 온 전승을 반영하고 있다.[204] 그러므로 이 왕의 개념에 부정적 시각이 있으며, 또 다윗의 혼합적 제의정책에서 궁중음모의 실상을 반영하고 있다. 가령 다윗은 그의 궁중에서 두 제사장을 도입하였는데 한 제사장은 실로에서 온 야웨의 제사장 아비아달(삼상14:22)이고, 또 한 제사장은 여부스 내지 가나안 제사장인 사독으로 말미암은 것이니 사독은 확실히 멜기세덱과 아도니세덱을 잇는 왕조에 속한 인물이었다.[205] 이 같은 두 계열의 제사장은 결국 왕권의 유지를 위한 궁중음모의 결과로 볼 수 있으며, 그 결과에 대한 예증은 예언자들로 하여금 왕국에 대한 빗발치게 들려온 예언의 목소리였다. 이처럼 왕이라는 명칭이 일반적으로 이스라엘 왕을 가리키는 경우가 많으나 때로는 다윗 왕을 가리키기도 한다.[206]

---

202) Larry A. Mitchel, A *Student's Vocabulary for Biblical Hebrew and Aramaic* (California: A Zondervan Publication), p.1.
203) 김철현, 하나님의 나라(上)(대구: 이문출판사,1985),pp.9-14,에서 각주 13-15참고바람.
204) *Ibid*, p.11.
205) 김철현, 예언자 연구 (대구: 이문출판사, 1983), pp.14-15.
206) *The New Brown Driver Briggs Gesenius Hebrew and English Lexico* "Melek"by Francis Brown.

이러한 관점으로 미루어 보아 왕의 리더십에 대한 복음적 이해
는 그리스도를 왕이라는 칭호보다 섬김의 왕으로 이해되어야 하는
것이 바람직하다. 섬김의 왕은 바로 왕의 리더십에 종의 리더십이
포함됨을 말한다. 이사야 53장은 종의 리더십에 대한 대표적 원형
으로 볼 수 있으며, 사도 바울은 자신을 그리스도의 종[207]으로 고백
하고 있다. 이처럼 하나님과의 종의 관계는 하나님과의 특별한 관
계를 가진 언약의 종임을 명심할 필요가 있다.[208]

② 다윗의 종의 리더십과 왕의 지도력 변질

이스라엘 왕정시대에 다윗만큼 지도력을 발휘한 왕도 없으며,
동시에 다윗만큼 그의 지도력의 변질을 가져온 왕도 없다. 그러함
에도 불구하고 다윗왕은 예수 그리스도의 육적 조상으로 성서는
언급하고 있으며(마1:1-17, 눅3:23-38), 유대인들이 다윗왕 같은
메시야를 기다리고 있다.[209] 이는 오늘날의 이스라엘의 국기가 다윗
을 상징하고 있으며, 이스라엘 민족의 상징적인 리더가 곧 하나님
이 세우신 다윗으로 믿고 있다.[210]

먼저 하나님의 종과 세상의 왕으로서의 리더십을 발휘한 다윗의
리더십을 살펴보고자 한다.

첫째, 하나님의 종으로서 리더십

하나님의 종으로서 리더십은 하나님으로부터 세우심과 부르심

---

207) 롬1:1등.
208) 출21:5-6.
209) 마21:9.
210) 삼하5:2; 대상11:2; 겔34:24; 행13:22.

을 받은 선택된 지도자라는 점이다. 사무엘하에서 보면 다윗은 이스라엘의 모든 장로들이 헤브론에서 여호와 앞에서 언약을 세우고 사무엘이 기름 부어 이스라엘의 왕을 삼음으로서 새로운 지도자로 세움을 받았다.[211] 다윗이 하나님의 세우심을 받은 것은 "다윗을 만나니 내 마음에 합한 사람"(행13:22)이였고, 관대하며 숭고한 인물로 백성들의 존경을 받은 인물이었으며, 놀라운 하나님의 능력을 힘입어 블레셋의 거인 골리앗을 물리친 점이다.[212]

다윗은 시편에서 자신을 스스로 하나님의 종이라고 했으며,[213] 하나님을 왕으로 불렀다. 하나님 역시 다윗을 나의 종으로 호칭하였음을 볼 수 있는데, 사무엘에서부터 역대기상까지만 해도 나의 종 다윗이란 말이 30여 회나 반복하여 언급하고 있다.

가령 " 내가 나의 종 다윗의 손으로 내 백성 이스라엘을 구원하여 블레셋 사람의 손과..."(삼하3:18). "오직 내가 이 나라를 다 빼앗지 아니하고 나의 종 다윗과 나의 뺀 이스라엘을 위하여 한 지파를 네 아들에게 주리라 하셨더라."(왕하11:13).

이처럼 하나님과 자신이 스스로 종으로의 고백에서 하나님의 지도력을 가시화하였다. 다윗에게는 어린 시절부터 그의 목자의 생활에서 근면과 겸손 그리고 사자와 곰으로부터 그의 양 새끼를 지키고 건져내는 목자의 생활에서 하나님의 마음에 합한 사람으로 훈련을 받았다. 다윗의 진솔한 인간미는 그의 지도력의 기초가 되었다. 가령 삼하 1장 19-27절을 보면 다윗은 사울과 그의 친구 요

---

211) 삼하5:3, 16:13.
212) 삼상17:11, 16:47-49.
213) 김희, *op.cit.*,p.11.

나단의 죽음을 슬퍼하고 그 두 사람의 미덕과 아름다움을 추모하는 애가에서 다윗의 애국심과 신실한 우정 그리고 넘치는 인간미를 느낄 수 있다. 뿐만 아니라 다윗에게서 위대한 종의 지도력은 세속적인 힘 있는 왕으로서의 지위에서 나단 선지자의 책망을 겸손하게 수용하며, 자신의 죄과를 하나님 앞에 철저히 회개하는 모습에서 종으로서의 다윗의 지도력을 볼 수 있다.[214]

또 시편에서는 다윗이 회개를 통한 하나님의 신뢰의 믿음을 엿볼 수 있으며, 언제나 하나님의 은혜를 구하고(삼하6:12-15), 백성들로 하여금 하나님을 찬양하도록 이끌었으며,[215] 철저한 하나님께 대한 예배의식이 또 하나의 종의 지도력이다(삼하6:13).[216]

아무튼 다윗의 종으로서의 부르심은 여호와의 신이 다윗에게 임함으로서 특별한 권능을 주셔서 그을 지도자로 세우셨기 때문이다(삼상16:13).

둘째, 왕으로서의 리더십과 그의 지도력의 변질

다윗의 왕으로서의 지도력은 위대했다. 그는 새로운 통치의 지도력을 집중시키기 위하여 그동안 헤브론이 중심이었던 수도를 예루살렘으로 정하고 이곳을 정치와 종교의 중심지로 삼았다. 그동안 여부스(예루살렘)는 여호수아 때부터 이스라엘 백성들이 그곳을 얻기 위해 무척이나 노력하였지만 영원한 발판을 구축하는데 실패하였다.[217] 예루살렘을 수도로 정한 이유는 동쪽으로는 기혼의

---

214) 삼하12장, 시51편.
215) 황위섭, 크리스찬 리더십(서울: 한국로고스 연구원, 1989), p.259.
216) 김순규, 크리스찬의 리더십(서울: 성음소리, 1987), pp.55-56.
217) Charles F. Pfeiffer, 김영배 역, 구약사개론(서울: 기독교문서선교회, 1986), p.74.

샘이 흐르고 있어 물 공급이 쉬울 뿐만 아니라 다윗이 태어난 고향이기도 하기 때문이다. 다윗은 이 예루살렘을 다윗성 또는 시온성이라 부르게 하였다(삼하5:7).

그는 이 다윗성에 그의 통치적 위력을 외형적으로 과시하기 위하여 궁성을 건축하였으며[218] 또 실로에 있는 법궤를 다윗성(삼하6:10-15)으로 옮기므로 훗일 예루살렘의 성전을 건축하는 기틀을 마련하게 되었다. 이처럼 다윗은 정치와 종교를 왕 아래 하나로 묶는데 정치적 지도력을 발휘하는데 성공하였다.

그의 군사적 지도력은 이스라엘에 숙적이었던 블레셋을 제압하므로서 이스라엘의 통치의 국토를 변경시키는 지도력을 발휘했다.[219] 이스라엘의 국토는 동북으로 유프라데스 강에서부터 남으로 에돔의 남단 애굽의 하수를 따라 홍해의 지경까지 이르게 되었다. 이 같은 국토의 확대는 아브라함에게 약속한 땅이며(창15:18, 민34:2-12), 에스겔 선지자가 말한 이스라엘의 전 영역이었다(겔48:16-20). 이 같은 다윗의 군사적 지도력은 당시 이웃의 애굽, 바벨론, 앗수르 등의 나라가 이스라엘을 넘보지 못하는 결과를 초래하였다.

다윗의 외교적 지도력도 대단했다. 삼하5:11에 보면 "두로 왕 히람이 다윗에게 사자들과 백향목과 목수와 석수를 보내매 저희가 다윗을 위하여 집을 지으니"라고 기록하고 있는데 이를 미루어 볼 때 다윗의 외교적 지도력을 높이 평가할 수 있다.

---

218) 왕상9:1, 10, 10:12.
219) 삼하5:25; Leon Wood, 김의원 역, 이스라엘의 역사(서울: 기독교문서선교회, 1989), p.274

그러나 다윗왕의 지도력에도 불구하고 그의 리더십은 변질을 가져왔다. 먼저 그는 자신의 왕권을 유지하기 위하여 정치와 종교를 하나로 묶는데 성공했다고 보이나, 종교적인 면에서 혼합제의 내지 모세전승에서 떠나므로 하나님이 세우신 그의 지도력에 변질을 가져왔다. 이미 전술한 바와 같이 야웨전승의 아비아달 제사장과 여부스 내지 가나안 제사장 사독 제사장을 혼합기용 함으로 결국 다윗왕조에서 혼합 범벅의 종교로 그 변질을 가져왔고, 결국 아비아달이 추방되고 사독 계열이 야웨전승의 대표자로 자처하는 결과를 초래하였으며, 다윗왕조의 멸망과 성전종교와 제사장의 변질을 가져왔다.

다음으로 그의 왕권을 이용한 밧세바 사건의 무서운 죄악이었다(삼하11:1-12:25). 지도자로서 그의 행위는 여호와 보시기에 악했으며(삼하11:27), 지도자인 다윗의 이중적인 인격을 적나라라하게 파헤치며, 동시에 왕권을 이용한 정욕의 범죄를 책망한 것이다(삼하12:1-6).

오늘날 교회의 지도자들의 지도력 상실이 여기에 있다. 진솔하지 못하고 외식과 이중적인 인격과 안목의 정욕과 육체의 정욕을 절제치 못함에서 오는 대 파국을 분명히 경고하고 있다.

또 하나의 다윗의 지도력의 변질은 자신의 명예의 과시와 자랑에 포로 된 지도력의 변질이다. 다윗은 금지된 인구 조사를 통해 자신의 세력과 영광스러운 번영을 과시하려 하였다. 이에 하나님은 선지자 갓을 보내어 세 가지 징계를 선택케 하였으니 곧 칠년간 기근과 대적에게 석 달 동안 쫓겨 다니는 신세, 혹은 삼일 동안의 온역을 선택케 하였다. 이에 대하여 다윗은 자신의 오만을 깨닫고

삼일의 온역을 택하므로 그 날에 단에서 브엘세바까지 온역을 내리시니 죽은 자만 칠 만이였다. [220]

이처럼 지도자 한 사람의 지도력의 변질은 칠만의 백성이 죽게 되는 결과를 가져왔다는 사실을 깨달아야 할 것이다.

5, 제사장의 지도력

1) 성전의 기원과 제사장의 지도력

성전종교의 기원은 언제부터인가? 아직까지 일치된 견해는 없으나, 왕국 이전에 이미 성전의 소재에 대하여 12곳 정도로 알려져 있다. [221] 그러나 이스라엘 민족의 종교생활의 구심점이 되고, 그 양식, 규모, 기능면에서 표준이 될 수 있는 가시적 성전의 효시는 예루살렘 성전으로 보아야 할 것이다. 이 예루살렘 성전은 다윗이 창안하였고(삼하7:20), 솔로몬 왕 때 완성한 것이다.

성전종교에서 중심적 지도력을 발휘한 직책이 바로 제사장이다. 제사장직의 생성과 기원에 대하여도 성전의 기원과 마찬가지로 시나이 계시 이전부터 백성의 종교지도자들이 존재했음을 볼 수 있고(출19:22-24), 또 이방 제사장도 존재했으며, [222] 그리고 족장사에 나타난 멜기세덱과 이드로와 미리암의 제사장 [223]이 존재하였음을

---

220) 삼하 24:10-15.
221) Michael Haran, *Temple and Temple Service in Ancient Israel* (London : Oxford University, 1978),pp28-31.
222) 창41:45, 47:22, 삼상5:5, 렘48:71; 49:3.
223) 창14:18; 출2:16, 3:1, 18:1.

볼 수 있다. 특히 멜기세덱(Melchizedek)은 시편과 창세기를 중심
으로 볼 때 메시야의 모형론으로 신성의 표상, 왕권의 표상, 제사
장의 표상으로 언급되고 있다.[224]

그러나 이스라엘 종교에서 가시화된 제사장직의 제도와 기원은
시나이 계시에서 야웨의 율법이 선포되고 제사장을 세우신 야웨의
말씀에서 출발함이 타당하다고 보여진다. P문서에 의하면 야웨는
회막과 부속품을 만들도록 명했고, 아론과 그의 네 아들을 제사장
으로 세웠으며(출28장), 위임식을 가졌기 때문이다(출29장). 이 제
사장은 히브리어로 "코헨"으로 이는 "서 있는 자"의 뜻을 지닌 "쿤"동
사에서 그 유래를 가지며, LXX에서는 "히에루스"로 번역되었으며, 라
틴권에서는 "사케르도스"로 사용되었다. 이는 제사장직을 수행한다는
"카한"에서 그 유래를 가진다. 이처럼 제사장은 여호와 앞에서 섬기
는 자로 그 직무를 수행키 위하여 세우심을 받았으며, 백성들을 야
웨 앞에서 성실히 살아가도록 도와주는 조력자요 중개자요 판단자
로 그의 지도력을 발휘하여야 한다. 그러므로 제사장의 지도력의
원천은 야웨에 있었음을 명심해야 한다.

첫째, 제의의 지도력

제사장은 하나님과 이스라엘 백성간에 생명의 교제와 속죄의 희
생제의를 주관하는 자로서의 지도력을 발휘하였다. 그들이 드린
제사는 번제(עֹלָה), 소제(מִנְחָה), 화목제(שֶׁלֶם), 속죄제(חַטָּאת), 속
건제(אָשָׁם)를 들 수 있다. 폰 라드(Von Rad)에 의하면 제사장들은
회중의 죄를 중보하는 자로서 세우심을 받았다고 언급한 바 있으

---

224) 시:110:1, 마22:41-46; 시110:4이하, 히5:6,10; 6:20등

며, 감사의 표현으로 하나님께 바쳐지고 또 하나님으로부터 용서
와 응답의 선물이 주어지는 제사의 주관자이다. 이처럼 제사장들
의 희생제의 지도력은 생명의 교제로서의 제의이며, 죄를 속죄 받
는 제의로서 그 지도력은 백성들에게 절대적이다. 이 제의는 신약
의 복음의 성례전(Gospel Sacramants)을 기초하였으며, 주의 만찬
의 교제(Communion of the Lord's Supper)를 표상하고 있다. 그러
나 예수 그리스도는 대제사장으로서 그의 의해 제사종교는 완성되
었다. (히10:10-14).[225]

둘째, 신의 뜻을 결정하는 지도력

제사장의 독특한 지도력은 야웨의 뜻을 결정하는 일이다. 사람들은
신의 뜻을 묻고 싶을 때 제사장을 통해 전달되었는데, 이 때 야웨의
뜻을 분별하는 주문으로 "우림"과 "둠밈"으로 조정했다.[226]
신명기 33장 8절에는 "주의 둠밈과 우림이 주의 경건한 자에게
있도다."로 언급되어 있고, 출 28장 15-30절에는 대제사장 아론의
옷에 판결 흉패가 달려있는데, 그 흉패 속에 둠밈과 우림이 있다.
삼상 28장 6절에는 하나님의 뜻을 아는 방법으로 꿈으로나 선지자
를 통해서나 우림으로 분별한다고 되어 있는데, 이는 하나님의 뜻
이 제비뽑기식 도구로 이루어지는 것이 아니라 야웨의 뜻을 알고
자 하는 한 방편이었던 것이다. 이처럼 제사장의 지도력은 신의 뜻
을 전달하는 자로서의 하나님의 도구임에 틀림없다.

---

225) C.H. Dodd, *The Sacrament of the Lord's Supper in the New Testament*,
"Christin Worship"(N. Micklem, 1980).
226) 삼상28:6, 신33:8.

셋째, 축복과 재판의 지도력

제사장의 고유한 지도력의 하나가 백성을 축복하는 특권과 위임 사항이다. 창14장 19절에는 제사장 멜기세덱이 아브라함을 축복한 사례가 있으며, 신명기 10장 8절에는 야웨가 레위지파에 축복한 사례가 나오고 있다. 또 민수기 6장 27절에는 아론이 축복할 때 야웨의 이름으로 축복했다.[227] 그러므로 제사장에게 부여한 축복의 근원은 야웨로부터 오며, 제사장은 축복전달의 도구임을 명심해야 한다.

또 제사장은 재판자로서의 지도력을 발휘했다. 신명기 17장 8절과 에스겔 24장에 보면 제사장은 송사하는 일을 재판하되 야웨의 규례도록 재판하도록 명하고 있다. 또 신명기 31장 9절 이하와 신명기 27장 14절에는 백성 앞에서 절기의 법률을 선포하였다.

넷째, 제사장의 지도력 변질

이상에서 제사장은 철저한 야웨의 도구로서 서 있을 때 그들의 지도력을 발휘할 수 있다. 그러나 그들이 드리는 희생제의, 신의 뜻 결정, 축복과 재판에서 자의적 카리스마를 이용하여 그 권한을 남발하고 횡포와 치부, 혼합화 함으로써 제사종교화로 성전종교화로 율법종교화로 그 변질을 가져왔으며, 그들의 지도력은 야웨로부터 상실되고 백성들로부터 외면당하는 결과를 가져온 것이다.

그 제사장들의 지도력의 변질은 이스라엘의 성전종교가 왕국종교가 되면서 왕과 제사장의 혼합과 타협과 뒤엉킴에서 비롯된다.

---

227) 황보갑, *op.cit.*,p.117.

포레(G. Fohrer)에 의하면 이 이스라엘의 성전은 왕국 안에 둘러싸인 복합 건물로 왕실의 "사적 예배실"의 성격이 강하며 폰 라드(G. Von. Rad)에 의하면 법궤 보관의 상징적 의미로 국가 성소적 의미가 강하다.[228]

이처럼 왕국과 더불어 시작된 성전종교는 왕국의 지도력에서 전술한 바와 같이 두 제사장의 시대를 맞이하게 됨으로서 야웨의 모세전승과 여부스 가나안 제의의 혼합으로 왕국종교화로의 변질을 초래하였다.

뿐만 아니라 야웨의 역동적 임재를 물리적 공간으로 제한하는 이른 바 성전종교화로 제사종교화로 왕국종교화로 변질되어갔으며, 제사장은 왕의 시녀로서 통치의 한 방편으로 그 존재 의미를 생각할 수 있다. 왕권의 본질은 왕권의 유지와 존속을 위해 필요에 따라 언제든지 그 본질을 떠날 수 있다. 왕국의 혼합정책의 결과 혼합종교(syncretism)로 변질됨으로서 야웨의 언약과 계명에서 떠나게 되었다.

그 양상은 예언자들의 빗발치는 예언으로 가시화되었다. 에스겔은 죄악이 가득한 성전에서 야웨의 영광이 떠나는 장면을 보았다고 예언했으며(겔48:35), 미가는 예루살렘 성전의 파괴를 예언했으며(미가4:1), 특히 아모스, 호세아, 이사야, 예레미야 등은 성전예배와 제사장의 계급에 대해 맹렬히 공격했음을 볼 때 그 당시 제사장들의 변질을 단적으로 말해주고 있다.[229]

예수 그리스도는 이사야서를 인용하여 "내 집은 만민의 기도하는 집"이라고 하였고, 예레미야서를 인용하여 성전을 "강도의 굴혈"로 만

---

228) *Ibid.*,p.92에 인용된 부분을 재인용함.
229) A Hall, 소외된 사회의 예수, 김희언 역(서울: 1983), pp.62-63.

든다고 책망하였다. 예수 그리스도는 변질된 성전종교와 제사장으로 부터 에클레시아를 선포했고, 성전에서 나온 복음적 지도자를 요 구하신 것이다.

6. 회당중심의 장로들의 지도력

회당의 기원에 대하여 아직까지 통일된 견해와 정확한 자료도 없다. 다만 고고학적으로 최초의 회당은 A.D. 1세기에 건설된 것 으로 추정되는 골란공원의 가물라(Gamla)와 맛사다(Massada).. 그리고 헤로디움(Herodium)으로 추정하고 있다.[230] F Josephus, Philo, H.R.Biesenthal, L.Finkelstein에 의하면 유대 전통으로 모 세나 족장시대까지 거슬러 올라가는 입장이다.[231] 그러나 J. Bright 는 그의 「이스라엘 역사(A. history of Israel)」 에서 그들이 유배 생활에서 기도를 드리고 또 교사들과 예언자들의 이야기를 들을 수 있는 장소로 모인것을 회당의 가시적 기원으로 보았다.[232]

본고의 입장은 브라이트의 견해에 동의하면서 회당의 존립목적 이 바벨론 포로에서 디아스포라 유대인들이 성전파괴와 성전제의 를 드릴 수 없는 상황에서 그들의 "토라"를 전승시키기 위함에서 세 워졌다.

회당이란 명칭은 히브리어로 "베잇트 케네세트"(Bayith-Keneseth)로 서 "모임의 집"이며, 희랍어로는 "수나고게"(Synagogue)로서 집회나 모 임, 인도함, 또는 함께 오다, 연합의 의미를 가진다. 회당은 성전종교

---

230) 주한 이스라엘 대사관, 성서고고학 유물전(서울 : 1995), p.20.
231) H. H. Rowley, *Worship in Ancient Israel* (London, 1962), pp.213-215.
232) 겔8:1, 20:1-3.

처럼 범국가적 민족적 차원의 종교행위라기 보다는 지방적, 마을 단위, 가정단위[233] 차원의 종교행위였다. 그러나 차차 그 기능이 확대되면서 마을회관이나 공회당으로 확대되어 갔다. Kittle에 의하면 이집트, 북아프리카, 스페인, 그리스, 이태리, 메소포타미아, 바벨로니아, 시리아, 갈릴리 등지에서 이미 150여개의 회당이 있었고, 티투스(Titus)에 의해 성전 파괴시에 예루살렘에서도 480여개가 존재하였다.[234] 회당의 기능 역시 예배만이 아닌 교육의 장소 또는 숙박의 기능까지 담당하였다.

이 회당과 성전종교와는 여러 면에서 차별성이 있다. 성전은 제의 중심의 예배이나 회당예배는 쉐마의 낭송, 기도, 율법의 낭독, 예언서 낭독을 하고 때로는 율법 중심의 예배로 볼 수 있다. 또 성전은 엄격한 형식과 율법에 의거한 제의 절차로 이루어졌으나 회당은 토의와 낭독과 예배로서 지극히 자연스러웠다. 성전에서의 모든 일은 제사장과 레위인이 중심이나 회당에는 회당장이 있었고 장로들이나 랍비 그리고 서기관 중심이었다.

회당에는 장로가 있으며, 장로들의 우두머리로 회당장을 뽑았다. 회당장 아래에는 2-3명의 장로가 있었으며, 이들은 주로 예배와 율법의 일을 관장했다. 또 회당 내의 모든 일을 주관했다. 특히 바벨론 포로기 시기에 변칙적으로 시작된 회당은 장로들로 하여금 전통적인 왕과 선지자직 그리고 제사장직을 겸하게 하였다. 그러나 장로들은 제사장처럼 엄격하거나 백성과의 거리를 둔 개념이 아니라 친절했으며, 성전에서처럼 법복을 입고, 제단을 차리고, 의식중심은 아니었다. 또 장로들은 대표적 기능의 리더십으로 주민

---

233) 겔8:1, 20:1-3.
234) *Gerhard Kittle, Theological Dictionary of New Testament* VoI (Michigan: Eerdmans Publishing Company, 1971),p.812.

120명이나 되는 도시의 경우는 지방의회 또는 "게루시아"혹은 "소산 헤드린"에 장로 23명의 정족수를 가졌으며, 그 이하의 경우는 3-7명의 장로로 구성되었다. 그리고 대산헤드린에서도 장로 24명이 참여하여 그들의 지도력을 가시화하였다.

문제는 장로들의 지도력 변질이다. 그 서기관과 바리새인들의 위선적 기도(막6:5), 야심(막12:39)으로 회당을 그릇되게 이용하였다. 뿐만 아니라 세속적 통치자와 야합하는 성소로 변질되었다.

G. Kittle은 이러한 회당을 여왕벌을 중심한 벌들의 집단의 모임으로 변질되었다고 지적한 바 있다.[235] 변질된 회당에서 예수님께서 사단의 세력과 싸우셨던 곳이 바로 회당이다(막1:23ff). 요한 계시록에는 변질된 유대인의 무리인 회당을 사단의 회(계2:9, 3:9)로 언급한 바 있다. 예수 그리스도는 변질된 회당의 장로들에게 "에클레시아"의 복음적 지도력을 요구하고 있다.

---

235) Gerhard Killel, *op.cit.*, pp. 810-841.

(THE EVANGELICAL LEADERSHIP OF JESUS CHRIST)

제 **IV** 장

예수 그리스도의 복음적인 지도자상과
지도력의 원리와 실제

인류와 성서는 지금까지 수많은 지도자를 배출했다. 그러나 역사 속에서 예수 그리스도 만큼 위대한 지도자는 없다. 지금까지 예수 전에 대하여 60,000권 이상 나오고 있으나, 그 모든 저서를 통해 예수 그리스도는 독특한 권위를 지닌 종결적 계시자(Concluding Revelation)이다.[236]

그의 신적 권위와 삶의 가르침과 지도력은 완벽한 선생으로 결코 실수함이 없는 분으로 R.E. Coleman은 언급한 바 있다.

예수 그리스도의 지도력은 소크라테스(Sokrates)의 철학적 권위와 다르며, 신학자 칼벵(Calvin)의 권위와도 다르며, 셰익스피어(W.

---

236) 황보 갑, *op.cit.*, pp.160-161.

Shakespeare)의 문학적 권위와도 다르며, 붓다(Buddha)의 사성제의 권위와도 다르다.[237] 예수 그리스도는 하나님 나라의 권세로서 사랑과 용서와 섬김으로 그의 지도력을 가시화 하였다.

1. 예수 그리스도의 지도력의 內 外證

예수 그리스도의 지도력의 권위는 세상으로부터가 아닌 하늘로부터의 계시이며, 내적, 외적 증거를 통해 그의 지도력이 가시화 되었다. 예수 그리스도의 지도력의 권위의 증거에 대하여 Michael Youssef는 「예수의 지도력(*The Leadership Style of Jesus*)」에서 예수 그리스도의 최소한 일곱 가지의 확증을 언급한 바 있다.[238]

첫째, 하나님으로부터 증거되었다(요5:37). 예수께서 요단강에서 세례요한에게 세례를 받을 때 예수의 리더십을 하나님이 공적으로 증거하셨다. "이는 내 사랑하는 아들이요 내 기뻐하는 자라"(마3:16-17).

둘째, 세례 요한으로부터 증거 되었다(요5:33). 요한은 자신에게 예수가 세례를 받을 때 성령의 비둘기가 하늘로부터 내려오는 것을 보았고, 요한은 이를 증거하였다.

"이튿날 요한이 예수께서 자기에게 나오심을 보고 이르되 보라 세상 죄를 지고 가는 하나님의 어린 양이로다"(요1:29)

셋째, 그리스도 스스로 증거하였다.[239] 예수는 자신을 아버지와 하나라고 증거하였다(요10:30). 또 "내게는 요한의 증거보다 더 큰 증거가 있으니 아버지께서 내게 주사 이루게 하시는 역사 곧 내가 하는 그

---

237) *Ibid.*
238) Michael Youssef, *The Leadership Style of Jesus*, Victor Books, 1986.
239) 요5:36; 10:30,33.

역사가 아버지께서 나를 보내신 것을 나를 위하여 증언하는 것이요"
(요5:36)로 자증(自證)하였다.

넷째, 성령의 증거이다.[240]

다섯 번째, 성서의 증거다.[241] 성서는 예수 그리스도에 대하여 증거한
책이다. 이사야는 그의 탄생(사9:6)과 고난(사53장), 그리고 종으로 오
신 그리스도(사42장)를 증거하고 있다. 특히 영생에 대하여 "너희가
성경에서 영생을 얻은 줄 생각하고 성경을 연구 하거니와 이 성경이
곧 내게 대하여 증언하는 것이니라 그러나 너희가 영생을 얻기 위하
여 내게 오기를 원하지 아니하는도다"(요5:39-40).

여섯 번째, 기적 사화의 증거다.[242] 예수 그리스도는 기적 사화를 통
해 그의 지도력을 가시화 하였다. 예수 그리스도는 38년 된 병자를 고
치시고 나면서 소경된 자와 앉은뱅이를 고치셨는데 이는 자신의 권위
를 자랑키 위함이 아닌 오직 하나님의 영광을 나타내기 위한 지도력
이었다.

마지막으로 그의 제자들의 증거이다.[243] 예수를 따르는 제자들은 대
부분 그리스도의 복음을 증거하다가 순교하였다. 그들이 순교할 수
있는 힘은 주님만이 영생을 주시는 분으로 확신했기 때문이다.

예수 그리스도의 지도력은 전술한 증거뿐만 아니라 그 자신의 칭호
속에 신적 권위가 계시되고 있다. 마울레(C.F.D.Moule)의 『기독교의
기원(The Origin of Christology)』에 의하면 예수 그리스도에 대한 칭

---

240) 요1:34; 마7:29; 막1:22-27; 눅4:36.
241) 사9:6; 53:4-10, 42:1-4, 40:3, 요5:39-40
242) 요9장, 요5:41.
243) 요6:68; 21:24.

호를 "하나님의 아들", "인자", "주", "그리스도"로 언급하였다.[244]

하나님의 아들이란 칭호의 권위는 그 자체만으로 신적 권위가 있으며, 어떤 연관도 특별한 신분도 필요치 않다. 마울레에 의하면 하나님의 아들이란 용어는 예수가 살던 시대에는 메시아의 특징 중에 하나로 인식되어 왔음이 분명하다.[245] 이 하나님의 아들이란 계시의 근거는 하나님으로부터(막1:11) 또 베드로의 입술을 통해서(마16:16), 또 천사와 대 제사장과 백부장과 귀신들린 자들을 통해 계시 증거되었다.[246]

인자(人子)란 칭호는 예수 그리스도의 인성의 함축(含蓄)을 나타내는 말로 하나님의 아들임에도 불구하고, 인자란 말을 자칭(自稱)한 것은 메시야의 비밀성을 함축하고 있으며, 섬김의 권위를 나타내는 독특한 칭호이다. 이 인자의 칭호는 예수께서 스스로를 그렇게 자주 부르신 칭호라는데 사복음서의 일치된 증거이다.[247]

주(Lord) (κυριος)란 칭호는 구약의 "야훼"를 번역할 때 쓰여진 칭호로, 야훼는 하나님께서 스스로 자신을 계시한 표현으로 하나님 자신을 계시한 어휘이다. 이 "주"라는 개념으로 예수는 현재적 구원의 대명사로 표상화 될 뿐만 아니라 하나님과의 항구적 중보자로서 예배, 축복, 기도, 성례전 등의 실제적 의미를 가지며, 또 구원받은 자들의 그리스도 됨이 본질적으로 표시된 주권적 개념이다.

메시아로서 그리스도의 칭호는 가이사랴 빌립보에서 베드로의 입술을 통해 고백되었다. 그러나 정작 예수 자신은 그리스도에 대한 비

---

244) C.F.D. Moule, *The Origin of Christology*(London : Cambridge University Press,1977),pp.12-46.
245) C.F.D. Moule, *op.cit.,pp.*27-28.
246) 눅1:35; 마14:31; 막3:11; 15:29.
247) Joachim Jeremias, *New Testament Theology* (London :SCM Press Ltd, 1971), p.259.

밀성을 지키고자하셨다. 그 이 유는 그가 메시아이시기 때문이다. H. Conzelmann에 의하면 그리스도는 메시아에서 온 말이다. "메시야"는 LXX에 "크리스토우"로 번역되었다. 메시야는 "기름을 붓다", 또는 "기름을 바르다"는 "마사"라는 동사에서 나온 말이며, 구약에서는 "기름부은 자"는 "왕", "선지자", "제사장"으로 표현한 바 있다.[248] 그러므로 예수 그리스도는 3직의 독특한 지도력을 가지신 분이다.

2. 바실레이아($\beta\alpha\sigma\iota\lambda\epsilon\iota\alpha$)의 선포와 에클레시아($\epsilon\kappa\kappa\lambda\eta\sigma\iota\alpha$)를 세우신 예수 그리스도의 지도자상

예수 그리스도의 복음의 시작은 "바실레이아"선포로부터 시작되었다(막1:15). 이 "바실레이아"는 복음의 본질인 동시에 예수 그리스도의 전 생애의 가르침(Teaching)의 중심(Center)이었다.[249] 예수님의 가르침을 기록한 공관복음서도 하늘나라 또는 하나님의 나라로 교차 사용되었는데 그 횟수가 무려 126회나 언급되어 있다.[250] 이 "바실레이아"라는 말은 구약에는 LXX으로 볼 때 Malkuth Shamayim를 η $\beta\alpha\sigma\iota\lambda\epsilon\iota\alpha$ $\tau\omega\nu$ $o\upsilon\rho\alpha\nu\omega\nu$로 번역되었으며, 영어권에서는 Kingdom of God으로 번역되었다.[251]

이 Malkuth는 구약과 유대문헌에서 언제나 왕적 통치를 의미하며, 왕이 다스리는 영토를 의미하는 "나라"로 사용하였다.[252] Alfred

---

248) 삼상26:11; 시89:20; 사45:1(왕), 왕상19:16(선지자), 출29:36(제단).
249) John Piper, *Love Your Enemies*(London : Cambridge University, 1979), p.69.
250) *C.T.D.T.*,pp.270-273.
251) 황보갑, *op.cit.*,pp.209-215.
252) G. E. Ladd, *Crucial Questions about the Kingdom of God*, 신성종 역 (서울: 성광문화사, 1982), p.84.

Plummer는 영토나 백성이 아니며, 그 백성에 대하여 주어진 영토에서 왕으로 "통치"를 말한다.[253] 그러나 황보 갑 박사는 그의 "에클레시아"에서 "바실레이아"를 하나님의 "통치"라는 개념보다 "권능성의 임재"로 보고 있다. 그 이유는 "통치"라는 개념은 세속적인 왕의 의미를 강하게 나타내는 말로서, 구약에서 야훼를 왕의 칭호로 언급된 것은 비교적 후기에 다신론적인 신화를 전제하고 있고, 또 고대의 제왕이념에 근거하고 있기 때문이다. 물론 $\beta\alpha\sigma\iota\lambda\epsilon\iota\alpha$는 $\beta\alpha\sigma\iota\lambda\epsilon\upsilon\omega$의 통치(Rule or Geverment) 적 의미가 있으나, 예수 그리스도가 언급한 "바실레이아"는 하나님의 "권능성의 임재"로 봄이 타당하다.[254] 이 "바실레이아"의 주는 하나님이다. 구약에서 하나님의 별칭의 하나인 "만군의 여호와"를 LXX에서 권능성인 "뒤나미스"($\delta\upsilon\nu\alpha\mu\iota\varsigma$)로 번역하고 있기 때문이다.[255]

예수께서 선포하신 말씀 가운데 하나님의 나라의 본질인 권능성의 임재를 여러 곳에 언급하고 있다.[256]

"내가 진실로 진실로 너희에게 이르노니 여기 서 있는 사람 중에는 죽기 전에 하나님의 나라가 권능으로 임하는 것을 볼 자들도 있느니라"(막9:1).

본고에서는 하나님 나라의 현재성, 비밀성과 미래성을 고찰하는 것이 아니고, 단지 하나님 나라의 주로서의 권능성의 임재로서의 리더십을 언급하는데 있다.

---

253) Alfred Plummer, *Critical and Exegetical Commentary on the Gospel according tos*, Luck(Edinburgh: T&t. CLARK, 1981),p.439.
254) 황보갑, *op.cit*., pp.209-228.
255) 대상29:11, 욥12:13.
256) 막9:1, 13:26, 눅11:20, 고전4:20, 롬1:4, 눅4:14, 살전1:5, 갈3:5.

다음으로 예수 그리스도는 "바실레이아"를 위한 "에클레시아"를 세우셨다. "에클레시아"를 세우신 예수 그리스도의 리더십은 유대주의 성전종교나 회당종교로부터 유출이 아닌 하나님으로부터 나온 것(Called Out)이며, 하나님 나라의 백성으로 구원하는데 있다. 또 어떤 인위적인 사회 공동체나, 교파나 어떤 조직체를 만들어 군림하려는 리더십이 아니라 오직 메시아십(Messiahship)으로서 저 창세로부터 죄(Sin & sins)와 고통과 죽음으로 부터 그의 영원한 사랑과 용서와 섬김의 복음으로 그의 "바실레이아"를 위한 "에클레시아"를 그의 의중(Mind)과 말씀(λoγoς)로 선포하시고 세우셨다(마16:18; 18:17).

그의 "에클레시아"의 지도력은 음부의 권세(The Power of Death)가 이기지 못할 뿐만 아니라 무엇이던지 매고 푸는 천국의 열쇠(The Keys of the Kingdom)의 권세를 가지고 있다. 그러므로 예수 그리스도의 지도력은 "바실레이아"의 주로서 그의 "에클레시아"의 세우심에서 이해되어져야 하며, 그 지도력의 본질인 영원한 길과 진리와 생명에 이르게 하는 사랑과 용서와 섬김의 복음에 있는 것이다.

1) 사랑

예수 그리스도의 제일가는 리더십은 그의 사랑이다. 나폴레옹은 힘의 논리로 세계제패를 꿈꾸었으나 실패하였다. 그러나 예수는 사랑으로 온 인류에게 길과 진리와 영원한 생명을 계시했다. 예수 그리스도는 사랑 그 자체이시다. "태초부터 있는 생명의 말씀에 관하여는 우리가 들은 바요, 눈으로 본 바요, 자세히 보고 우리의 손으로 만진바(요일1:1) 된 사도요한은 하나님은 사랑이라(God is Love)"라고 증거하였다. 그러므로 예수 그리스도가 선포한 복음의 본질은 사랑이며, 그의 성육신(聖肉身;Incarnation)도 인간 사랑의 결정체이며(요3:16), 그의 십자가의 죽으심도, 그의 "바실레이아"도 사랑으로 충만 되어진 나라 이기 때문이다. Victor Paul Furnish는 예수 그리스도가 선포한 "바실 레이아"는 하나님의 용서와 명령되어지는 사랑으로 충만 되어 진다고 언급한 바 있다.[257]

Adams는 예수 그리스도의 중심에 위치한 속성은 사랑이며, 사람 들을 자신에게 묶은 것은 바로 사랑이었다고 언급한 바 있다.[258] 예 수 그리스도의 행적을 기록한 사복음서에는 예수 그리스도의 가 르침을 두 물줄기로 요약할 수 있다. 그것은 대 계명(The Great Commandment)[259]과 대 명령(The Great Commission)[260]이다. Leonard Sanderson은 대 계명이 먼저이고, 대 명령은 수직의 관계로 보았다.[261] 예수 그리스도의 대 계명은 하나님 사랑(love to God), 원수 사랑을 포함한 이웃사랑(love to neighbor)을 말한다.

예수 그리스도의 사랑의 리더십은 첫째로 구원의 완성이다.

그는 인류의 구원을 위해 어떤 힘이나 세력이나 율법으로서가 아니 라 오직 그의 십자가의 사랑으로 그의 구원을 완성하신 것이다.

이 "아가페"의 Leadership은 세상의 어느 지도자도 할 수 없는 죄

---

257) Victor Paul Furnish, *The Love Command in the New Testament*(London : SCM Press,1973), pp.194-195., 황보갑, *op.cit.*,pp.174-178.
258) A.M. Adams, *Effective Leadership for Today's Church* (Philadelphia :The Westminster Press, 1978),p.7.
259) 마22:34-40, 막12:28-34.
260) 마28:18-20.
261) Leonard Sanderson & Ron Johnson, *Evangelism for All God's People* (Nashville : Broadman Press, 1990),p.49.

인 된 인류를 구원한 것이다.[262] 예수 그리스도의 십자가 사랑은 우주적이고 세계적인 사랑으로 민족과 국경과 인종과 계급과 교파와 종교까지 넘어 누구든지 주를 믿는 자에게 값없이 주시는 하나님의 사랑 즉 "아가페"(αγαπη)이다. 이 "아가페"는 사랑할 가치가 없음에도 불구하고 사랑하는 것(롬5:8; 눅23:34)이며, 주고받는 사랑이요 love 가 아닌 like의 결정체인 "에로스"와 다르며, 또 선택과 기호와 한정적 의미를 지니며 배려와 우정의 나눔의 사랑인 "필리아"와도 다르며, 혈연과 인도주의적 관계에서 언급되는 "스톨케"와도 다르다. 뿐만 아니라 불교의 자비와도 다르며, 유교의 인(仁)의 사랑과도 다르다.[263]

둘째, 고난의 종으로서 리더십이다.

참된 사랑은 언제나 고난을 동반한다. 예수 그리스도는 인류를 구원하시기 위하여 절대자가 상대적인 인간의 몸으로 성육신함에는 반드시 고난이 동반된 사건이었다. 예수 그리스도가 종의 리더십으로 이 땅에 오심은 이미 구약 이사야 53장에 예수 그리스도의 "고난의 종"의 모습을 표상하였으며, 사도바울은 빌립보서에서 예수 그리스도의 성육신은 하나님이 종의 모습을 지닌 인간의 몸으로 오셨음을 증언하고 있다(빌2:5-11).

예수 그리스도의 종의 리더십의 요소로서는 순종, 희생, 겸손이다. 이 세 요소는 예수 그리스도가 죽으신 십자가에서 가시화 되었다. 예수 그리스도의 십자가의 예고 원리는 "순종"과 "복종"의 삶이었다. "내 아버지여 만일 할 만하시거든 이 잔을 내게서 지나가게 하옵소서, 그

---

262) 요3:16, 행4:12. 롬3:23-24.
263) 더 깊은 연구는 황보 갑 박사의 "에클레시아"pp.174-178.를 참조하시기 바람.

러나 나의 원대로 마시옵고, 아버지의 원대로 하옵소서... 내 아버지여 만일 내가 마시지 않고는 이 잔이 내게서 지나갈 수 없거든 아버지의 원대로 되기를 원하나이다"(마26:39, 42). 그가 세상에 오셔서 십자가를 지심은 아버지의 뜻에 따라 절대적인 복종을 이루고자 함이었음을 스스로 고백하였다(마26:42). 이를 사도 바울은 예수 그리스도의 십자가의 죽으심은 죽기까지 복종하였다고 증거하였다(빌2:8). 또 하나의 십자가의 예고의 원리는 자신을 팔자를 미리 아시고 계시면서도 끝까지 그를 책망하거나 출교하거나 정죄하지 않고 오히려 함께 만찬하며 발을 씻기며 자신의 행위를 스스로 느끼게 하고 반성케 하고자 했던 예수 그리스도의 종의 리더십이다. 이야말로 위대하지 않을 수 없으며, 끝까지 하나님의 뜻에 순종과 복종하는 모습을 볼 수 있다.

다음으로 예수 그리스도의 그의 십자가의 길이다.

예수가 십자가를 지고 가 신길 "비아돌로로사"(Via Dolorosa)는 "슬픔의 길"또는 "고난의 길"이요 "희생의 삶"의 본을 보여주신 현장이었다. 그는 무죄한 분이다. 이를 빌라도는 증거했다(마27:22-24). 예수 그리스도의 희생은 온 인류를 구원하는 종으로서의 리더십을 아낌없이 발휘하신 것이다. 예수 그리스도의 희생적 리더십은 "비아돌로로사"의 길에서 구레네 시몬을 통해 그 모습을 재현했으며 이를 표증 시켰다(마27:32). 끝으로 십자가 지심의 원리는 겸손의 리더십을 가시화하였다. 바울의 증거처럼 "그는 근본 하나님의 본체시나 하나님과 동등됨을 취할 것으로 여기지 아니하시고 오히려 자기를 비워 종의 형체를 가지사 사람들과 같이 되셨고"(빌2:6-7)라고 증거 하였다.

오늘의 교회와 교회 지도자들은 예수 그리스도의 십자가의 예고와 십자가의 길과 십자가의 원리의 리더십을 배워야 한다. 다시 말하면 순종과 복종 그리고 희생과 겸손으로 하나님의 뜻을 이루어 드리고 사랑의 리더십을 따라야 할 것이다.

셋째, 온유와 용기와 율법을 완성하는 지도력이다.

예수 그리스도는 온유한 지도자였다. 온유란 말은 헬라어로 프라우스(Praus)로서 분노할 때 분노하지만, 긍휼의 눈으로 자제력을 갖춤을 뜻한다. 예수 그리스도의 온유한 지도력은 모든 사람에게 언제나 사랑의 목자였으나 불의나 비 복음에 대하여는 단호했다. 외유내강(外柔內剛)이란 말이 예수 그리스도의 온유한 지도력에 함축적인 말이다. 예수 그리스도의 분명하고 단호한 지도력을 살펴보자. 가령 요8장에 유대인 지도자들이 예수가 마귀들이었다고 비난 했을 때 "나는 귀신 들린 것이 아니라 오직 내 아버지를 공경함이거늘 너희가 나를 무시하는 도다"(요8:49). 또 제자들을 꾸짖는 모습이 언급되었다. 최후의 만찬석상에서 제자 베드로의 발을 씻기려고 할 때 베드로는 "내 발을 절대로 씻기지 못 하리이다."라고 거절했다. 그때 예수께서 분명히 말씀하셨다. "내가 너를 씻어 주지 아니하면 네가 나와 상관이 없느니라"(요13:8).

반면에 예수의 긍휼하신 온유의 지도력을 살펴보자.

가령 요한복음 8장에 현장에서 간음하다 잡힌 여인을 율법주위 지도자들이 세워놓고 예수를 시험했다. 율법주의 지도자들은 율법에 의하면 현장에서 간음하다 잡힌 여인은 돌로 쳐 죽이도록 되어있다. 그러나 예수 그리스도의 사랑의 지도력은 온유함으로 나타났으니 곧 그 여인에 대하여 부 도덕성을 훈계하지 않았으며, 그의 부도덕성으로 인한 이웃과 가족의 피해도 묻지 않았으며, 그리고 그 부도덕성에 대한 원인을 묻지 않았다.

다만 한 가지 "여자여 너를 고소하던 그들이 어디 있느냐? 너를 정죄한 자가 없느냐? 대답하되 주여 없나이다. 나도 너를 정죄하지 아니하노니 가서 다시는 죄를 범치 말라"는 그의 사랑의 온유함의 지도력은 용납과 용서와 관용의 복음의 지도력 이었다. 잠언기자는 "자기 마음을 다스리는 자는 성을 빼앗는 자보다 나으니라"(잠언16:32) 고 하였고, 모세의 지도력은 온유한 지도력으로 나타나고 있다(민12:3).

오늘의 교회와 교회 지도자들에게 예수님의 온유한 지도력이 요구된다. 양들을 향한 긍휼과 관용과 용서의 돌봄이 요구되며 잘못된 길을 가는 양들에게는 단호하고 분명한 입장의 표명이 되어야 할 것이다.

예수님에게는 용기 있는 지도력이 있었다. 예수님은 제자들에게 용기를 가지라고 명령하지 않았다. 그는 용기의 지도력을 본을 통해 가시화 하였다. 요한복음2장에서 "성전 안에서 소와 양과 비둘기 파는 사람들과 돈 바꾸는 사람들의 앉은 것을 보시고 노끈으로 채찍을 만드사 양이나 소를 다 성전에서 내어 쫓으시고 돈 바꾸는 사람들의 돈을 쏟으시며 상을 엎으시고 비둘기 파는 사람에게 이르시되 이것을 여기서 가져가라 내 아버지 집으로 장사하는 집으로 만들지 말라"[264] 고 꾸짖는 용기 있는 지도력을 볼 수 있다.

또 예수님은 "예"와 "아니오"를 분명히 하신 용기 있는 지도자였다.[265] 예수는 종교적인 훈련을 받은 유대인의 지도자인 니고데모가 밤중에 찾아와서 예수께 질문을 할 때 그의 말을 다 들으시고 난후 예수는 니고데모에게 세상적인 방법으로 타협이나 명령이나 최선을 다하도록

---

264) 요2:14-16.
265) 마5:37, 고후1:17, 18, 약5:12.

명하지도 않고 단지 "거듭나야 한다."는 말씀만 하셨다. 그는 진리만 말하는 용기 있는 지도력이다.

우리는 16세기 종교개혁자 Martin Luther의 용기를 배울 필요가 있다. 그는 당시 교회와 교황 그리고 웜스(Worms)국회에서 행한 그의 용기는 예수 그리스도의 용기의 지도력을 증거하는 한 일면으로 볼 수 있다.[266]

오늘의 교회와 교회 지도자들에게는 예수님의 용기 있는 지도력이 필요하다. 타협의 관문을 통과하여 진리에 서서 "예"와 "아니오"를 하고 불의를 향해 용기 있는 결단의 태도가 필요한 것이다.

끝으로 예수님의 율법에 대한 새로운 해석을 부여하였다.

다시 말하면 잘못된 율법의 해석과 심화 내지 원칙적 성격을 부여하는 지도력을 보였다. 정통 유대인들은 율법을 613가지(248가지 의무 조항이고, 365가지는 경한 조항)로 규칙의 조항을 만들어 놓고 날마다 지키도록 명하였다. 또 가르침의 근본을 모세나 하나님의 법 보다 유명한 랍비 힐렐(Rabbi Hillel) 선생이 가르친 바에 의하면 하고 언급하였다. 따라서 요5장 1-15절에 예수님께서 38년 된 병자를 고치신 것에 대하여 종교지도자들은 안식일의 규례를 범한 것으로 기쁨과 축하 보다는 오히려 분노하였다.

그러나 예수님은 이들의 잘못된 율법의 인식을 가르치시고 안식일 주인은 인자이며 안식일은 사람을 위해 있는 것임을 말씀하셨다. 그러나 예수 그리스도는 율법을 거부가 아니라 언제나 구약과 연관을

---

266) T. M. Lindsay, *A History of the Reformation* (Charles Scribners Sons), p.257.

맺되 원칙적 성격 부여 내지 새로운 해석을 제시했다. 가령 "나는 들었다 …그러나 나는 너희에게 말한다"이다. 오늘의 교회에는 그 나름대로의 전통이 있으며, 또 관습이 전해져 오고 있다. 교회의 지도자는 그 전통과 관습이 비 복음적일 때는 그 내용을 심화 내지 새로운 해석을 부여하여 잘못된 관습을 타파하는 지도력이 요구된다.

2) 용서

하나님의 사랑은 용서가 전제된 사랑이다. 하나님이 이 세상을 이처럼 사랑하셔서 그의 독생자를 보내신 것은 이미 용서가 전제된 사랑이었다(요3:16).

태초에 하나님은 범죄한 인류의 시조 아담(Adam, Man, Mankind)과 하와를 부르심도(창3:9) 용서가 전제된 사랑의 부르심이요, 아담에게 가죽옷을 입히심은(창3:21) 예수 그리스도의 피를 통한 온 인류이 죄를 용서하시는 하나님의 사랑의 행위의 표상이다.

모세를 통해 주어진 율법은 하나님께로 향하게 하는 몽학선생이나, 그 기능은 죄를 폭로하고 정죄하고 심판하는 것이다. 때문에 바리새인 지도자들은 율법의 기능성을 강조하면서 율법의 완전이행을 주장하며, 용서보다 정죄와 폭로와 심판의 자리에 스스로 서는 변질을 가져왔다.

예수 그리스도의 성육신은 용서가 전제된 사랑의 계시였고,[267] 그의 복음은 변질된 율법종교와 종교지도자들로부터 Calling Out하여 용서의 복음으로 초대한 것이다. 따라서 예수 그리스도의 가르침은 칸트(I.Kant)나 공자처럼 도덕적인 가르침이 아니라 하나님 나라로 초청

---

267) 황보갑, *op.cit.*,p.179.

하는 죄의 용서의 복음이었다.[268] 하나님은 온 인류를 향하여 용서받을 수 있는 길을 제시하였으니 곧 길과 진리와 생명 되신 예수 그리스도의 복음을 믿음과 그의 나라의 초대이다. 용서의 근원과 출발은 하나님이요, 그 용서는 죄에 대한 값을 치름이니 곧 하나님이신 예수 그리스도의 십자가의 죽으심이다. 그러므로 용서의 본질은 죄에서 자유함이요. 사망에서 영생이며, 율법에서 복음이요, 정죄에서 용서인 것이다.

예수 그리스도의 용서의 리더십의 원리는 다음 몇 가지로 고찰할 수 있다.

첫째, 용서의 원리

주님은 용서받은 자는 반드시 용서하여야 함을 가르치고 있다. 이 용서의 능력은 하나님으로부터 용서를 경험한 자를 말하는 것이며, 그 용서의 경험은 원수를 포함한 이웃 용서를 말하는 것이다. 예수님은 이 용서의 원리를 복음서 여러 곳에서 주님이 말씀하셨다. 먼저 제자들에게 가르치신 주님의 기도(Lord's Player)에서 볼 수 있다.

"우리가 우리에게 죄 지은 자를 사하여 준 것 같이 우리 죄를 사하여 주옵시고"(forgive us our debts, as we forgive our debtors)[269] 라는 말씀이다.

또 마6장과 눅6장에도 같은 원리의 말씀이 기록되어 있다.

"너희가 사람의 잘못을 용서하면 너희 하늘 아버지께서도 너희 잘못을 용서하시려니와 너희가 사람의 잘못을 용서하지 아니하면 너희

---

268) *Ibid.*,p.181.
269) 마6:9-13,

아버지께서도 너희 잘못을 용서하지 아니하시리라"(마6:14-15).

"비판치 말라 그리하면 너희가 비판을 받지 않을 것이요 정죄하지 말라 그리하면 너희가 정죄를 받지 않을 것이요 용서하라 그리하면 너희가 용서를 받을 것이요"(눅6:37).

그러므로 용서의 지도자는 주님의 용서의 능력을 충만히 경험하고 확신이 있어야 한다. 그래야 피 지도자를 용서 할 수 있다.

둘째, 용서는 희망의 산실

주님의 용서는 단순히 죄 자체의 용서로 끝나는 것이 아니라 가시적 죄의 원인 결과까지를 용서하며 더 나아가서 죄 용서함을 받은 자들로 하여금 희망의 새 출발을 제시하는 독특한 용서의 지도력이다. 흔히 우리들을 상대방의 가시적 죄의 결과를 용서하기에는 참으로 어려운 것이며, 용서 보다 정죄하고 빌라도 재판을 하고 종교재판을 하고 세상 법정에 재판을 하는 경우가 오늘의 교회 지도자들의 모습이다.

주님은 요한복음 8장에 나타나는 현장에서 간음한 여인에 대하여 바리새인의 지도자의 시각과는 전혀 다른 용서를 통해 희망의 새 출발을 말씀하고 계시고 있다. "나도 너를 정죄하지 아니하노니 가서 다시는 죄를 범하지 말라"(요8:11)고 말씀하셨기 때문이다.

셋째, 용서는 우주적인 복음
주님의 복음은 우주적(Universal)이고 카톨릭(Catholic)적이다. 복음의 본질인 용서도 우주적인 용서를 전제한다. 바로 끝없는 용서의 삶을 말하고, 원수를 사랑함을 말하고, 더 나아가서 원수를 위해 하나님께서 기도드리는 용서까지를 말한다.

주님은 십자가상에서 자신을 향해 창을 겨누고, 채찍질하고, 침을 뱉고, 조롱하고, 그의 옷을 제비 나누는 원수들을 향해 "아버지여 저들을 사하여 주옵소서 자기들이 하는 것을 알지 못함이니이다"(눅 23:34)고 기도하신 모습이 우주적인 용서의 복음의 표증이다. 뿐만 아니라 제자 베드로의 용서의 질문에서 다음과 같이 용서의 원리를 말씀하셨다.

"그때에 베드로가 나아와 이르되 주여 형제가 내게 죄를 범하면 몇 번이나 용서하여 주리이까 일곱 번까지 하오리이까 예수께서 이르시되 네게 이르노니 일곱 번뿐 아니라 일곱 번을 일흔 번까라도 할지니라"(마18:21-22).

마5장에서는 원수를 향한 용서를 넘어 기도하라고 주님은 우주적인 용서의 복음을 가르치고 있다. "네 이웃을 사랑하고 네 원수를 미워하라 하였다는 것을 너희가 들었으나 나는 너희에게 이르노니 너희는 원수를 사랑하며, 너희를 박해하는 자를 위하여 기도하라"고 말씀하셨다(마5:43-44).

넷째, 용서는 인간 사랑

주님은 인류의 죄 때문에 십자가를 지시고 그 값을 치루셨다. 때문에 죄는 주님의 적이요 아픔이요 미움의 대상이요 고통이었다. 그러나 주님은 죄를 지은 인간을 끝없이 사랑하신 인간 사랑 그 자체였다. 하나님은 인간을 만물의 왕으로 창조하셨고, 그의 영을 불어 넣으사 하나님의 형상으로 만드셨기 때문이다. (창1:27, 2:7)

시편 8편에는 인간을 사랑하시는 하나님을 찬양하고 있다. "사람이 무엇이 관대 주께서 저를 생각하시며 인자가 무엇이 관대 주께서 저를 권고 하시나이까 저를 천사 보다 조금 못하게 하시고 영화와 존귀로 관을 씌우셨나이다 주의 손으로 만드신 것을 다스리게 하시고 만물을 그 발 아래 두셨으니"라고 노래하고 있다.[270]

인간을 사랑하시는 하나님은 우리의 약함을 아시고 계시며, 죄의 자리에서 끝임 없는 화해의 중보자로 하나님과의 바른 관계를 이끄심은 바로 용서하시는 인간 사랑이다.

"나의 자녀들아 내가 이것을 너희에게 씀은 너희로 죄를 범하지 않게 하려 함이라 만일 누가 죄를 범하여도 아버지 앞에서 우리에게 대언자가 있으니 곧 의로우신 예수 그리스도시라"(요한1서 2:1).

죄는 분명히 하나님을 대적하며, 죄는 사단으로부터 오며, 죄의 삯은 사망이다.(롬6:23) 그리고 죄를 짓는 자는 인간이다. 이 땅에 의인은 없나니 하나도 없다(롬3:10). 주님의 죄인의 용서는 바로 인간 사랑인 것이다. 이것이 예수 그리스도의 용서의 리더십이다. 더 나아가서 용서를 넘어 죄에서 자유 하는 인간으로 사랑하셨다.

오늘의 교회와 교회 지도자들은 예수님의 용서의 리더십을 배워야 한다. 오늘의 교회 지도자로 칭하는 목사와 장로, 목사와 목사, 장로와 장로 그리고 교회와 교회 사이에 서로 물고 물리는 끝없는 분열과 쟁투, 미움과 질투와 모함과 빌라도 재판은 마치 바벨론의 포로 된 모습이라 감히 말하고 싶다. 때 아닌 성전종교나 회당종교나 성당종교나 율법종교의 형식과 외식과 전통과 파벌과 지역주의와 계급과 계층주의에서 나온, 또 바리새인이나 서기관이나 랍비의 리더십로 돌아가

---

270) 시8편 4-6.

는 것이 아니라 복음으로 돌아가서 예수 그리스도의 용서의 리더십 즉 죄는 미워하되 인간을 사랑하는 것을 말한다.

그러므로 복음의 지도자는 언제나 열린 마음과(요1:51) 화목의 직책(고후 5:17-19)으로 타인을 심판이나 정죄하기에 앞서서 자신을 용서해 주신 예수 그리스도의 십자가를 바라보는 눈을 가진 지도자를 말한다. 따라서 이웃을 향해 타오르는 격정을 스스로 자제할 수 있는 자기용서의 능력을 가진 지도자를 말한다. 이 같은 자기용서의 능력을 가진 지도자는 이웃을 용서하는 지도자로 가시화되며, 그 지도력의 열매는 사랑과 용서가 넘치는 복음이 충만한 "바실레이아"가 이루어져 가는 교회가 될 것이다.

3) 섬김

예수 그리스도의 독특한 리더십의 하나가 섬김의 리더십이다. 예수 그리스도의 섬김과 겸손의 삶은 세상의 어느 지도자와 비길 대 없는 독특한 리더십이다. 흔히들 리더십은 지배의 도를 연상하여 정복하고 다스리고 세력화하여 그 힘을 상징화 하였다. 그러나 예수 그리스도는 지배의 도가 아닌 섬김의 도로서 그의 "바실레이아"를 이루어 갔다.

따라서 예수 그리스도를 세속적인 왕이란 칭호를 붙이는 데 거부감이 있다. 왜냐하면 전술한 바와 같이 왕이란 어휘의 생성은 가나안 여부스 족속에서 유입이 거의 확실하며, 예수 그리스도는 세속적인 유대인의 왕이 아니기 때문이다. 또 예수 그리스도가 성육신 사건은 하나님이 종의 형체를 지녀 인간이 되신 겸손과 섬김의 사건이다.

박창환 박사는 "절대자가 상대적인 사람이 되셨다는 사실이 절대적인 고통을 동반하는 것"[271]이라고 언급한 바 있다. 예수 그리스도의 십자가의 죽으심은 섬김의 절정이요 그의 사역이 왕이 아닌 섬김의 결정체라고 할 수 있다(빌2:6-8). 뿐만 아니라 예수 그리스도는 이 땅에 오신 목적이 "섬김을 받으려 함이 아니라 도리어 섬기려 하고 자기 목숨을 많은 사람의 대속물로 주려 함이니라"는 선언은(막10:45) 바로 세속적인 왕의 칭호에 어울리지 않는 섬김 그 자체의 왕임을 나타낸 말이다. 그는 스승으로 제자의 발을 씻기시며, 세리와 창기와 가난한 자의 친구가 되셨기 때문이다.

예수 그리스도는 섬김의 리더십은 이미 구약에서 표상적으로 계시되었는데 구약에서 종의 개념이 이스라엘과 메시아를 지칭할 때 사용되었으며, 이스라엘에서 사용될 때는 특별한 선택의 의미를 지니고 있다(사44:1-2). 신약성서 공관복음서는 섬김의 종에 대하여 다음과 같이 언급하고 있다.

"예수께서 불러다가 이르시되 이방인의 집권자들이 그들을 임의로 주관하고 그 고관들이 그들에게 권세를 부리는 줄을 너희가 알거니와 너희 중에는 그렇지 않을지니 너희 중에 누구든지 크고자 하는 자는 너희를 섬기는 자가 되고 너희 중에 누구든지 으뜸이 되고자 하는 자는 모든 사람의 종이 되어야 하리라. 인자가 온 것은 섬김을 받으려 함이 아니라 도리어 섬기려 하고 자기 목숨을 많은 사람의 대속물로 주려 함이니라"[272]

"그때에 제자들이 예수께 나아와 이르되 천국에서는 누가 크니이까 예수께서 한 어린아이를 불러 그들 가운데 세우시고 이르시되 진

<hr>

271) 박창한, 신약성서해설(서울: 대한예수교 장로회 총회,1991), p.64.
272) 마20:25-28, 병행 막10:42-45, 눅22:25-27.

실로 너희에게 이르노니 너희가 돌이켜 어린아이들과 같이 되지 아니하면 결단코 천국에 들어가지 못하리라. 그러므로 누구든지 이 어린아이와 같이 자기를 낮추는 사람이 천국에서 큰 자니라"(마18:1-4).

예수께서 언급하신 섬김이란 말을 살펴보면 "섬김"이란 헬라어로 디아코노스($\delta\iota\alpha\kappa o\nu o\varsigma$) 와 라트류오($\lambda\alpha\tau\rho\epsilon\upsilon\omega$)이다. 이 "디아코노스"는 영어권에서는 Servant 또는 Minister 또는 Serve로 번역되었다. "라트류오"는 Worship 또는 Serve로 번역되었다.

예수 그리스도의 "디아코노스"로 가장 적절한 표현은 "둘로스"($\delta o\upsilon\lambda o\varsigma$)의 개념으로 그 표징적 의미는 그의 몸을 인류구원을 위한 대속물($\lambda\upsilon\rho o\nu$)[273] 되심과 하나님이 사람이 되신 인자(Son of Man)되신 그리스도이다.

예수 그리스도께서 본으로 보여주신 섬김은 하나님의 섬김과 백성 상호간의 섬김의 원리를 계시하신 것이다.

먼저 하나님과의 섬김이다. 헬라어'디아코노스'에서 Serve 또는 Worship으로 번역에서 볼 수 있듯이 하나님을 향한 섬김은 예배와 봉사 그리고 "아콜루데오"($\alpha\kappa o\lambda o\upsilon\theta\epsilon\omega$)로서 예수를 따르는 것(Follow Jesus Christ)을 말한다. 예수 그리스도를 예배하고 봉사하고 따름에는 24시간 내내 모든 재능과 힘과 시간을 하나님을 위해 드리는 것을 말한다. 사도 바울은 그리스도의 섬김을 "디아코니아"에서 둘로스($\delta o\upsilon\lambda\epsilon\upsilon\omega$)로 신학화 하였다.

다음으로 백성 상호간의 섬김의 원리이다. 백성 상호간의 섬김은 예배나 따름의 개념이 아니고 봉사 즉 Serve 또는 Service의 차원으로

---

273) 막10:45, 마20:28.

서 그 본질적 정신은 이기적인 봉사가 아니라 사랑과 용서에서 비롯되어야 한다.

그러므로 예수 그리스도의 리더십은 변질된 율법이나 제국이나 성전이나 회당이나 성당종교의 지배의 도와 계급의 도를 거부하며, 이들의 종교와 종교지도자로부터 Call in이 아닌 Called Out를 선언하신 것이다. 이것이 "바실레이아"의 선포가운데 말씀과 의중(Mind) 가시적 또는 불가시적으로 선포하신 "에클레시아"이다.

Paul Ceader는 「종의 리더십(*Servant Leadership*)」에서 크리스찬의 리더십은 섬기는 지도자가 되어야 한다고 말하면서 섬기는 자의 모델을 3가지 모델로 제시한 바 있다. ① 크고자 하면 섬기는 자가되고 ② 으뜸이 되고자 하는 자는 종이 되어야 하고 ③ 우리는 예수님의 모델을 따라야 한다고 언급한 바 있다.[274]

4) 예수 그리스도의 3직의 지도자상

예수 그리스도는 어떤 모습을 지닌 지도자인가? 예수를 따르든 제자들 조차도 예수에 대한 올바른 지도자 상을 갖지 못했다. 예수께서 가이사랴 빌립보에서 "사람들이 인자를 누구라 하느냐?"라고 질문하였을 때 더러는 세례요한, 더러는 엘리야, 어떤 이는 예레미야나 선지자 중의 하나이다(마16:14) 라고 대답했기 때문이다. 뿐만 아니라 예수는 그의 선교사역에서 때로는 율법을 해석하고, 또 토론하기도 하였으며, 회당에서 설교도 하심으로 유대인들과 사람들에 의해 "랍비"라는 칭호로 불리기도 하였다.[275] 신학적 입장에서 본 예수의 칭호가 19세기

---

274) Paul Ceder, *Servant Leadership* (Pasadena :Avenue Congregation Church), 제5부 참조.
275) 막9:5; 11:21; 14:45; 마26:25, 요한복음서의 여러 구절등.

에서는 예수를 "나사렛의 랍비"로 불리어지는 경향이 있었으며, 루돌프 불트만(R. Bultmann) 조차도 그렇게 언급한 바 있다.[276] 이처럼 예수를 랍비로 칭하는 데는 랍비의 생성과정에서 볼 때 예수에 대한 바른 이해가 아니었다. 가령 랍비 또는 서기관은 유대전통에 의하면 대략 7세에서 10세까지 예비 랍비의 학생으로서 서기관과 상주하면서 서기관의 가르침을 받고, 그 실무를 배우게 되면 서기관의 임명 예비자(ready for ordinance)로 임명되고, 그 후 그 서기관의 직책 위임을 받게 된다. 예수는 이러한 과정이 전혀 없었으며, 오히려 서기관과 대조를 이룬다(막1:22). "랍비"라는 칭호는 A.D. 1C에 존경에 대한 표시로서 일반적 표시로 사용되었다(마23:8).

예수 그리스도는 랍비나 선지중의 한 사람으로 국한되어서는 안된다. 그의 사역의 지도력을 비추어 볼 때, 구약에서 기름 부음을 받은 왕, 제사장, 선지자의 3직을 완성하는 3직의 지도자 상을 예수 그리스도를 통해 볼 수 있기 때문이다.

첫째, 선지자로서의 예수 그리스도

이는 예수를 구약의 선지자와 동일선상에 두려는 것이 아니다. 다만 그의 사역에서 구약의 선지자 사역이 예수 그리스도를 통해 본질적으로 선포되었기 때문이다.[277] 예수는 사람들이 자신을 선지자 반열에 포함시키는 것을 거부하지 않았다. 때문에 예수가 백성들의 사이에서 선지자로 불리어졌고(막6:15 병행; 8:28; 병행 마:21:11, 46; 눅7:16; 요4:19; 6:14; 7:40, 52; 9:17). 심지어 바리새인과 회의주의자 사이

---

276) Joachim Jeremias, *New Testament Theology*, 정충하 역, 신약신학 (서울 : 새순 출판사, 1990), pp. 123-128.
277) 눅13:33; 마23:31절이하; 34-36병행, 막6:4병행, 눅4:24; 요4:44등.

에서도(눅 7:39; 막8:11 병행) 호칭되었으며, 예수를 따르는 제자들도 예수를 선지자로 칭하였다(눅24:19). 특히 유대인들이 예수를 죽이기 위하여 거짓 선지자로 조롱하고 부른데서도 그 호칭이 당시에 대중적으로 사용되었음을 분명히 알 수 있다(막14:65).

예수 그리스도가 선지자가 되는 것은 하나님의 영을 소유했기 때문이다.[278] 여기서 예수가 선지자와 영을 소유하였다는 것은 구약의 사자들과 연결고리를 가졌음을 의미하는 것은 아니다. 이스라엘의 죄 때문에 말라기 선지의 죽음과 더불어 이미 영은 끊어졌다. 예수 그리스도의 영의 시작은 요단강의 세례를 받은 시부터 하나님으로부터 시작되었다.

이처럼 예수는 선지자로서 영을 지니고 있었으며, 그의 하나님 나라의 사역을 통해 어느 지도자도 흉내를 낼 수 없는 독특한 지도력을 가시화 하였다. 그의 지도력은 성령을 힘입어 귀신을 쫓아내고(마12:28), 누구든지 성령을 훼방하는 자는 사하심을 얻지 못한다는 말씀(막3:28) 등은 모두 선지자로서의 독특한 권위로 볼 수 있다. 특히 마5:12, 눅6:23, 26이 이를 뒷받침하고 있다.

둘째, 대 제사장으로서의 예수 그리스도

구약에서 가시화 되었던 제사장 직분은 야훼로부터 섬김의 직분(출28:1)으로 하나님의 백성들 앞에서 조력자로, 중개자로, 판단자로 세우심을 받았다. 그러나 이들 제사장은 하나님의 제사장 직분과 멀어져서 왕국종교와 더불어 혼합되고, 뒤섞임으로 전술한 바와 같이 제

---

278) 마12:28; 병행 눅11:20, 눅4:18-21, 마5:3; 병행 11:5, 이사야 61:1 등 참고.

사장의 지도력의 변질을 가져왔다. 이를 뒷받침하는 근거는 당시 성전 종교와 제사장들에 대한 예언자들의 빗발치는 목소리다.[279]

가령, 아모스는 "나는 너희 제물을 기뻐하지 않는다"(암5:21-22)라고 하였고, 호세아는 "나는 인애를 원하고 제사를 원치 아니하며 번제보다 하나님을 아는 것을 원하노라"(호6:6, 마9:13, 12:7)고 하였다. 이처럼 변질되고 불완전한 제사장직에 대하여 예수 그리스도는 성전보다 큰 이가 예수 그리스도 자신임을 선포했으며(마12:6), 또 내 교회인 "에클레시아"를 선포하였다(마16:16, 18:17). 뿐만 아니라 예수 그리스도는 율법의 완성자로서 사랑의 계명을 선포하였다.[280] 히브리서 기자는 구약에서 언제나 제물을 가지고 지성소에 들어가는 불완전하고 변질된 제사장에 비하여 근본적이고 본질적이며 완성적인 대 제사장이신 예수 그리스도를 증거하고 있다. "염소와 송아지의 피로 아니하고 오직 자기의 피로 영원한 속죄를 이루사 단번에 성소에 들어 가셨느니라"고 증언하였다(히9:11-12). 이사야 선지는 예수 그리스도의 십자가 사건을 바로 죄 사함을 위한 공의적 행동으로 예언한 바 있다(사53:4-6).

예수 그리스도의 대제사장으로서 리더십은 제물이나 제단으로서의 구원이 아닌 자신이 단번에 제물이 되어 죄로부터 결코 정죄함(롬8:1)이 없는 완전한 구원함을 말한다.

셋째, "바실레이아"의 왕으로서의 예수 그리스도

---

279) H. Hall, 소외된 사회의 예수, 김희언 역(서울: 1983), pp. 62-63.
280) 갈5:14, 롬13:8-10.

예수 그리스도를 왕이라고 칭함은 세속적인 왕이나 다신교에서 유입된 왕적 칭호가 아니고 "바실레이아"의 왕을 말하며, 그 왕의 본질은 지배나 통치나 정복의 세상적인 왕의 개념이 아니라[281] 사랑과 용서와 섬김의 Leadership으로 "바실레이아"의 권능성의 임재로 보아야 할 것이다. 결국 "바실레이아"의 권능성의 임재는 온 인류의 구원에 있으며, 그 구원은 섬김의 왕으로 가시화되었기 때문이다. 이 "바실레이아"의 권능성의 상태는 자유와 평안과 믿음으로서, 사도 바울은 의와 평강과 희락으로 신학화한 바 있다. 이 바실레이아의 가시적인 권능성의 임재 상태는 성서 여러 곳에 언급되어 있다.

가령 막12:25에는 "사람이 죽은 자 가운데서 살아날 때에는 장가도 아니 가고 시집도 아니 가고 하늘에 있는 천사들과 같으리라"고 말씀하셨다. 막14:58에는 "우리가 그의 말씀을 들으니 손으로 지은 이 성전을 내가 헐고 손으로 짓지 아니한 다른 성전을 사흘에 지으리라 하시고"라고 기록되어 있다. 이 말씀은 새 성전을 계시하고 있으며, 또 하나님 나라의 백성에게 새 이름이 주어지고(마5:9), 영원한 유월절 잔치가 베풀어지며(눅22:16) 하나님 나라 백성이 받게 될 상급을 계시하고 있다(막10:30-31). 눅16:19에는 영원한 처소(eternal tents)라는 말이 표현되고 있는데, 이는 광야에서 유랑하던 회막(Tent of Meeting)의 영원한 표상으로 지상성소(earthly Sanctuaries)의 문이 닫히고, 성소의 논쟁이 종결되며(요4:21), 하나님의 백성들이 하나님 앞에 경배하는 존경의 때를 말한다(요4:23). 막14:25과 눅22:30에는 하나님 나라에서 새것으로 먹고 마시는 잔치의 날을 계시하고 있다.[282]

---

281) 마27:11, 29, 37.
282) 마14:28, 눅22:30.

5) 예수 그리스도의 복음적 지도력의 원리와 실제

예수 그리스도의 복음 지도력의 원리와 실제는 "바실레이아"와 "에클레시아"에서 찾아야 한다. 왜냐하면 주님은 "바실레이아"와 "에클레시아"의 주이시기 때문이다. 예수 그리스도는 "바실레이아"와 "에클레시아를 위하여 그의 제자들을 직접 부르심과 세우심과 보내심으로 그의 제자들을 양성하였다.

A. 예수 그리스도의 지도력의 원리

복음서에서 언급된 예수 그리스도의 지도력의 원리는 하나님 나라에 들어가는 원리이다. 이를 위해 예수는 "바실레이아"를 선포했고 "에클레시아"를 세우셨다. 예수 그리스도는 그의 복음의 선포에서 하나님 나라에 들어가는 방법으로 "회개하고 복음을 믿으라" 라고 하였고, 또 헤드십 또는 선한목자로서 "나를 따르라"는 지도력을 가시화하였다.

① "회개하고 복음을 믿으라"

예수 그리스도의 지도력의 목적은 온 인류에게 "바실레이아"에 들어가게 하는데 있는 것이다. 때문에 그의 최초의 선포된 메시지는 "때가 찼고 하나님의 나라가 가까왔으니 회개하고 복음을 믿으라"(막1:15)고 선포하셨다.

구약에서 "말쿠트"로 가시화 된 나라, 통치, 현세의 왕이나, 묵시문학에서의 이원론적 메시야 사상이나 그리고 랍비문학에서 나타난 현세적이고 정치적인 다윗의 나라는 예수가 선포한 하나님 나라를 간절히 표상하고는 있으나 그 본질은 아니며, 세례요한의 예비적 운동과도 그 본질적 계시면에서 분명히 구분된다.

예수가 선포한 "바실레이아"는 구약이나 유대종교나 회당종교나 묵시문학의 전승이나 모방이나 유출이 아니고, 또 낡은 전통이나 해묵은 철학이나 장로의 유전이나(마15:2), 신화나 족보(딤전1:4)가 아닌 전무후무한 새로움의 나라를 말한다. 이 새로움이란 헬라어로 "카이노스"(καινος)로서 영어권에서는 New or Unused로서 번역하였는데, 이는 내적 외적으로 전적인 새로움을 뜻한다. 구약에서는 이 "카이노스"적 의미를 나타내는 말로 새 영(New Spirit, 겔18:31), 새 신(New Spirit., 겔11:19), 새 노래(New Song, 시40:3, 96:1, 98:1), 새 언약(New Covenant, 렘31:31), 새 일(New thing, 사42:9, 43:19, 렘31:12)으로 표상하였으며, 신약에서는 예수님의 새 계명(요13:34), 새 생명(롬6:4), 새 피조물(고후5:17), 오순절 성령강림으로 새로움의 "카이노스"가 증거 되었다(행2:1-12). 그 외에도 새 예루살렘(계3:12), 새 노래(계5:9), 새 이름(계2:7), 새 하늘과 새 땅(New Heavens and a New earth) (계21:1) 등이 증거 되었다.

이 같은 "카이노스"의 표상과 증거는 예수 그리스도 안에서 완성되며 종결된다.

J. Jeremias는 주님은 옛 이스라엘(Old Israel)을 일소하고 새 이스라엘(New Israel)로서 그의 "바실레이아"를 선언하였다고 언급하였고,[283] R. N. Flew는 예수 그리스도의 새 이스라엘 사상은 분명하다고 언급하였다.[284]

283) Joachim Jeremias, *New testament Theology*, Tr, John Bowden (London :SCM Press, 1971), p. 168.
284) R. Newton Flew, *Jesus and His Church* (London : The Epworth Press, 1938), p. 36.

주님이 선포한 하나님의 나라는 권능성의 임재로 가시화 되었는데, 하나님의 능력으로 귀신을 쫓아내고,[285] 말씀이 있게 하며,[286] 성령의 감동으로 친히 말하고,[287] 가난한 자에게 복음이 전파되고 포로된 자에게 자유를 얻게 하고 눈먼 자에게 다시 보게 함을 전파하며, 눌린 자를 자유케 하며,[288] 성령을 통해 진리 가운데로 인도하는,[289] 이 같은 권능성의 가시화는 구원을 향한 변화를 동반하였다. 이 변화인 '알락소'(αλλασσω)는 내적인 변화는 물론 외적인 옛사람의 변화를 동반하는 전인적인 변화를 가져옴으로서 그리스도 안에서의 새로운 피조물이 되는 것이다(고후5:17).

특히 성령의 권능성의 임재는 물의 표상으로 죄를 씻고,[290] 바람의 표상으로 신비의 능력이 임하고,[291] 호흡의 표상으로 생명을 소생케 하고,[292] 불의 표상으로 정결케 하고,[293] 비둘기의 표상으로 순결과 평화를 상징한다.[294] 이 같은 하나님 나라의 백성의 모임이 변화 받은 신실한 모임으로서 "에클레시아"이다.

그러므로 "에클레시아"는 "바실레이아"의 임재가 있어야 하며, 그 임재의 역동적 가시화가 사랑과 용서와 섬김의 복음이 넘치는 하나님의

---

285) 마12:28.
286) 막13:11, 눅12:12
287) 시110:1, 막12:36
288) 사21:1, 눅4:18
289) 요14:16-18
290) 요3:5, 시51:7
291) 요3:8, 행2:2
292) 창2:7
293) 행2:3-4, 출3:2
294) 마3:10, 10, 16, 눅3:22, 요1:32

나라이다.

예수 그리스도는 하나님 나라에 들어가는 조건을 두 가지, 즉 회개하고 복음을 믿으라고 말씀하셨다. 본문에서 회개는 "메타노에오"(μετανοεω)로서 "메타"(μετα)는 "달리"라는 뜻이고, "노에오"(νοεω)는 "깊이 생각함"을 말하는 것이니, 지금까지 유대종교나 율법종교나 구약종교나 성전종교나 회당종교에서 율법과 전통과 규칙과 신조에서 불완전하고 변질된 생각을 바꾸는 것이며, 그리스도에서 빗나간 과녁에서 그리스도의 중심으로 돌아오는 것을 말하는 것이다. 그리하여 율법의 완성이요 종결적 계시자인 예수 그리스도의 복음을 믿을 때 "바실레이아"에 들어가는 것이다. 이 같은 복음적 회개는 바로 믿음의 자리에 이르게 하는 능력이 있으니 곧 정죄나 심판이 아닌 용서가 동반된 사랑의 회개를 말한다.

왜 예수 그리스도는 하나님 나라에 들어가는 조건으로 복음을 믿으라고 말씀하셨는가? 지금까지 율법종교이나 제사종교나 회당종교의 가르침과 제사행위로는 도저히 구원의 자리에 이를 수 없기 때문이다. Michael Green은 그의 "Evangelism Now & Then"에서 이 "유앙겔리온"이 지난 10년 동안 추한 단어(dirty word)에 지나지 않았으나 1990년대에 들어서면서 가시적 교회에서 복음으로 충만하게 되어지는 경향이 있다고 언급한 바 있다.[295]

복음(기쁜 소식) 즉 "유앙겔리온"(ευαγγελιον)은 동서남북으로 퍼져 나가는 예수 그리스도의 기쁜 소식이자 길과 진리와 생명을 주는 살리는 소식으로, "알케"의 복음임을 복음서 서두에서 일제히 언급하고

---

295) Michael Green, *Evangelism New & Then* (Cambridge shire :Cambridge, 1973) 황보갑, op.cit., p. 173.

있다.[296] 그러므로 예수가 복음을 믿으라는 것은 지금까지의 유대 율법종교나 성전종교나 회당종교나 그들의 종교지도자들의 가르침에서 나와서(Called Out) 예수 그리스도의 복음을 믿으라는 것이다.

이 믿음은 그가 선포하신 사랑과 용서와 섬김의 복음을 믿고 경험하고 따르는 삶 까지를 말하다. 그러므로 예수 그리스도의 지도력의 원리는 완벽한 구원에 이르게 하는 복음을 믿으라고 하는 놀라운 신적 권위와 확신에서 볼 수 있다.

그러므로 오늘의 교회와 교회 지도자들에게 가장 중요한 지도력은 바로 복음의 확신에 있다. 예수님처럼 복음을 믿으라고 할 수 있는 영적인 권위가 있을 때, 즉 사랑과 용서와 섬김의 권위가 말씀과 삶의 본으로 가시화 될 때 하나님의 나라의 도구로 쓰임 받는 지도력을 발휘할 수 있다.

② "나를 따르라"

예수 그리스도의 리더십의 절정은 "믿으라"의 차원을 넘어 "나를 따르라"에 있다. 이 땅에 예수님처럼 "나를 따르라"고 말할 수 있는 지도자가 어디 있으랴! 이 같은 지도력은 오직 그리스도만이 가지신 신적 권위인 것이다. 예수님이 "나를 따르라"하신 말씀 속에는 다음 두 가지의 리더십을 계시하고 있다.

첫째, 선한 목자

예수님이 "나를 따르라"하신 말씀은 자신이 "선한 목자"이시기 때문

---

296) 요1:1, 눅1:2, 막1:1, 창1:1의 "레쉬트"는 LXX에서 "알케"로 번역되었음.

이다.[297)]

　요한복음에서는 "에고 에이미"(εγω ειμι)의 용법을 통해 자신이 양을 전제로 한 목자임을 스스로 말씀하고 있다. 가령 "나는 양의 문이라"[298)]등이다. 구약에서 모세는 하나님을 그 백성의 목자라 불렀고,[299)] 다윗은 그의 시편에서 "여호와는 나의 목자"로 노래하였으며,[300)] 이사야는 하나님이 목자의 마음을 가지고 계심을 즐거워했다.[301)]

　선한 목자의 지도력은 언제나 흩어진 양떼를 모으시는 이미지를 통해 그의 사명을 나타내고 있으며,[302)] 언제나 자신의 양을 알아야 하며,[303)] 잃어버린 양을 찾으며,[304)] 양으로 하여금 생명을 풍성하게 얻도록 인도하며,[305)] 최후에는 양들을 위하여 목숨까지 바치는 리더십이다.[306)]

　선한목자이신 예수 그리스도는 요한복음 8장에서는 "예수께서 일러 가라사대 나는 세상의 빛이니 나를 따르는 자는 어두움에 다니지 아니하고 생명의 빛을 얻으리라"[307)]고 말씀하였다. 더 나아가서 예수 그리스도는 나를 섬기려면 먼저 나를 따르라고 말씀하셨다.[308)]

　선한 목자이신 예수 그리스도는 그의 제자들을 부르시고 자신을 따르도록 말씀하셨다. 예컨대 "이 말씀을 하심은 베드로가 어떠한 죽음으로 하나님께 영광을 돌릴 것을 가르키심 이러라. 이 말씀을 하시고

---

297) 요10:11.
298) 요10:7
299) 창49:24
300) 시편 23편
301) 사40편
302) 마10:6,;15:24, 눅19:10, 겔34등
303) 요10:3
304) 눅15:4
305) 요10:10
306) 요10:11-12
307) 요8:12.
308) 요12:26

베드로에게 이르시되 나를 따르라 하시니”309) 또 “나를 따라 오너라 내가 너희로 사람을 낚는 어부가 되게 하리라,310) 그리고 “곧 부르시니 그 아비 세베대를 삯꾼들과 함께 배에 버려두고 예수를 따라 가니라”311)라는 말씀들에게서 찾을 수 있다.

선한 목자의 리더십에는 언제나 제자들만이 아닌 수많은 무리가 따른다. 성경에서도 그 내용을 찾을 수 있는데 “앞서고 뒤에서 따르는 무리가 소리 질러 가로되 호산나 다윗의 자손이여 찬송하리로다. 주의 이름으로 오시는 이여 가장 높은 곳에서 호산나 하더라”312)라든가 “큰 무리가 따르니 이는 병인들에게 행하시는 표적을 봄이러라”313)라는 말씀에서 수많은 무리의 따름이 있었음을 볼 수 있다.

예수를 따르는 제자들과 무리들을 통해 큰 표적이 일어나기 시작했다. 이것은 곧 하나님 나라의 권능성의 임재였다.

예수를 믿고 따르고 세례를 받는 사람들이 구원을 얻게 되었고,314) 또 예수의 제자들이 말씀을 확실히 증거하는 역사가 일어났으며,315) 표적과 기사는 “내 이름으로 귀신을 쫓아내고 새 방언을 말하며, 뱀을 집으며 무슨 독을 마실지라도 해를 받지 아니하며, 병든 사람에게 손을 얹은 즉 나으리라 하시더라.”316)라는 선언은 예수 그리스도의 하나님 나라의 권능성의 임재를 나타내는 것이었다.

---

309) 요21:19
310) 막1:17
311) 막1:20
312) 마21:9
313) 요6:2
314) 막16:17-18
315) 막16:20
316) 막16:17-18

하나님은 목자가 양을 목양하는 일에 실패했을 때 주권적인 권위로 간섭할 것임을 여러 곳에 언급하고 있다.[317]

오늘날 교회와 교회지도자들은 분명히 주님께서 세우신 목자이다. 목자는 선한 목자이신 예수님의 리더십에 있어야 한다. 양을 향해 나를 따르라고 할 수 있는 선한목자상이 절실히 요구된다. 오늘날 목회자의 리더십의 실패는 목자가 양을 사랑하고 양육하고 치료하고 풍성하게하고 양을 위해 목숨을 버림이 없이 양을 자신을 위해 이용하고 지배하고 종속하고 이른 바 삯꾼 목자로 변질되었기 때문이다. 이러한 목자상에 대하여 예언자들의 빗발치는 예언이 있었다.[318]

선한 목자의 삶의 우선순위는 목자를 세워주신 하나님을 향한 헌신이 있어야 하며, 다음으로 맡겨준 양의 생명을 풍성하게 하여야 하며, 끝으로 자신을 돌보아야 한다.

둘째, 교회의 머리

전술한 바와 같이 예수 그리스도는 "나를 따르라"는 리더십을 가지고 그의 "바실레이아"의 선포와 그의 "에클레시아"를 세우셨다. 사도 바울은 예수 그리스도의 "에클레시아"의 리더십을 "교회의 머리"(του σωματος της εκκλησιας)로 신학화 하였다. 그는 골로새서에서 교회의 머리되신 그리스도를 다음과 같이 언급했다.

"그는 몸인 교회의 머리라 그가 근본이요 죽은 자들 가운데서 먼저 나신 자니 친히 만물의 으뜸이 되려 하심이요"[319]

---

317) 렘23:4, 겔34:11, 슥10:3.
318) 렘23-25장, 슥11장, 사59:9-12, 겔34:23.
319) 골1:18

바울은 머리(Head)는 모든 육체의 으뜸(πρτευω)의 자리에 있는 바 유기체적 의미를 지닌 동시에 헤드십(headship)의 지도력을 가진다. 여기서 지도력의 의미와 헤드십의 의미는 다소 차이가 있다. 지도력은 헤드십의 의미를 포함하는 광범위한 개념으로 일정한 목적을 달성하기 위하여 집단 또는 개인을 통해 그들의 능력을 합리적으로 배열하고 발휘하는 일종의 기술로서 능력을 말한다. 반면에 헤드십은 어떤 집단에 공식적으로 부여되는 최고 관리자로서의 직권력을 말한다. 따라서 교회의 머리되신 예수 그리스도는 교회의 최고의 헤드십으로 모든 만물이 그의 발아래 복종케하는 이른 바 신적 헤드십이다. 이 헤드십은 오직 예수 그리스도만 가질 수 있는 권세이다.[320] 유기체로서의 머리는 교회의 머리되시는 주님과의 생동적인 관계를 유지할 때만이 그 존재적 의미를 찾을 수 있다. 에베소서 4:15-16을 통하여 바울이 보았던 교회가 그리스도 중심의 유기체적인 조직체로 보고 있음을 알 수 있다. "오직 사랑 안에서 참된 것을 하여 범사에 그에게까지 자랄지라 그는 머리니 곧 그리스도라 그에게서 온몸이 각 마디를 통하여 도움을 입음으로 연락하고 상합하여 각 지체의 분량대로 역사하여 그 몸을 자라게 하며 사랑 안에서 스스로 세우느니라"

바울은 교회를 그리스도 중심의 유기체적 조직체로 보고 있다. 이 유기체는 그리스도 안에서만 성장하고 자라가서 그리스도에까지 자라야 함을 말하고 있다. 그러므로 예수는 어떤 일반적인 리더십을 넘어 주권적이고 절대적인 헤드십을 계시하고 있다. 주경 신학자 이상근 박사는 머리와 몸의 관계를 창조자와 피조물, 또는 통치자와 피치자의 관계 이상의 긴밀함을 말하며, 머리는 몸의 가장 중요한 부분이요 지배하는 부분인 동시에 생명과 의지의 중심이요 나아가서 양 부분의

---

320) 엡1:22-23; 4:15; 5:23; 골1:18.

연결이 됨으로서 피차 생명을 유지하는 것으로 보았다.[321]

렌스키는 "머리는 구속론의 표현으로 보면서 모든 교회의 영적인 생명과 능력은 머리되신 그리스도로부터 나온다고 언급한 바 있다.[322]

그러므로 교회는 하나의 기관이라는 개념이 아니라 생명의 유기체이다. 이 유기체는 가시적 조직체의 의미가 아니라 살아있는 유기체로서 머리는 오직 하나만 가질 수 있고, 머리의 기능은 다른 지체에 결코 위임할 수 없다.

다음으로 헤드십으로서의 머리를 살펴보고자 한다. 이 헤드십은 집단이나 무리가 전제된다. 그러나 그 무리나 집단이 하나님의 부르심을 받은 "피스토이"(πιστοι, Faithful followers, NIV)의 모임이므로 어디까지나 그리스도 중심의 모임이다. 따라서 그리스도의 말씀에 복종과 순종과 섬김만 있을 뿐이다. 여기서 "헤드십"의 지도력이 가시화 된다.

바울의 몸으로서의 교회는 "헤드십"의 가시화로 모름지기 신본주의이며, 인본주의를 배격한다. 구약시대에 모세 교회는 신정(Theocracy)과 민정(Democracy)이 공존하는 묘한 정치원리를 전술한 바 있는데, 이 같은 원리는 헤드십에 의한 민정의 모임이었고 그 민정의 지도 원리는 철저한 헤드십에서 이행되었다.

오늘의 교회는 헤드십에 의한 신정과 민정이 공존되어야 하나 헤드십에서 떠나고 생명의 유기체적 교회에서 떠나 인본주의적인 사회 공동체 내지 기관으로 그 변질을 가져오고 있다. 뿐만 아니라 교회와 교

---

321) 이상근, 옥중서신 (서울 : 총회교육부: 1977), p. 271.
322) R.C.H. Lenski, 장병일 역, 골로새서 주석 (서울 : 백합출판사, 1975), pp. 246-248

회 지도자인 목사는 헤드십과 지도력을 상실한체 세력과 힘과 돈으로 타협과 협상의 목회를 하는 경향을 진단하지 않을 수 없다.

목사는 "포이멘"(ποιμην)으로 사람들을 마음으로 사랑하고 그들을 중재하며, 그들을 돌보는 사람으로서 목양자(牧羊者)임에도 불구하고 잎만 무성한 무화과나무처럼 교회의 직분의 하나로 자리를 지켜가고 있음은 슬픈 일이다.

목사는 주님으로부터 받은 고유한 영적직분으로 "예수 그리스도의 목사직"이며, 영어권에서는 minister로 번역하는 것이 바람직하다. 이는 "하나님의 목사"또는 "주님의 목사"를 말하는 것이다. 가령 All Minister of God,[323] Minister of Lord,[324] Minister of God,[325] Minister of Christ Jesus[326]이다.

이처럼 목사는 예수 그리스도로부터 부르심(Called)[327]과 세우심,[328] 과 교육의 훈련을 받고,[329] 그의 나라를 위해 보내심을 받고,[330] 또 땅 끝까지 예수 그리스도를 증거토록 대 명령을 위임받았으며,[331] 아버지와 아들과 성령의 이름으로 세례를 주고 그가 분부한 모든 복음을 가르쳐 지키게 하는 자이기 때문이다.[332]

주님은 목양을 원하고 계신다. 그리고 양들을 향해 "나를 따르라"고 할 수 있는 헤드십과 지도력을 가진 목사를 간절히 요구하고 있다.

---

323) 고후6:4
324) 엡6:21
326) 딤전4:6
327) 요15:16
328) 막3:13-14
329) 마5:7
330) 막3:15;마10:1-15.
331) 마28:16-20
332) 마28:16-20.

B. 12제자들의 지도자 양성원리의 실제

예수님의 지도자 양성원리는 어느 지도자의 양성원리와 비교할 수 없는 탁월한 지도력이었다. 그것은 마치 유능한 조각가가 볼품없는 돌덩어리로 멋진 예술 조각품을 조각해 내는 모습과 Peter Marshall의 "진흙 같은 제자들"(Disciples in Clay)이란 설교에서는 제자들의 모습을 다음과 같이 묘사하고 있다. 베드로는 고기냄새를 풍기고 거칠고 세련되지 못하고 충동적이며 성급한 분위기를 풍기며, 안드레, 야고보, 요한도 비린내를 풍기며 세련되지 못한 모습을 드러내며, 엉거주춤한 빌립, 냉소적 도마, 조국의 반역자 마태, 혁명가 시몬, 도둑의 모습 유다이다. 예수님은 도무지 성공할 수 없는 집단으로 묘사된 이러한 사람들을[333] 3년이라는 짧은 기간 동안 이들을 훈련시키고 변화시켜서 영적이고 우주적인 복음 사역을 위한 위대한 지도자들로 12사도의 훈련(The Training of the Twelve)을 시켰다.

A. B. Bruce는 그의 「12사도의 훈련(*The Training of the Twelve*)」에서 예수님께서 진흙 같은 제자들을 변화시킨 모습을 다음과 같이 기록하고 있다.

"그들은 지성에 있어서도 새로워졌으며, 모든 인류를 품을 수 있을 만한 넉넉한 사랑을 부여받았으며, 모든 의무와 요구에 대해 민감한 양심을 가졌으며, 관습과 전통과 인간의 계명의 굴레로부터 자유함을 받았고, 자만과 자기의지, 인내하지 못함, 혈기, 복수심 그리고 무자비함으로부터 깨끗하게 정화된 새로운 기질의 소유자들로 변화되

---

333) LesIieb. Flynn, *The Twelve*, 최기운 역, 열두사도(서울: 파이디온출판사, 1992), pp24-25.

었다." [334]

뿐만 아니라 예수의 열두제자들, 예를 들어 사상적 반(反)로마 투사인 열심당 시몬과 로마정부에 봉직하고 있는 세리 마태와 같이 심리적, 기질적, 지리적, 환경적으로 도저히 하나가 될 수 없는 상황 속에서도 하나가 되어 우주적인 복음의 동역자가 되게 하신 예수님의 지도력은 신적 권위에서 나온 것이다. [335]

J. O. Sanders는 "예수 그리스도께서 제자를 육성할 때 친히 모범을 보여 주셨으며, 그의 가르침은 형식에 치우치기보다 상황적이었다. 뿐만 아니라 제자들과 함께 생활하는 삶속에서 경험을 통하여 영적인 원리와 가치를 깨우치고, 실제 적용시키는 방법을 가르쳤으며, [336] 또 성공뿐만 아니라 실패를 통하여서 믿음의 훈련을 시켰다." [337]고 예수 그리스도의 이론에서만 아니라 실천적인 지도력을 강조했던 것이다. [338]

Kerreth O.Gargel은 예수 그리스도는 리더십의 중점을 어디에 두셨는가에 대하여 다음과 같이 언급한 바 있다. [339]

첫째, 예수 그리스도는 개개인에 중점을 두셨다.

요한복음 21장에서 예수와 베드로와의 대화는 예수가 베드로 개인에게 중점을 두고 있다. 베드로의 생활과 전도에 관심을 가지면서 그의 생애가 어떻게 될 것인지를 가르쳐 주고 있다.

---

334) *Ibid.*,p.32.
335) 요17:22
336) 눅17-24장
337) 막9:14-29
338) J.O. Sanders, *Spiritual Leadership*, 이동원 역, 영적지도력 (서울: 요단출판사, 1982), pp. 77-78.
339) Ted W. Engstrom, *The Making of a Christian Leader* (Grand Rapids, Michgan Zondervan Publishing House, 1977), pp.41-42.

둘째, 예수 그리스도는 말씀에 중점을 두었다.

예수 당시의 유대의 지도자들은 율법에 계시된 하나님의 뜻을 어겼으나 예수 그리스도는 "내가 율법이나 선지자나 폐하러 온 줄로 생각지 말라 폐하러 온 것이 아니요 완전케 하려 함이로라(마5:17)"하시고 "...하늘에 계신 너희 아버지의 온전하심 같이 너희도 온전하라"[340] 고 말씀하셨다.

셋째, 예수 그리스도는 자신에게 중점을 두었다.

요한복음에서 빌립과의 대화 속에서 가르침의 중심이 자신에게 있음을 볼 수 있다. "내가 이렇게 오래 너희와 함께 있으되 네가 나를 알지 못하느냐 나를 본 자는 아버지를 보았거늘 어찌하여 아버지를 보이라 하느냐"(요14:9)
예수그리스도는 복음의 중심이 자신임을 분명히 가르치셨다.
넷째로, 그는 "하나님 나라"를 위한 분명한 목표와 의도를 가지시고 그의 제자들을 양육했다.

그는 의중(Mind)과 말씀가운데 끊임없이 하나님의 나라를 선포했고, 그를 위해 그의 제자들을 양육하였다. 또한 3년간이란 짧은 시간 속에서 그의 목표를 성취했다.
Lawrence O. Richards는 예수 그리스도의 본받아야 할 Leadership으로 겸손과 순종, 사랑과 희생을 통하여 섬기는 종으로서 리더십을 보이며, 그를 따르는 제자들도 그의 본을 받아 섬기는 종의 신분의 제

---

340) 마5:21-48.

자가 되었음을 지적한다.

그러나 필자는 예수 그리스도의 제자양육 원리는 말씀으로, 인격으로, 본으로 전 생애를 가르치신 분으로 본다. 그는 언제나 삶의 자리로부터 출발하셨다. 그리고 궁극적으로는 영혼의 문제를 해결하는 제자양육의 목표로 삼았다. 예수 그리스도는 신, 인적인 권위의 교사로서 사랑과 용서와 섬김의 복음을 가르쳤다. 그 가르침의 방법은 언제나 삶의 자리에서 개인 또는 집단적인 만남과 교제[341] 그리고 개인적 존중과 칭찬[342] 때로는 잘못을 즉각 책망하셨다.[343] 또 예수의 독특한 교수법은 비유적 방법이나[344] 실물적 교수법 그리고 실제적인 본을 보이시면서 훈련시켰다.[345]

① 부르심

예수 그리스도의 지도자 양성은 그의 12제자들을 선택과 부르심에서 비롯된다. 예수 그리스도가 12제자를 양성함에는 분명한 의도가 있었고, 또 하나님 나라의 복음 사역을 위한 새로운 지도자 양성이 필요하였다. 주님이 양성하고자 하는 지도자는 율법이나 회당종교나 제사종교의 서기관이나 랍비나 바리새인과 같은 지도자 상으로는 그의 나라의 가르침을 위임할 수 없기 때문이다.

R. N. Flew에 의하면 예수 그리스도의 새 이스라엘 사상은 분명하

---

341) 예수님은 제자들과 교제를 많이 가지셨다. "필로스"의 교제와 공동식탁교제, 주의 만찬교제, 부활 후 식탁교제 등은 바울이 언급한 "코이노니아"의 원형이다.
342) 눅19:1-10, 7:36-50, 요4:1-30.
343) 요18:11.
344) 예수님의 비유적 가르침은 그의 가르침에 3분의 1를 차지할 많큼 많은 비유를 사용하셨다. 전경연, 예수의 비유(서울 : 종로서관, 1962), p.4.
345) 요13:1-15.

다. 그는 새 이스라엘의 핵심자들인 제자들을 모우고[346] 그 제자들을 통해 천국복음을 선포케 했으며, 하나님의 나라의 권능성을 제자들에게 부여하여 병든 자와 죽은 자를 살리며 문둥병을 깨끗하게 고치며, 귀신을 쫓아내는 권세로서 그의 나라를 가시화 하였다.[347]

　J. Jeremias는 주님은 옛 이스라엘(Old Israel)을 일소하고 새 이스라엘(New Israel)로서 "바실레이아"를 선포함과 동시에 새 부대인 "에클레시아"를 선언하였다.[348] R. Bultmann도 예수 그리스도는 종말론적인 공동체로서 참 이스라엘로 이해하였다.

　이처럼 새 이스라엘 또는 새로운 지도자로의 12제자의 선택과 부르심은 주님의 의도적인 지도자 양성이었다. 주님은 왜 12명을 부르시고 선택하셔서 지도자로 양성하셨는가에 대하여 여러 면에서 상징성이 주어지고 있다.

　먼저 이들의 부름은 단순한 연합적 차원 보다 우주적인 영적 부름이다. 왜냐하면 12제자의 구성 요소가 전술한 바와 같이 그들은 "클레토이"와 "에클레토이"와 "피스토이"한 그 자체가 인종과 지역과 사상과 환경을 초월한 부르심과 선택하심의 모임이기 때문이다.

　다음으로 12제자는 이스라엘의 12지파 동맹인 "암픽티오닉"(Amphictyony)과 이스라엘 이름을 상징화하는 의미가 있다. 이 지파연합은 모세의 유언(신33:1-29)과 여호수아를 통한 지파연합의 가시화이며(수24:1-28), 단순히 연합적 차원 보다 영적 연합이었다. 또 엘리야가 갈멜산의 대결가운데서 이스라엘의 이름으로 상징되는 12돌을 취

---

346) R.Newton Flew, *Jesus and His Church* (London : The Epoworth Press, 1938),p.36.
347) 황보갑, *op.cit.*, p.298.
348) J. Jeremias, *op.cit.*,p.168.

한 것도 12제자의 상징성이다(왕상18:31).

또 12제자는 영원성과 능력성의 의미를 상징화하고 있다 "…크고 높은 성곽이 있고 열 두문이 있는데 문에 열두 천사가 있고 그 문들 위에 이름을 썼으니 이스라엘 자손 열두지파의 이름이라"

"그 성에 성곽은 열두 기초석이 있고, 그 위에 어린 양의 십이사도의 열두 이름이 있더라"[349]

어떤 성경학자들은 12라는 숫자에 대하여 세상의 수인 4와 하나님의 수인 3을 곱한 것으로 하나님이 인간가족에 개입한 것의 상징화로 주장하고 있다.[350] 또 열둘(the Twelve)를 "한몸"(Corporate body)으로 언급하고 있다는 점이다.[351] 때문에 그들은 함께 일했고, 함께 사람들에게 세례를 베풀었으며, 함께 유월절을 지냈으며, 다락방에서 함께 부활하신 예수 그리스도를 만나기도 하였다.[352]

예수님께서 12제자를 부르심과 선택하심에는 독특한 의미가 있다. 늙은 사람도 아닌 20대 정도의 젊은이들이었다. 요한은 10대 후반이고 베드로는 아마 서른에 가까운 어부였다. 대개 하류 또는 중류 계층의 평범한 직업을 가지고 생계를 유지하였다. 주님이 이들을 부르실 때에는 대부분 자기의 직업에서 열심히 일하는 가운데 부르심을 입었다.[353]

이처럼 평범하고 불완전한 자들을 선택하시고 부르셔서 훈련시키고 변화시켜 그리스도의 교회를 조직하고, 세계복음화의 사명을 감

---

349) 마19:28; 계21:12, 22:2.
350) Leslieb. Flynn, *op.cit.*,p.20.
351) *Ibid.*
352) *Ibid.*
353) 마4:18-22; 막1:16-20; 2:13-14.

당하는 위대한 지도자들로 양육하셨다.

② 세우심

예수 그리스도는 평범하고 실수투성이인 12인을 부르시고 선택하시고 훈련시키시고 변화시켜서 그를 12제자로 세우셨다.

"이에 열둘을 세우셨으니 이는 자기와 함께 있게 하시고 또 보내사 전도도 하며 귀신을 내어 쫓는 권세도 있게 하려 하심이러라(막13:14-15)."

12사도의 세우심은 예수 그리스도의 대리자들로서 특별한 권위와 사명이 수반되는 자들이다.[354] 그러므로 이들에게는 특별한 자격요건이 수반되었다. Leslie B.Flynn는 The Twwlve에서 12사도의 세우심의 자격 요건이 다음과 같이 수반됨을 말하고 있다.

첫째, 처음부터 예수님과 동행한 자들이었다.

예수님의 12제자들은 예수님과 함께 생활하면서 교육과 훈련을 받았고 늘 동행한 사람들이다. 이를 입증하는 근거는 사도행전에서 예수를 판 가룟 유다 대신에 보충할 사도의 선택과정에서 베드로가 "요한의 세례로부터 우리 가운데서 올리어 가신 날까지 주 예수께서 우리 가운데 출입하실 때에 항상 우리와 함께 다니던 사람 중에서" 선택해야 한다고 언급한 데서 알 수있다.[355]

---

354) 마10:1, 눅6:13, 행1:2, 2:38, 42-43.
355) 행1:21-22

둘째, 부활의 주님을 목격한 자들이어야 한다.

전술한 바와같이 주님과 동행은 물론 "우리와 더불어 예수의 부활하심을 증거 할 사람"[356] 즉 예수의 부활하심을 증거할 증인이 되어야 함을 베드로 사도는 맛디아 사도 선택의 과정에서 말하고 있다.

셋째, 교회의 교리적 기초를 세운 사람으로 보았다.

즉 성령에 의한 계시된 영감을 받은 사도들의 말씀을 후대에 정경(Canon)으로 인정하였다는 점이다.[357]

R. N. Flew는 12사도가 일반적으로 소유한 탁월한 점을 4가지로 소개하고 있다. 첫째, 예수 생전에 매우 친밀한 관계를 갖고 있어야 하며,[358] 둘째, 예수의 부활을 목격하고 증거 할 수 있어야 하며,[359] 셋째, 예수 생전에 전도자로 파송 받은 사실이 있어야 하고,[360] 넷째로 귀신을 쫓아낼 수 있는 권능을 예수로부터 받은 사실이 있어야 한다. 이 같은 사실이 맛디아(Matthias) 보선(補選)할 때에 입증 되었다.[361]

예수의 12제자가 주님으로부터 사도로 세우심을 받은 것은 그리스도의 대리자로서 그 독특한 위치가 주어졌고 또 신적 권위로 앉은뱅이를 일으키며,[362] 귀신을 쫓아내며, 하나님 나라의 복음을 담대히 전한 것이다.[363]

---

356) 행1:22
357) Leslie B.Flynn, *op.cit.*, p. 17.
358) 막3:14;행1:21
359) 행1:21,고전9:1
360) 막3:14, 15
361) 행1:21-26
362) 행3:6
363) 막13:13-15

③ 보내심

예수 그리스도는 그의 12제자를 부르시고 선택하시고 세우셔서 그의 나라의 복음 사역을 위하여 보내셨다. 사도(Apostle)란 헬라어로 "아포스톨로스"($\alpha\pi o\sigma\tau o\lambda o\varsigma$)로서 그 뜻은 "보냄을 받은 자"를 뜻한다. 이 "아포스톨로스"는 히브리어 "솨라흐(שלח)"와 그 뜻을 같이하나 불트만은 유대주의에서 한시적 직책으로서의 "솨라흐"와는 근본적으로 다르다고 본다. 이 사도란 말은 예수님이 직접 사용하신 말이다.[364]

J.D.Douglas는 사도란 말은 예수 그리스도에 의해 부르심과 보내심(Sendfoth)을 받은 자들로[365] 거룩한 성 새 예루살렘에 새겨진 열두 주춧돌을 의미한다.[366]

그러므로 사도는 주님의 복음을 위임받은 자들이다.[367] 요한복음 20장 21절에 "아버지께서 나를 보내신 것 같이 나도 너희를 보내노라" 마태복음 10장 40절에는 "너희를 영접하는 자는 나를 영접하는 것이요, 나를 영접하는 자는 나 보내신 이를 영접하는 것 이니라"고 말씀하심으로 주님이 보내신 사도는 주님의 대리자이심을 말씀하셨다. 주님은 승천 시 그의 제자들에게 대 명령(The Great Commission)을 분부했다.

"너희는 가서 모든 족속으로 제자를 삼아 아버지와 아들과 성령의 이름으로 세례를 주고 내가 너희에게 분부한 모든 것을 가르쳐 지키게 하라 볼찌어다 세상 끝 날까지 너희와 항상 함께 있으리라 하시니라"(마28:19-20)

---

364) 눅6:13
365) J. D. Douglas, *The New International Dictionary of the Christian Church* (the Paternoster Press, 1977), p. 58.
366) 계21:14
367) 마10:5, 16, 40, 21:1, 막14:13, 눅11:49, 22:8, 요17:18 등.

주님의 제자들은 주님의 지상명령을 신실히 수행하였으며, 사람의 영혼을 구원하는 위대한 지도자들이었다. 그들의 지도력은 전 세계의 복음화를 구상하여 전도여행을 하였으며, 가는 곳마다 그리스도의 교회를 조직하고 하나님의 복음을 전파하였다.

구전에 의하면 그들은 사명을 감당하기 위하여 대부분 순교로서 그의 생을 마감하는 사명의 지도자요 충성된 하나님의 대리자였다. 베드로는 그의 마지막 생애를 로마에서 장식하면서 십자가에 거꾸로 매달려 순교하였으며, 야고보는 예루살렘에서 목 베임을 당하였으며(행 12:2), 요한은 도미티안 황제의 박해 때 끓는 가마솥에 던져졌다가 기적적으로 목숨을 건졌다. 그 후 밧모섬에서 유배되어 요한 계시록을 기록한 후 에베소에서 수명이 다하여 장사되었으니 살아서 순교한 이이다. 안드레는 그리스 파트래에서 순교했는데 그는 X형의 십자가에 매달려 죽었으며, 빌립사도는 소아시아에서 돌에 맞았거나 십자가에 매달려 죽었고, 바돌로매는 아르메니아에서 산채로 살 껍질을 벗기고 목 베어 죽임을 당했으며, 마태는 에디오피아에서 칼에 찔려 살해당했고, 도마는 인도와 아시아 지방의 사도가 되어서 복음을 전하다가 인도에서 창에 몸이 찔려 순교했으며, 작은 야고보 사도는 예루살렘의 한 탑 꼭대기에서 던져진 후 돌에 맞고 몽둥이에 맞았으나, 거기서 다시 회복되어 후에는 결국 온 몸을 톱으로 베임을 당하였다. 유다 다대오는 메소포타미아에서 화살을 맞아 죽었으며, 열심당 시몬은 페르시아만 근처에서 폭도들의 공격을 받고 순교했으며, 유다는 자살했다. [368] 젊은 마가는 뒤에 200년 동안이나 기독교의 선봉이 되어 콥틱교회(The Coptic Church)와 알렉산드리아교회(The Church of Alexandria)를 세웠다.

---

368) Leslie B. Flynn, *op.cit.*,pp.33-34.

(THE EVANGELICAL LEADERSHIP OF JESUS CHRIST)

제 V 장

변화된 12제자의 지도력

예수 그리스도는 그가 부르시고, 세우신 그의 12제자를 변화시켰다. 예수 그리스도의 복음은 인식에 있지 않고 변화에 있었다. 이 변화는 물리적 변화나 화학적인 변화를 말하는 것이 아니고, 영적이고 전인적인 변화로서 태도와 삶의 변화였다. 예수 그리스도는 3년 동안 진흙 같은 제자들을 가르치고 훈련시켜서 그들을 변화시켜 위대한 지도자로 지도력을 발휘케 했다.

Michae Youssef의 "지도자는 과거에 따라서 사는 존재가 아니라 새롭게 만들어지는 존재"라고 말한 것처럼 예수 그리스도는 그의 제자를 새롭게 만드신 것이다. 예수님은 과거의 보잘 것 없는 제자들에게 "가능성과 비전을 심어준"지도자였다. 요14:12-13절 에서 "내가 진실로 진실로 너희에게 이르노니 나를 믿는 자는 나의 하는 일을 저도 할 것이요 또한 이보다 큰 것도 하리니 이는 내가 아버지께로 감이니

라. 너희가 내 이름으로 무엇을 구하든지 내가 시행하리라 이는 아버지로 하여금 아들을 인하여 영광을 얻으시게 하려 함이라"

이처럼 도무지 성공할 수 없는 집단으로 묘사된(Leslie B. Flynn) 개인 제자들의 변화된 지도력의 모습을 살펴보고자 한다. 12제자들의 자료의 출처는 사복음서와 사도행전과 제자들이 기록한 것으로 보이는 성경에서[369] 의존한다.

1. 시몬 베드로

시몬 베드로는 3가지 이름을 가진 인물이다. 그는 갈릴리 가버나움에 살면서 고기잡이하는 어부였다. 본명은 요나의 아들 시몬(Simon)[370] 이고 예수님께서 주신 새 이름은 아람어 "게바"(Cephas) 인데 이를 헬라어로 번역하면 "베드로"(Πέτρος) 로 그 뜻은 반석(Rock)이다.

"네가 요한의 아들 시몬이니 장차 게바라 하리라 하시니라 게바를 번역하면 베드로라"(요1:42)

예수 그리스도는 전능의 눈으로 충동적이고, 다혈질이고, 비겁하고, 거칠고, 조급하고, 지나친 열정으로 이리저리 "쓸려 다니는 모래"(Shifting Sand) 같은 존재를 예수 그리스도를 만나고 훈련받고 가르침을 받아 반석(Solid Stone)같은 위대한 지도자로 지도력을 발휘케 했다.

---

369) 벧전후서, 요한1,2,3서, 계시록, 야고보서 유다서등.
370) 막1:16, 요1:40-41.

A. 옛 사람 시몬

시몬은 베드로로 변화받기 전의 본명이요 그의 원래의 모습이다. 그의 성품은 모래 같고 진흙 같은 사람으로 그의 내적 외적인 모습을 통해 살펴 볼 수 있다. 그는 어부로서 다듬어지지 않는 성격이 그대로 노출되었다. 예수께서 잡히시던 날 밤 기드론 시내에서 대제사장의 종이 나사렛 예수를 찾을 때 옛사람으로서 베드로는 어떤 사람이었는가를 나타내는 성경이 있다.

"이에 시몬 베드로가 검을 가졌는데, 이것을 빼어 대제사장의 종을 쳐서 오른편 귀를 베어 버리니 그 종의 이름은 말고라"(요.18:10)

그러나 자그마한 계집종 앞에서 예수를 결코 본적이 없다고 부인하였다. 또 무덤 속에 안치된 예수님의 몸이 없어졌다는 소식을 듣고 자기보다 무덤에 더 빨리 도착해서 기다리고 있던 요한을 두고 겁 없이 먼저 무덤 속으로 들어갔다. 뿐만 아니라 그는 쉽게 실망하고 절망하는 자로서 예수 그리스도의 십자가 이후 실망하여 다시 어부로 돌아감을 볼 수 있다. 그는 변덕이 심한 사람이었다. 예수님이 자기 발을 씻을 수 없다고 하면서 곧장 자기 몸 전체를 씻어 달라고 간청하기도 하였다. 그러나 시몬은 베드로라는 지도자로서 세움 받을 수 있는 잠재력을 소유하고 있었다. 예수님은 그것을 이미 감지하고 계셨다.

B. 변화된 베드로

예수님은 해변에서 그물 던지는 시몬의 모습을 보시고 그를 부르셨다.[371] 시몬은 갈릴리 바다에서 어부의 수장으로 언제나 리더격이었으며,

---

371) 막1:16

용감하게 바다위로 걸어 가다가 물에 빠지는 모습에서 적극적인 성격을 유추할 수 있다.[372]

뿐만 아니라 그는 솔직했다. 자기의 모습을 스스로 시인하기도 하였으며, 삶의 열정의 사람이며, 다시 시작하는 용기의 사람이었다.[373]

시몬은 주님을 잘 따랐다. 그리고 3년간 최고의 스승으로부터 훈련을 받았다. 어부라는 신분은 오히려 예수님으로부터 배움의 열정과 순종의 사람이 될 수 있었다. 주님은 언제나 시몬의 약점보다 가능성을 보셨으며 처음 만남에서부터 시몬이라 부르지 않고 "반석"이라고 부름에서 그것을 알 수 있다.

주님이 베드로를 지도자로 훈련시킨 주된 메시지는 사랑과 용서와 섬김의 복음이었다. 주님이 베드로에게 보여준 사랑은 요21장에서 부활의 주님의 모습에서 절정을 이룬다. 스승을 배반하였지만 주님은 베드로를 찾아와서 그것도 빈 배 인생에게 153마리의 고기를 가득 잡게 하셨고, 그 마지막의 3번 물음은 "네가 나를 사랑 하느냐?"이다.

주님의 용서의 가르침은 베드로가 예수님께 한 질문에서 볼 수 있다.

"주여 형제가 내게 죄를 범하면 몇 번이나 용서하여 주리이까? 일곱 번까지 하오리이까? 예수께서 가라사대 네게 이르노니 일곱 번 뿐 아니라 일흔 번씩 일곱 번이라도 할지니라"(마18:21-22) 일만 달란트 빚진 자가 탕감을 받고, 자기는 백 데나리온 빚진 동관을 용서해 주지 않음을 예를 들면서 "너희가 각각 중심으로 형제를 용서하지 아니하면 내 천부께서도 너희에게 이와 같이 하시리라"(마18:21, 35)

주님은 베드로에게 섬김의 본을 가르쳐 주셨다. 요13장 예수가 제자

---

372) 마14:22-23
373) 요21장 참조

들의 발을 씻기시는 장면에 베드로가 주연이 된 것이다. 이 섬김의 본은 시몬을 감동시키기에 충분했다. "주께서 절대 제 발을 씻기실 수 없습니다"라고 거절했다. 예수께서 말씀하시되 "내가 너를 씻기지 아니하면 네가 나와 상관이 없느니라"이때 시몬이 "주여 내 발 뿐만 아니라 손과 머리도 씻겨 주옵소서"(요13:8-9)라고 말하였다. 그러나 예수께서는 이 섬김의 교훈을 가르치시면서 이렇게 교훈 하셨다.

"내가 주와 또는 선생이 되어 너희 발을 씻겼으니 너희도 서로 발을 씻기는 것이 옳으니라"(요13:14)

예수 그리스도의 지도력은 시몬을 베드로로 변화시켰고, 그의 모난 인격은 잘 다듬어져 갔다. 주님으로부터 변화 받은 베드로는 그의 이름처럼 위대한 지도력을 발휘하였다.

첫째, 그는 영생의 말씀을 확신한 지도자였다.

예수님은 디베랴 바다 건너편 산에서 장정 5000명을 먹이신 사건 이후 무리들이 예수를 임금으로 삼으려는 줄을 아시고 산에 가신 후 무리가 다 떠나간 뒤에 "예수께서 열두제자에게 이르시되 너희도 가려느냐 시몬 베드로가 대답하되 주여 영생의 말씀이 계시매 우리가 뉘게로 가오리까 우리가 주는 하나님의 거룩하신 자신 줄 믿고 알았삽나이다"(요6:68-69)

둘째, 예수 그리스도에 대한 분명한 신앙고백의 지도자였다.

베드로는 가이사랴 빌립보에서 예수 그리스도로부터 3년간 지도자

훈련을 받은 결과를 묻는 예수의 질문에 합격했다. 베드로는 예수 그리스도를 주(κύριος) 와 그리스도(Χριστὸς)와 살아계신 하나님의 아들(ὁ υἱὸς τοῦ θεοῦ τοῦ ζῶντος)로 고백하였다.

셋째, 예수 그리스도의 복음의 증인이 된 지도자였다.

눅22:61에서 베드로가 주를 세 번 부인한 후 "주께서 돌이켜 베드로를 보시니"에서 베드로는 주님의 사랑의 눈길이 그의 가슴에서 떠날 수 없었다. 그 후 베드로는 부활의 주님을 디베랴 바닷가에서 만나고 주님으로부터 자신이 주님을 사랑함을 고백하였다. "내가 주를 사랑하는 줄 주께서 아십니다"주님은 베드로에게 "내 양을 치라. 내 양을 먹이라"[374]는 새로운 사명을 부여하였다. 그 후 베드로는 그리스도의 복음의 증인의 삶을 위해 세 차례나 옥중의 생활을 하였고 구전(口傳)에 의하면 로마에서 십자가를 거꾸로 지고 순교했다.

넷째, 겸손하고 복음의 열정이 있으며 용기 있는 지도자였다.

베드로는 자기의 잘못을 지적한 후배인 바울의 말을 겸허히 받아들이는 겸손을 볼 수 있다. 베드로는 안디옥에 있는 이방인 성도와 자리를 같이 하다가 유대인들이 오자 두려워하여 피한다. 바울이 베드로에게 그 잘못을 지적하였을 때 베드로가 잘못을 인정하는 겸손을 보였으며,[375] 그가 순교하기까지 예수 그리스도의 복음을 전하는 열정 그리고 좌절과 실망에서 다시 시작하는 베드로의 용기는 변화 받은 지도자로서 지도력이다.

374) 요21:15-18
375) 갈2:11-14

끝으로 베드로는 행정의 능력과 복음의 능력을 나타낸 지도자였다.

사도행전의 증언을 통하여 볼 때 오순절 성령강림 이후 베드로는 12사도 가운데 확고한 리더십의 위치를 점하였다. 다락방에서 기도회를 인도하였고, 가룟 유다를 대신할 맛디아를 뽑는 회의를 주재하는 행정적 능력을 보였다. 그의 복음의 능력은 오순절 이후 그의 설교를 통해 3000명을 그리스도에게로 인도하였으며, 기적을 일으키며, 아나니아와 삽비라의 거짓을 폭로하며, 점쟁이 시몬을 바로잡고, 고넬료 가정을 구원으로 인도하였으며, 세 차례의 옥중생활 가운데서 주님께 간절히 기도하니 천사가 그의 옆구리를 쳐서 깨우고 옥문을 열어 자유케하는 역사가 일어나기도 하였다.
물론 베드로에게 큰 실수도 있었다.
저주를 동반한 강력한 그리스도의 부인(좀認)[376]과 위대한 신앙고백 이후 주님으로부터 사탄으로 책망을 받기도하였다.[377] 그러나 베드로의 마지막은 주님을 위한 순교였다. 그는 로마에서 복음을 전하다가 주님의 십자가를 거꾸로 지고 순교했다.[378]

오늘의 교회와 교회 지도자들에게 주님은 시몬이 베드로가 된 것처럼 변화된 지도력을 간절히 바라고 계신다.

---

376) 마26:69-75
377) 마16:23
378) 요21:18

2, 안드레

안드레는 복음서와 사도행전에서 13회 나타나고 있다. 그는 벳세다 사람으로 태어나 가버나움에 살았다.[379] 베드로와 같이 한 형제이나 전혀 다른 성격의 소유자였다. 그는 적극적이고 열정적인 베드로에 비해 소극적이고 보수적이었다. 그는 '폭발하는 화산'보다 '지글 거리는 불꽃'이라는 표현이 합당할 것 같다. 그는 앞에 나서는 것 보다 뒤에서 소리 없이 묵묵히 일하는 성격의 소유자였다.

안드레는 원래 세례요한의 추종자였다. 그의 회심은 세례요한의 예수를 향한 "보라 세상 죄를 지고 가는 하나님의 어린 양이로다"(요 1:29)의 가르침에 의해 예수의 제자가 된 것이다.

안드레는 예수의 제자 가운데 제일 먼저 부름을 받았으며, 초대교회에서는 "프로토클레테"(protoclete) 즉 "처음 부름 받은 자"(First-Called)라 칭하였다.

A. 위대한 전도자 안드레

안드레는 소극적이고 보수적인 성격의 소유자였으나, 그가 예수 그리스도의 제자로 훈련받은 후에 위대한 전도자로서의 지도력을 가시화 하였다. 그의 전도 사역은 베드로에 비해 개인적 사역자(personal worker)로 봄이 타당하다. 그는 설교자라기보다 한 영혼을 사랑하는 인도자(Introducer)로 볼 수 있다. 위대한 전도자로서의 안드레의 지도력은 다음과 같다.

---

379) 요1:44-45, 막1:29, 마4:18

첫째, 지위나 위치 보다 복음 전도의 관심을 가진 지도자

안드레는 예수의 사도로 최초의 인물이다. 그러나 그는 위치나 지위에 관심 보다 본래적 사명에 헌신했다. 그는 지위나 위치를 시기하거나 질투하며 탐하는 소인배(小人輩)가 아니었다. 오직 사도(ἀπόστολος)로 "보냄을 받은 자"로서 그의 사명은 선교(Mission)였다. 그의 선교는 가족으로부터 시작했다. 먼저 형 시몬을 예수께로 인도했다.[380]

그리고 어린 소년을 예수께 인도했다.[381] 그리고 주님이 십자가를 지시기 며칠 전 헬라인 몇 명이 제자들을 찾아와서 예수 뵙기를 청할 때, 빌립을 비롯한 제자들은 이방인을 내버려 두라고 하였다. 그때 안드레는 주님의 복음의 우주성을 깨닫고 이들을 주님께 인도함으로서 이방전도자가 되었다.[382]

이것은 국내 전도의 차원을 넘어 세계 선교의 지도력을 가시화 한 것으로 볼 수 있다. 오늘의 교회와 교회 지도자들은 안드레처럼 지위와 감투에 관심보다 오직 영혼을 구원하는 사역에 몰두하는 목회자를 주님은 간절히 바라시고 있다.

둘째, 소금과 빛 같은 지도자

복음이 임하는 곳에는 언제나 빛처럼 소금처럼 소리 없이 녹고 비취고 스며들며, 그 어두움을 밝히고 부패를 방지하며 언제나 새로움으로 가시화 되는 역사가 있다. 그리고 울리는 꽹과리처럼 요란함도

---

380) 요1:41-42
381) 요6:5-9
382) 요12:20-33

없다. 안드레는 바로 소금과 빛 같은 지도자이다. 그는 불평 없이 조용히 자기 일에 진력하는 사람이다. 조용히 불평 없이 자기 일에 진력한 다는 것은 참으로 훌륭한 인격이다. 그의 후배요 자신이 인도한 베드로와 야고보와 요한에게 예수를 가까이 모시는 일을 양보하고 소리 없이 묵묵히 예수님의 사역을 도운 사람이다.

셋째, 사랑과 믿음의 눈을 가진 지도자

갈릴리 바다 건너편 벳세다 광야에서 5000명을 먹인 사건이 있다.[383] 예수는 빌립에게 이들을 먹을 수 있는 방법을 간구토록 명했다. 그 주위는 아무것도 먹을 것이 없는 상황에서 제자들은 이들을 마을로 보내어 먹이도록 제안했고, 빌립은 이들을 먹이는 데는 200데나리온이 들며, 또 시장도 멀다고 부정적 견해를 피력했다.[384]

이에 안드레는 어린 소년에게로부터 보리떡 5개와 물고기 2마리를 가지고 와서 결과를 주님께 맡기는 믿음의 눈을 소유하였다. 주님은 말씀하셨다. "할 수 있거든이 무슨 말이냐 믿는 자에게는 능치 못할 일이 없느니라"(막9:23)

주님은 그 떡과 물고기를 통해서 오병이어의 기적을 나타내셨다. 안드레가 이처럼 이 소년이 물고기와 보리떡을 가지고 있는 것을 발견할 수 있었던 것은 평소에 당시의 소외층인 어린이에게 관심을 가진 사랑의 지도자였기 때문이다. 전승에 의하면 안드레의 마지막 생애는 헬라의 아가야 지방에서 복음 전도를 하다가 X형의 십자가로 순교하였다고 한다.

---

383) 눅9:10
384) 요6:7

주님은 오늘도 이 같은 사랑과 믿음의 지도자를 간절히 찾고 있다.

3. 요한

성경에 요한이란 이름을 가진 자가 5명 나온다. 세례요한, 베드로의 아버지 요나 또는 요한(요1:42, 21:15-17), 마가 요한(행12:12, 25), 공회 회원인 요한(행4:5,6), 사도요한이다. 요한은 아버지 세베대와 어머니 살로메, 형 야고보가 있으며, 베드로처럼 갈릴리 어부였으나 부유한 어부의 가정이었다. 그가 그물을 깁다가 예수로부터 부르심을 입었다.

A. 우뢰의 아들 요한

우리는 요한을 사랑의 사도로 이해하고 있다. 예수님도 요한을 사랑하는 제자로 말씀하셨다. 그러나 요한이 처음부터 사랑의 제자는 아니었다. 요한이란 뜻은 "하나님의 은혜로운 선물"로 그는 하나님의 크신 사랑을 받고 훈련을 받아 변화된 사랑의 사도가 된 것이다.

첫째 그는 "우뢰의 아들"이란 별명처럼[385] 과격하고 도량이 좁은 사람이요 지나친 우월감을 가진 야심가였다.

요한은 다른 제자들 보다 가정이 부유하고, 또 예수와 친 인척이란 점을 과시하면서, 그의 어머니를 통하여 예수님이 세상적인 왕으로 오실 때 예수님의 좌와 우를 차지하도록 부탁한 점을 미루어 볼 때 그

---

385) 막3:17.

는 대단한 야심가였다.[386]

둘째 그는 과격한 기질의 소유자였다.

예수께서 예루살렘으로 가신다는 말을 듣고는 사마리아 인의 한 촌에서 예수를 맞아들이지 아니하자 야고보와 요한이 이를 보고 가로되 "주여 우리가 불을 명하여 하늘로 좇아내려 저희를 멸하라 하기를 원하시나이까"[387]

셋째, 관용성이 부족한 좁은 마음의 소유자이다.

누가복음 9장 49절에서 요한은 자기의 집단이 아닌 사람이 귀신을 좇는 것을 시기하였다. "주여 어떤 사람이 주의 이름으로 귀신을 좇는 것을 우리가 보고 우리와 함께 따르지 아니하므로 금하였나이다" 이 같은 편협한 행위는 다른 사도들과 비교하여 최고의 승리자가 되고 싶어 하는 야망과 좁은 마음의 한 단면을 보여주고 있다. "예수께서 가라사대 금하지 말라 너희를 반대하지 않는 자는 너희를 위하는 자니라 하시니라"또 "내 이름을 의탁하여 능한 일을 행하고 즉시로 나를 비방할 자가 없느니라"(막9:39), 비록 그들이 주님의 제자는 아니었지만 주님의 이름으로 주의 능력을 행하는 것을 금하는 것은 요한의 관용성이 부족한 마음이기 때문이다.

---

386) 마20:20-21.
387) 눅9:54.

B, 사랑의 사도 요한

우뢰의 아들이란 별칭처럼 과격하고 좁쌀 같은 마음의 소유자인 요한이 예수 그리스도를 만나고 훈련받아 사랑의 사도로 온유한 사람으로 변하게 되었다. 그의 야망도 야심도 복음의 용광로 안에서 녹아져서 사랑과 용서와 섬김의 사도로 변화되었다. 그는 일생토록 사랑의 복음을 증거 하는 일에 최선을 다하였다. 그는 언제나 예수의 오른편에서 사랑받는 사도였다. 사도 요한은 주님이 "사랑하는 자"라고 묘사된 유일한 사도로서 예수 그리스도와 가장 가까운 자리에서 예수의 품에 기대어 누울 정도로 사랑받는 사도였다(요13:23). 따라서 종종 요한을 "에피스테디오스"(The Epistethios)라고 기록하기도 한다. 예수 그리스도가 십자가에서 운명 시 그의 육신의 어머니를 요한에게 부탁하였으며, 요한은 아들처럼 효도했다. 뿐만 아니라 예루살렘 교회의 기둥이 되는 지도력을 발휘하게 되었다.

복음서에 나타난 요한의 모습은 화를 잘 내고, 야망과 조급함으로 가득한 우뢰의 아들의 모습을 보는듯하나 요한 1,2,3서와 계시록에서의 요한의 모습은 변화된 사랑의 사도 요한이다.

첫째, 예수를 끝까지 사랑한 용기 있는 지도자

사랑은 오래참고 사랑은 두려움을 극복하며, 사랑은 죽음을 넘는 용기를 가진다. 요한은 죽음과 두려움 속에서도 예수님을 끝까지 사랑하였으며, 그의 심문과 십자가와 그의 사랑을 끝까지 증거한 사랑의 사도였다.

예수께서 대제사장이 심문하는 뜰로 끌려가실 때 베드로는 멀찍이 뒤따랐지만 요한은 용감하게 대제사장의 뜰까지 들어갔다.[388] 요한은 예수님과 함께 심문하는 방까지 들어갔다.[389] 그리고 베드로는 예수를 세 번 부인하고 울면서 그 자리를 떠나갔지만 요한은 끝까지 그 자리를 지키며 결코 예수를 부인하지 않은 용감한 사도였다.

그는 십자가상에서 주님을 끝까지 지켜보았고, 주님의 십자가상의 칠언을 마지막까지 듣고 또 예수님과 말씀을 나눈 유일한 사도였다. "여자여 보소서 아들이니이다" 그리고 요한에게 어머니를 가리키면서 "보라 네 어머니라" "다 이루었다"라고 말씀하신 것을 기록한 증인이기도 하였다. 뿐만 아니라 요한만이 "한 군병이 예수님의 옆구리를 찌를 때 거기서 피와 물이 쏟아져 나온 사실"과 니고데모와 요셉에 의해 장사되신 사실을 전할 뿐이다.[390] 요한은 베드로와 함께 산헤드린 앞에서 함께 심문을 받으면서 예수의 이름으로 가르치지도 말고, 말하지도 말라는 협박에 "우리는 보고 들은 것을 말하지 아니할 수 없다"[391] 참으로 요한은 용기 있는 사랑의 사도였다.

둘째, 예수님의 사랑을 전승한 지도자

주님께서 이 땅에 성육신하심은 사랑 그 자체였다. 사랑의 본체이신 주님은 그의 사랑을 제자들에게 가르치시며 또 새 계명을 분부했다. "네 마음을 다하고 뜻을 다하고 힘을 다하여 주 너의 하나님을 사랑하라 하신 것이요, 둘째는 이것이니 네 이웃을 네 몸과 같이 사랑하

---

388) 요18:15-16.
389) 요18:15 (글자를 10포인트로 수정)
390) 요19:38-42.
391) 행4:20, 행3장-4(장 삭제).

라 하신 것이라 이보다 더 큰 계명이 없느니라”[392]

뿐만 아니라 주님은 그의 사랑을 십자가에서 재현했다. 제자들에게 “내가 너희를 사랑한 것 같이 너희도 서로 사랑하라 너희가 서로 사랑하면 이로써 모든 사람이 너희가 내 제자인 줄 알리라”[393] 하셨다 요한은 그의 서신에서 50회 이상 “사랑”이란 어휘를 언급하였다.

주님의 이 사랑을 전승한 지도자가 바로 사도요한이다. 사도요한은 주님의 사랑을 요한서신에서 “우리가 눈으로 본 바요 주목하고 우리 손으로 만진 바”로 증거하고 있다.[394] “하나님은 사랑이심이라”(요일 4:8)고 선언 하면서 하나님이 이같이 우리를 사랑하셨은 즉 우리가 서로 사랑하는 것이 마땅하다고 말한다. (요일4:11)

그의 말년의 설교는 언제나 “형제들이여 서로 사랑합시다”라고 설교 하면서 주님이 부탁하신 이것만 행하면 넉넉하다고 하였다. 전승에 의하면 그가 에베소를 방문했을 때 젊은 한 청년을 감독에게 부탁하였는데 어느 날 돌아와 보니 그 청년이 깡패 두목이 되어 온갖 악한 일을 행하는 것을 보고, 그는 자신의 옷을 찢으면서 “내가 감독에게 맡긴 것은 내 형제의 영혼을 부탁하였소”하며 괴로워했다. 그 후 요한은 그 청년을 찾아 가서 “너는 아직 희망이 있다 필요하면 그리스도가 우리를 위하여 죽으신 것처럼 내가 너를 위하여 목숨을 버리겠다”고 함으로서 그 사랑에 감동된 청년이 주님께로 돌아오게 되었다.

그의 사랑의 능력은 하나님의 놀라운 은혜를 입었다. 제롬에 의하면 로마의 박해 시 끓는 가마에 던져졌으나 그는 전보다 더 거룩하고 빛이 났으며, 독약을 먹여도 그는 결코 상하지 않았다. 그는 도미티아누스 황제 때 밧모섬에 유배되어 마지막 인생을 보내면서 요한계시록

---

392) 마22:34-40, 막12:30-31.
393) 요13:34-3
394) 요1서 1:1

의 말씀을 계시 받았다. 요한복음에는 다른 복음서와는 달리 주님에 대한 특별한 사랑을 볼 수 있는데 주님의 말씀을 절반 이상을 기록하고 있으며, 그리스도의 찬란한 영광을 묘사하고 있다. 그의 생애는 에 베소에서 마감되었으며, 그의 무덤에 대하여 어거스틴이 전하는 바에 의하면 그 성자의 숨기운이 덮인 흙이 움직이는 것을 보고 그가 아직 살아있다고까지 묘사되어 있다.

예수 그리스도의 지도력은 그토록 야심차고 거친 성격 그리고 좁은 마음을 가진 우뢰의 아들 요한을 사랑의 사도로 변화시켰다. 그 변화의 주된 요인은 주님의 사랑과 용서와 섬김의 지도력이다.

셋째, 예루살렘 교회의 지도자

사도 요한은 사랑의 사도로서 주님의 교회에 지도자로 봉사했다. 사도행전에서는 사도 요한의 기사가 없지만 요한이 예루살렘 교회의 지도자였음을 밝히고 있다. 바울이 예루살렘을 방문했을 때 베드로와 야고보 그리고 예루살렘의 기둥의 하나인 "요한"을 만났다고 기록하고 있다.[395]
오늘의 교회와 교회 지도자들은 바로 사도 요한과 같은 사랑의 지도력을 지닌 지도자를 요구하고 있다.

4. 야고보

베드로와 요한과 야고보는 예수 그리스도의 특별한 사랑을 받은

---

395) 갈2:9

제자들이다. 때문에 주님은 이들에게 독특한 체험을 하게 하셨다. 예수님께서 죽은 자를 살리시는 주님의 권능을 보게 하셨고, 영광스러운 변모의 사건, 그리고 겟세마네의 고뇌의 현장을 목도케 하셨다. 이 사건들은 야고보에게 순교에까지 이르게 하는 준비의 과정으로 볼 수 있다.

야고보는 남다른 복수심이 가득한 열정의 사람이었고,[396] 교만과 분노의 냄새가 뒤범벅되어 있었으며,[397] 과도한 야망으로 가득한 인물이었다.[398] 이런 야고보도 주님의 사랑과 용서와 섬김의 지도력에 변화를 받아 수많은 무명의 순교자들의 선구자가 되었으며, 용기와 용서와 자제력을 지닌 지도자로 변화 받았다.

전승(傳承)에 따르면 야고보가 체포되었을 때 그를 기소한 담당관이 야고보의 자제력과 용기에 감화를 받아서 자신도 세례를 받고 교회의 일원이 되어 야고보와 함께 순교했다. 사형을 집행하기 위하여 가는 도중에 그는 자신을 용서해 달라고 간청하였을 때 야고보는 기쁜 마음으로 그를 껴안고 "형제에게 주님의 평화를 빕니다."라고 말하였다. 그는 주님의 가르침인 용서의 복음을 실천한 지도자였다.

야고보는 복음을 위해 순교했다.[399] 그리고 그는 용서의 사도로, 용감한 사도로, 자제력이 있는 영원한 순교자로서의 지도자로, 세우심을 받았다. 그에게는 야망도 과격한 성격도 사라졌다. 전승에 따르면 지중해 지역을 여행하였으며, 그 후 상당한 기간 동안 스페인에 머물면서 많은 교회를 세웠다고 전해지고 있다.

---

396) 눅9:54
397) 마10:14-15
398) 마20:20-28, 막10:35-45.
399) 행12:1-2

5. 빌립

빌립을 향해서는 실증주의 인물로 묘사한다. 아마 그는 오늘의 과학시대, 이성시대, 실증주의 시대에 사는 현대인들이 요구하는 인물일지도 모른다. 그는 현실성과 계산 감각이 뛰어난 인물이나 믿음의 시야가 좁은 사람이었다. 요한복음의 오병이어 사건에서 그는 철저한 현실론적 인물이었다. 그는 이들 무리에게 식사를 제공하는 데는 200데나리온의 돈이 필요하며, 또 거리적으로나 시간적으로 불가함을 말했다. "이 많은 사람들에게 떡 하나씩이라도 먹이려면 거의 일 년 동안의 품삯이 요구됩니다. 또 설령 우리가 지금 돈을 가지고 있다고 해도 이렇게 많은 양의 떡을 이 짧은 시간 동안에 어떻게 구할 수 있겠습니까?" 라고 하면서 스스로 실증주의적 인물임을 나타내었다.

그는 아버지를 보여 달라고 하는 실증주의적 사람이었다. "주여 아버지를 우리에게 보여 주옵소서 그리하면 족하겠나이다."[400]고 하였다.

빌립은 하나님을 외적이고, 신비적인 아버지로 착각했으며, 주님으로부터 3년간의 배움에서도 변하지 않는 눈의 소유자였다. "빌립아 내가 이렇게 오래 너희와 함께 있으되 네가 나를 알지 못하느냐. 나를 본 자는 아버지를 보았거늘 어찌하여 아버지를 보이라 하느냐. 나는 아버지 안에 있고, 아버지는 내 안에 계신 것을 네가 믿지 아니하느냐. 내가 너희에게 이르는 말이 스스로 하는 것이 아니라 아버지께서 내 안에 계셔 그의 일을 하시는 것이라"(요14:9-10)

그는 또한 우유부단한 인물이었다. 명절에 예배하러 올라온 사람 중에 헬라인이 몇이 있는데 그들은 진리를 애타게 갈망하는 그리스 철학의 대가들의 후예였다. 그들이 예수의 소문을 듣고 예수를 만나

---

400) 요14:8

기 위하여 헬라 이름을 가지고 또 벳세다 사람인 빌립을 찾아와서 "선생님, 우리가 예수를 뵙고자 합니다."(요14:21)라고 요청했을 때 빌립은 그들을 바로 예수께 인도하지 않고 또 안드레에게도 이들과 예수의 대면을 신중하게 고려해야 한다는 우유부단함을 보였다.

그러나 빌립은 자신의 변하지 않는 사고 속에서도 계속적인 예수 그리스도의 가르침과 능력의 가시화 속에서 믿음이 싹트게 되었으며, 그의 논리적 사고 속에 하나님을 포함시키는 법을 배웠다. 그는 오병이어의 기적에서 자신의 우둔하고 계산적인 모습의 결과가 창조적이지 못함을 깨닫게 된 것이다. 하나님이 함께하실 때 아무리 작은 것이라도 큰 것임을 깨닫게 되었다. 전승에 의하면 빌립은 브루기아에서 전도하다가 하에라볼리에서 순교한 것으로 전해지고 있다.

6. 나다나엘(바돌로매)

예수의 열두 제자 가운데 바돌로매(Bartholomew)는 또 하나의 이름이 언급되어 있는데 바로 나다나엘(Nathanael)이다. 바돌로매의 바(Bar)는 "아들"이란 뜻이며, "돌로매"는 삼상에서 언급된 달매(Talmai)와 관련이 있는 듯하며,[401] 또 애굽왕 톨레미(Ptolemy)와 관련이 있는 듯하다. 그러나 이 이름의 관련성에 비추어 보아 모두 왕가와 관련이 있는 것으로 사료되나 확실한 근거는 없다. 그러나 나다나엘은 예수님이 직접 부르신 점을 미루어 보아 예수님께서 붙여준 이름인 듯 하며, 그 뜻은 "하나님의 선물"이라는 의미를 지닌다. 그런데 "바돌로매'라는 이름은 공관복음서와 사도행전에서 열두 제자의 명단에서 6-7회

---

401) 삼상3:3

가 언급되어 있으나, 나다나엘은 없고,[402] 반면에 요한복음에서는 바돌로매의 전혀 언급이 전혀 없고 오직 나다나엘만이 사도의 이름에 포함시키고 있다.[403] 이 같은 사실을 미루어 보아 두 이름은 각각의 다른 사람을 칭하는 것이 아니고 동일한 이름인 것으로 보인다.

요한복음에 의하면 나다나엘은 갈릴리 가나 출신이며,[404] 빌립에 의해 예수께 인도함을 받았으며, 빌립과 친구인 듯 하며,[405] 사도들의 명단 세 곳에 모두 빌립과 바돌로매가 함께 짝을 이루고 있다는 점이다. 그는 베드로나 안드레처럼 어부 출신이 아니며, 교부들에 의하면 율법에 능숙한 사람이고 학자이며, 예언가로 믿어지고 또는 여겨지고 있다.

이 같은 사실을 뒷받침할 수 있는 근거는 빌립이 나다나엘을 전할 때 율법에 나타난 메시야를 만났다고 전함에서 볼 수 있다. 나다나엘에 대해서는 그와 예수 그리스도와의 만남에서 여러 가지 위대한 점들이 많이 언급되고 있다. 주님은 성경을 묵상하는 경건한 사람으로 주님은 그를 칭하셨다.[406] 또 그 속에 간사가 없는 참 이스라엘이라 칭했으며,[407] 하나님 나라의 이상을 보리라고 말씀하셨다. 또 "내가 너를 무화과나무 아래서 보았다 하므로 믿느냐 이보다 더 큰일을 보리라. 진실로 진실로 너희에게 이르노니 하늘이 열리고 하나님의 사자들이 인자 위에 오르락내리락 하는 것을 보리라"[408]하셨다.

이처럼 나다나엘은 다른 제자와 달리 예수를 통해 칭찬을 받은 인격의 소유자였으며, 예수 그리스도를 만난 후에 사도로서 부르심을 받

---

402) 마10:3, 막3:18, 눅6:14, 행1:13.
403) 요1장.
404) 요21:2
405) 요1:45-46
406) 요1:49
407) 요1:47
408) 요1:50-51

고 예수 그리스도의 복음을 위한 그의 지도력을 발휘했다. 나다나엘은 예수를 만난 후 예수가 하나님의 아들이며 이스라엘의 임금으로 분명한 신앙을 고백하였다.[409] 그는 신앙고백 이후 그리스도의 십자가를 끝까지 따랐으며, 예수가 십자가에 못 박힐 때도 그는 끝까지 예수 그리스도가 왕임을 믿었다.[410]

전승에 의하면 나다나엘은 브루기아와 히에라볼리, 아르메니아, 그리고 더 나아가서 인도에까지 복음을 전한 것으로 알려졌으며, 몽둥이에 맞고 살 껍질이 벗겨진 후에 산 채로 거꾸로 십자가에 못 박혀 순교한 것으로 전하고 있다.

7. 도마

예수의 열두 제자 가운데 도마는 의심 많은 도마(doubter)라는 별명을 가지고 있으나, 그 별칭의 명칭을 그대로 의미하는 것은 아니다. 오히려 예수 그리스도의 부활에 대한 그의 진솔한 의심(questioning mind)은 예수 그리스도의 부활을 의심하는 수많은 지적인(intelligent) 이들에게 부활의 확실한 증거를 보여주는 계기가 되었다.

도마에 대한 자료는 공관복음서의 열두 제자 이름 가운데 언급이 되어 있고, 부활 후 다락방에 모였던 제자들 중 여섯번째로 언급이 되어 있으며,[411] 요한복음에는 디두모라 하는 도마의 다른 이름으로 언급되어 있다.[412]

---

409) 요1:49
410) 요21:2.
411) 마10:3; 막3:18, 눅6:15. 행1:13.
412) 요11:16

　　도마는 히브리말이며 디두모는 헬라어로서 그 뜻이 구별을 나타내는 이름으로 "쌍둥이"란 뜻이다. 따라서 쌍둥이 도마라는 뜻을 뒷받침해 주는 것은 막6장 3절에 의존할 수 있다.

　　도마는 독특한 성격을 소유한 사람이었다. 낙천주의자라기보다는 염세주의자였다. 이같은 경향의 사고 구조를 가진 사람은 긍정보다는 의문적 경향이 많고, 최선보다는 최악의 상태를 생각한다. 따라서 선뜻 믿음을 가질 수 없다. 믿기 전에는 반드시 보아야 한다.

　　다음으로 도마는 확실한 지식을 얻기 위하여 올바른 문제의식을 가지는 성품의 소유자였다. 예수님께서 다락방에서 최후의 십자가를 앞두고 그의 제자들에게 십자가 이후에 대하여 언급하셨다. "내가 어디로 가든지 그 길을 너희가 알리라"고 말씀하셨을 때, 도마는 즉시 "주여! 어디로 가시는지 우리는 모릅니다. 어떻게 그 길을 알겠습니까?"라고 물었고, 이 도마의 질문에 주님은 놀라운 해답을 말씀하셨다. "나는 길이요 진리요 생명이다"(요14:1-6).

　　또 도마에게는 용감한 기질도 있었다. 요한복음 11장에서 보면 나사로의 죽음으로 예수는 예루살렘으로 가야만 했다. 당시 유대권력자들은 예수를 죽일 음모를 꾸미고 있었고, 따라서 예수가 예루살렘으로 간다는 것은 자살행위와 다름이 없었다. 그 전에도 그들은 두 번이나 예수를 돌로 쳐 죽이려고 했기 때문이다.[413] 그 때 침묵을 지키던 도마가 "우리가 선생님과 함께 죽고 말자"(요11:16)고 했다. 흔들리기 쉬운 열한 제자들에게 충성심에 용기를 불러일으킨 자이다.

　　부활의 주님을 만난 후 도마는 위대한 사도로 변화되었다. 그의 신앙 고백은 신약성서 가운데 베드로의 신앙 고백처럼 위대했다. "나의 주 나의 하나님이시다"(요20:26-28). 그는 그의 고백처럼 주와 하나님

---

413) 요8:59, 10:31

을 위해 순교했다.

역사가 유세비우스에 의하면 도마는 오늘날 이란 북부지역의 "파르데아"(Parthea)을 선교지로 배정받았다. 이 파르데아 사람들은 독립국으로서의 민족성이 강한 민족으로 로마인들에게도 존경과 두려움의 민족이었다. 교부 제롬에 의하면 도마는 파르데아에서 전도했으며, 인도에 까지 복음을 전하다가 인도의 칼라미아에서 순교했다고 전해지고 있다. 또 다른 전승에는 중국까지 복음을 전했고 돌아오는 길에 인도의 브라만들의 시기와 박해로 돌로 맞고, 창에 찔려 순교했다고 전해 지고 있다.

8. 열심당 시몬

성경에는 두 명의 시몬이 언급되어 있다. 한 사람은 시몬 베드로이고 또 한 사람은 "열심당 시몬"(Simon, the Zealot)이다. 이 열심당은 Zetotes에서 온 말이다. 열심당(Zetotes)은 유대종파 가운데 하나로서 격렬한 극우자들이다. 헤롯이 죽기 전에 영토를 분할하였는데, 유대와 사마리아는 "아켈라오"가 주도하였을 때 이 열심당의 봉기로 갈릴리를 중심으로 폭동이 일어났고(행5:37), 세포리스(Sepphoris) 궁전에 쇄도하였으나 로마 군에 의해 섬멸되었다. 여기서 소위 열심당의 출현을 보게 된다. 그러나 그 결정적인 원인으로는 유대의 민족과 신앙을 말살하려는 안티오커스 에피파네스(Antiochus Epiphanes)의 야만적인 행동에 마카비 일가가 일어나 유대민족의 구세주적 인물로 등장했던 것을 들 수 있다. 마카비의 아버지 "마타티아스"(Mattathias)가 죽을 때 그의 자식들에게 남긴 말이 유명하다. "아들들아 율법을 열심히 지키고 우리 선조의 언약을 위하여 몸과 목숨을 바쳐라"[414]

따라서 열심당은 광신적인 유대 애국자였고, 율법에 열심이며, 외국 세력을 극히 적대시했다. 특히 로마의 지배 하에서도 로마를 인정치 않았고, 화산처럼 폭발의 기세로 도사리고 있는 세력이었다. 역사가 요세퍼스에 의하면 이들의 암살 대상은 로마 사람과 유대인과 로마 타협자이며, 전투 방법은 게릴라 전법으로 불을 지르는 것이었다. 이들의 로마에 대한 항전의 정신은 A.D 70년 로마의 장군 티토에 의해 예루살렘이 완전 포위 되었을 때 결코 항복하지 않았으며, 오히려 화해하려는 자를 광분하여 죽였다는 것에 잘 나타난다. 그들의 최후는 마사다(Masada)에서였고, 당시의 지도자 엘리아잘(Eleazar)은 최후의 연설을 한 후 그의 아내와 아들을 죽이고 자결하였으며 당시 함께 자결한 사람이 960명이었다. 생존자는 두 여자와 다섯 아이만 동굴에서 숨었다가 살았다.

시몬은 바로 이 열심당 또는 시카리에 소속된 인물이다. 이 같은 국수주의자요 율법에 온 몸을 바친 시몬이 어떻게 예수의 제자가 되어 복음의 지도자가 되었을까? 여기에 예수 그리스도의 복음적 지도자 양성 비결이 있다.

먼저 시몬은 예수 그리스도의 사랑의 지도력에 감화되었다. 제자의 발을 씻기시는 주님의 사랑은 물론 그의 용서의 가르침과 섬김의 본에 의해 미움과 증오와 비타협과 살인의 눈이 변하여 복음의 사도가 되었던 것이다. 뿐만 아니라 이른 아침부터 밤늦게까지의 예수의 성실성과 가난과 압제와 고통과 세금이 없는 하나님의 나라에 시몬은 감화받았다. 그리고 예수님이 행하시는 기적과 이적 그리고 유대 예언자들

---

414) 마카비서 2:50.

이 선포한 거룩한 인자가 땅에 내려와서 평화를 선포하리라는 말씀에서 예수 자신이 곧 인자임을 선포함을 시몬은 믿었기 때문이다.[415]

시몬의 변화는 적대자를 화해하고 사랑하며(마태), 그의 열정은 하나님 나라의 열정으로 승화되어 그리스도의 복음을 위해 순교의 길을 가게 되었다. 전승에 의하면 소아시와 아프리카 그리고 바벨론까지 선교한 것으로 전해지고 있으며, 페르시아에서 복음을 전하다가 폭도들에 의해 살해된 것으로 전해지고 있다.

때문에 시몬은 제자 가운데 있는 로마의 앞잡이였던 세리 마태와도 한 공동체가 될 수 있었다.

예수 그리스도의 십자가의 용서와 사랑을 본 시몬은 그의 품 속에서 칼을 버렸다. 오늘의 교회와 교회 지도자들에게는 바로 시몬의 변화의 지도력이 요구된다. 미움과 증오의 칼을 버려야 한다. 자기를 적대하는 자를 사랑하고 용서하고 섬기며, 자신의 최후까지 자신의 열정을 복음을 위해 성화시키는 지도력이 간절히 요구된다.

9. 세리 마태

마태는 원래 이름이 레위로 불리는데 그 때 그가 세관에 앉아 있었으며, 나중에 마태로 불리어졌다.[416] 예수님이 마태라고 부르셨음을 볼 때 아마 그의 회심 후 마태라는 이름을 주신 것 같다. 마태복음에서는 그의 이름이 마태라 불리며,[417] 마가복음에서는 알패오의 아들이라

---

415) 요3:13
416) 막2:14, 3:18, 눅5:27, 6:15.
417) 마9:9, 10:3

고 불린다.[418]

예수의 부름을 받기 전의 마태는 멸시와 증오의 대상으로 지도자라기보다는 지탄의 대명사였다. 탈무드(Talmud)에 의하면 당시 일반 대중에게 철저하게 외면당한 직업이 카바이(gabbai)[419]와 미크사(mikhsa)[420]였다. 마태는 미크사를 담당하면서 온갖 부정과 착취로 부를 챙겼다. 그는 가버나움에 사무실을 차려놓고 예루살렘과 다메섹으로 향하는 모든 대상(caravan)들에게 세관통행료를 징수하였으며(약 2-12%), 또 갈릴리 어부들로부터도 어업세를 징수하였다. 밀수품을 찾기 위하여 막대기로 짐을 찌르기도 하고 뒤지기도 하였다. 그리고 그가 징수한 세금은 로마 정부에 모두 바쳐진 것이 아니라 부당이득과 착취였다.

다음으로 세리는 로마의 정부의 앞잡이로서 유대 민족주의자들 특히 열심당의 증오 대상이 되었다. 이처럼 세리는 당시의 이방인이나 창기와 같이 취급된 무리였다.[421] 그들은 법정에서 증언할 자격도 없으며, 일종의 사회적 문둥병자(Social Iepers)로 취급되었다. 그들은 오직 황금을 신(神)으로 생각하는 수전노요 현대판 마피아와 다름이 없었다.

이처럼 사회적으로 증오의 대상인 사람이 예수를 만나 위대한 지도자로 그의 지도력을 가시화했다. 마태는 그의 이름의 뜻인 "하나님의 선물"로서 많은 은혜를 받았다. 예수는 세관에 앉아서 장부를 정리하

---

418) 막2:14
419) gabbai: 일반 세리집단으로 술, 과일 등의 세금을 징수하는 세리이다.
420) mikhsa: 일종의 세관공무원으로 마태는 이에 속한다. 특히 세리는 통관절차를 담당하므로 모든 물건이 세리의 감찰대상이 되었다.
421) 마18:7, 21:31.

고 있는 그에게로 다가가서 다른 사람처럼 "세리"또는 사기꾼 레위라 부르지 않고 "나를 좇아라"(마9:9)라고 하셨고, 그는 검사대를 정리하고 예수를 따랐다.[422]

마태는 결단력이 있는 지도자였다. 그는 예수를 만남으로 자기의 소유에 집착하지 않았고 또 그의 직업을 버렸다. 먼저 "예수를 위하여 자기 집에서 큰 잔치를 하니 세리와 다른 사람이 함께 앉았다."[423] 그리고 그의 동료들에게 이제 자신의 직업을 포기한다고 선포했다.

마태는 영감 있는 성경을 기록한 지도자였다. 마태는 총명했다. 수려한 용모뿐만 아니라 그는 헬라어와 라틴어에 능통했다. 때문에 그는 예수 그리스도를 따라 다니면서 예수님의 말씀을 기록하였는데 바로 그것이 마태복음이다. 특히 마태는 그 유명한 산상수훈(마5장-7장)과 천국의 비유(마13장)와 천국의 삶의 모형을 아이들이 들어가는 곳으로 비유하는 예수님의 복음을 놓치지 않고 기록하고 있으며, 끝 부분에서는 예수 그리스도의 재림과 종말을 언급하였다(마24장-25장).

마태는 그리스도의 복음을 위하여 순교한 지도자였다. 전승에 의하면 마태는 에디오피아에서 순교했다고 전해지고 있다.

마태는 그리스도를 위하여 황금과 소유욕을 버린 위대한 지도자로서 그의 지도력을 가시화했다. 오늘의 교회와 교회 지도자들은 바로 황금욕과 소유욕에서 떠나야 한다. 그리스도를 만남으로 허락하신 사도직을 명예로움으로 생각하고 목양의 보람을 느끼는 지도자가 요구된다. 아울러 예수님의 말씀을 배우고 정리하는 마태와 같은 지도력이 오늘의 목양 현장에서 간절히 요구된다.

---

422) 눅5:27-28
423) 눅5:29

10. 작은 야고보와 유다

예수 그리스도의 열두 제자 가운데 성서에 잘 알려지지 않는 인물이 바로 작은 야고보와 유다이다. 유다는 마가 다락방에서 단 한 번 예수께 질문한 것으로 언급되어 있고, 신약에 나타난 야고보는 요한의 형제 야고보,[424] 예수의 형제 야고보,[425] 그리고 작은 야고보이다.[426] 작은 야고보는 알패오(Alphaeus)의 아들로서 마가 기자는 작은 야고보로 별칭을 붙여준 것이다.[427]

우리는 작은 야고보라는 이름에서 흔히 열등하고, 보잘 것 없는 사도로 또는 신체적으로 열등함으로 이해하는 경향이 있으나, 작은 야고보는 예수의 형제 야고보와 구분하기 위한 것으로 볼 수 있다.

열두 사도의 충성을 인정하시는 주님은 열두 사도의 높고 낮음이 없으며 모두 새 예루살렘의 기초석에 똑같은 크기의 이름으로 기록되어 있다.[428] 작은 야고보는 전승에 의하면 돌에 맞은 후에 톱에 잘려 순교했다고 전해지고 있다.

유다라는 이름을 가진 사람은 성경에 두명이 있다. 마태가 별칭으로 언급한 "레바이오"와 그 성은 "다대오"인 유다이다.[429] 마가 기자는 단지 그를 유다로 기록했다.[430]

또 한 명은 그 악명 높은 가룟 유다이다. 레바이오 유다는 제롬

---

424) 행12:2
425) 행1:14, 15:13, 갈2:9,12.
426) 마10:3, 막3:18, 눅6:15, 행1:13.
427) 막15:40
428) 계21:14
429) 마10:3
430) 눅6:16,행1:13

(Jerome)에 의하면 세 가지 이름을 가진 자의 뜻으로 "트리노미누스"(Trinominus)라 불렀다.

유다에 대한 언급은 요한복음에서 예수와의 대화 뿐이다. 요한복음 14장에서 유다는 예루살렘으로 입성하신 예수가 왕권으로 자신들을 다스릴 것으로 생각하였다. 그래서 유다는 주님께 질문한다. "가룟인 아닌 유다가 가로되 주여 어찌하여 자기를 우리에게는 나타내시고 세상에게는 아니하려 하시나이까"로 질문할 때, 예수께서 대답하여 가라사대"사람이 나를 사랑하면 내 말을 지키리니 내 아버지께서 저를 사랑하실 것이요 우리가 저에게 와서 거처를 저와 함께 하리라"[431]

유다에게 언급하신 예수 그리스도는 하나님 나라의 왕으로 나타날 때가 올 것이다. 그러나 그 하나님 나라의 영광의 왕으로 임재하기 전에 먼저 십자가를 져야만 한다는 것을 가르치신 것이다. 이를 깨달은 유다는 예수를 따라 복음을 위해 그리스도의 십자가를 묵묵히 지고 가는 순교의 반열에 서게 되었다.

전승에 의하면 그는 유프라테스강 근처에 있는 에데사(Edessa)에서 복음을 증거하였으며, 아르메니아에 교회를 세우는데 수고를 아끼지 않았고, 쿠르디스탄에서 복음을 전하다가 화살에 맞아 순교했다고 전해지고 있다.[432]

유다와 야고보의 지도력에서 오늘의 교회와 교회 지도자들은 두 사도의 묵묵히 주님의 십자가를 지고 가는 모습과 빛도 없이 이름도 없이 주님의 나라를 위해 헌신하는 지도력을 배워야 할 것이다.

---

431) 요14:22-23.
432) Leslie B. Flynn, *op.cit.*,pp.198-199.

11. 가롯 유다

비극의 대명사 가롯 유다는 신약성서에서 "예수를 팔 자"혹은 "배반자"로 언급되고 있다.[433] 유다에게 붙은 "배신자"(The Traitor)라는 별칭은 역사의 종말까지 따라다닐 수치스러운 별명이다. 가롯 유다는 "이스 카리웃"(Iscariot)에서 와전된 것으로 사료된다.

그는 갈릴리 출신이 아닌 유다 출신이었다. 때문에 처음부터 갈릴리 출신의 사도들과 친근하지 못했을지도 모른다. 반면에 서기관과 바리새인들과 친밀하게 지낸 것이 예수를 판 원인일지도 모른다.

그는 당시 유다 마카비(Judas Macedonian) 출신으로 민족의 지도자였다. 그에게 준 예수의 부름은 영광스러운 자리였다. 그는 3년간 예수와 함께 지내면서 예수의 신임이 두터웠다. 심지어 예수 대신에 전도의 여행을 하기도 하였다.[434] 그는 예수의 사도들 가운데서 세리 출신인 마태가 있음에도 가롯 유다는 회계의 직책을 담당하였다. 그는 정직했고 유능한 지도자였다. 그의 지도력의 변질은 어떻게 가시화 되었는가?

첫째, 유다는 그리스도의 복음을 완전히 받아들이지 못했고, 그에게는 "쥬다이즘"의 찌꺼기가 남아있었다. 그는 유대인들처럼 지상의 왕국을 꿈꾸었던 현실주의자였다. 그는 예수를 로마의 압제에서 유대민족을 해방시킬 지상의 왕으로 이해했다. 그러나 예수 그리스도는 왕이 아니었다. 그는 언제나 사랑과 섬김과 용서의 복음을 선포했기 때문이다. 유다는 변질되기 시작했다. 예수는 이를 감지하고 그에게 경

---

433) 마10:4, 26:15, 17:3, 막3:19, 눅6:16, 요6:71, 12:4, 18:2,5.
434) 눅10:17-20

고했다.[435)]

요한은 이 말씀에서 열둘 중의 하나는 시몬의 아들 유다를 가리킴이라 했다.[436)]

둘째, 탐욕의 마음이 지도력의 변질을 가져왔다. 야고보 기자가 쓴 "욕심이 잉태하면 죄를 낳고 죄가 장성하면 사망을 낳는다."는 말씀이 바로 유다에게 적용됨을 볼 수 있다.[437)]

유다의 마음속에는 욕심이 잉태하기 시작했다. 그는 마리아의 값비싼 향유를 예수의 발에 부었을 때 낭비라고 말했다. 그것은 낭비라는 것은 외식이고 그는 그것을 탐하였을 것이다.[438)] 예수님은 유다에게 돈을 사랑하지 말 것을 여러 곳에서 경고하셨다.[439)] 이같은 예수의 가르침에도 불구하고 유다에게 사탄이 들어가니 결국 스승을 팔고 자신의 목숨을 스스로 끊는 불행을 초래하였다.[440)]

예수는 유다에게 자신을 팔 것에 대하여 세 번이나 경고했다. "이미 목욕한 자는 발밖에 씻을 필요가 없느니라 온 몸이 깨끗하니라 너희가 깨끗하나 다는 아니니라 하시니 이는 자기를 팔 자가 누구인지 아심이라"하시면서 유다를 경계하셨던 것이다.[441)]

또 유월절 식사 때 "제자 중 한 사람이 그를 팔리라"고 언급하셨다.[442)] 특히 유다가 예수를 향하여 "내가 그입니까?"물을 때 예수께서

---

435) 요6:70
436) 요6:71
437) 약1:15
438) 요12:4-6.
439) 마6:24, 눅16:13.
440) 요22:3
441) 요13:10-11
442) 마26:21, 막14:18, 눅22:21, 요13:21.

"네가 말하였도다"[443]하셨고, 그리고 예수와 제자들 사이에 식사하는 과정에서 예수께서 떡 한 조각을 찍어다가 가룟인 유다에게 주시면서 유다가 자기를 팔자임을 암시하셨다.[444] 결국 그대로 가룟 유다는 예수를 팔게 될 때 "예수께 나아와 랍비여 안녕하시옵니까"하고 입을 맞추었고,[445] 그 입맞춤은 당시의 랍비를 맞이하는 입맞춤의 관례를 통해 비극의 신호탄이 된 것이었다.

유다는 영원한 지도자의 자리를 상실했다. 그는 은 30에 스승을 판 자로서 스스로 목매어 자살했다. 유다의 죽음에 대하여 또 다른 기록은 "몸이 곤두박질하여 배가 터져 창자가 다 흘러나온지라."[446]고 전승되었으며 사도 베드로는 다락방에서 설교하면서 "유다는 제 곳으로 갔나이다."[447]라고 역설 하였다.

그는 주님의 영광스러운 사도의 자리에서 떠난 인류 최대 수치의 사람이 되고 말았다.

오늘의 교회와 교회 지도자들은 가룟 유다의 길에서 Called Out하여 복음의 지도자로 세움을 받아야 한다. 명예욕에서 나오고, 영웅심에서 나오고, 금전욕에서 나와서 유혹과 탐심을 초월하는 그리스도의 리더십을 배워야 한다.

---

443) 마26:25
444) 요13:23-26
445) 마26:46-49
446) 행1:18
447) 행1:25

제 VI 장

결 론

　본고는 지금까지 예수 그리스도의 복음적 리더십을 연구하기 위하여 그 리더십의 본질적 표상으로 언급된 구약에서 아브라함의 지도력, 모세의 지도력, 사사들의 지도력, 성전종교의 제사장과 회당종교의 회당장의 지도력을 역사적, 이론적, 신학적, 성서적으로 고찰하였다.

　그리고 본 논문의 중심인 예수 그리스도의 복음적 지도자상과 그 원리의 실제를 논급한 후에 열두 제자의 변화된 지도력을 고찰하였다.

　구약에서 시대별, 인물별 지도력을 언급하면서 아브라함은 하나님의 부르심과 세우심으로 그의 지도력을 가시화한 인물임을 보았다. 그는 열국의 족장으로, 하나님의 사랑의 리더십으로, 때로는 정치적, 군사적, 경영적 리더십을 발휘하였다.

모세는 하나님의 권위 아래서 소위 국가교회(Church-State)의 형태를 이루어 갔다. 신정(Theocracy)과 민정(Democracy)이 공존하는 독특한 국가 민족 집단을 이루면서 영적 지도력과 입법, 사법, 행정 삼권의 지도력을 가시화하였다. 특히 신정의 위임으로 제사장직과 천부장과 백부장, 오십부장, 십부장제를 두어서 사법직과 행정직을 위임처리하였다. 또 장로직과 대의제도를 태동시키는 지도력을 가시화하였다.

사사들의 지도력은 지파동맹(amphictyony)을 중심으로 종교적, 정치적 장으로서 그들의 지도력을 가시화하였다. 특히 사사들은 야훼의 불연속적인 부르심에 기인된 지도력으로 야훼는 사사를 세워 이스라엘 백성들이 종교적, 혼합적 위기에 이르게 되었을 때 야훼를 향한 신앙으로 그의 지도력을 발휘케 했다. 사사들은 제사장과 예언자, 그리고 용장으로까지 그 지도력을 발휘하였다.

왕국시대와 왕들의 지도력은 예수 그리스도의 전통적인 삼직의 하나인 왕을 표상하고 있으나, 신학적으로 예수 그리스도는 세속적인 왕이 아니며, "바실레이아"의 왕이요 섬김의 왕이다. 때문에 가나안 여부스족에서 유입된 것이 확실한 왕이란 어휘의 도입은 왕국시대부터 야훼 종교와 지도력의 변질을 가져왔다. 특히 다윗은 자신의 왕권을 유지하기 위하여 야훼 전승의 아비아달 제사장과 여부스 내지 가나안의 사독 제사장을 혼합 기용하였다. 결국 이로 인해 다윗 왕조에서 혼합 뒤범벅의 종교로 변질되었고, 결국 아비아달이 추방되는 결과를 초래함으로써 야훼 신앙의 정통성에 변질을 가져온 큰 우를 범하게 되었다.

성전시대, 성전종교의 중심적 지도력의 위치는 제사장이다. 제사장의 기원은 시나이 계시에서 출발함이 타당하며, 그들은 야훼 앞에서 섬기는 자로 그 세움을 입었다. 특히 백성들로 하여금 야훼 앞에서 성실히 살아가도록 도와주는 조력자요, 중계자요, 판단자로서 그 지도력을 발휘하였다. 때문에 제사장의 본질적 지도력은 제의의 지도력과 신의 뜻을 결정하는 지도력과 또 축복의 전달자와 재판의 지도력으로 가시화하였다. 그러나 이같은 제사장은 지도력의 변질을 가져왔다. G. Fohrer에 의하면 이스라엘의 성전은 왕국 안에 둘러싸인 복합 건물로 왕실의 "사적 예배실"의 성격이 강하며, G. Von. Rad는 법궤 보관의 성소적 의미가 강하다고 진술한 바 있다. 이처럼 왕국 성소적 성격에서 제사장은 야훼의 제사장의 지도력에서 떠나서 왕의 시녀로서의 제사장으로 전락되었다.

회당시대의 회당장들의 지도력은 성전종교 시대의 범국가적 또는 연합적 의미의 제사장의 지도력에 비하여 지방적 마을 단위 또는 가정 단위 차원의 지도력이었다. 성전에서는 모든 일을 제사장이나 레위인이 그 지도력을 가시화 하였으나, 회당에서는 회당장 중심으로 회당이 운영되었다. 특히 회당에는 장로들이 있었으며, 장로들의 우두머리로 회당장을 뽑았다.

회당장은 전통적인 왕과 선지자 그리고 제사장직을 겸하게 되었다. 이 회당의 특징은 성전처럼 엄격하거나 법복을 입고, 제단을 차리고, 의식 중심이 아니라, 주민의 대표격인 지방의회 또는 "게루시아"또는 "소산헤드린"을 통해서 그들의 지도력을 가시화하였다는 것이다.

문제는 회당의 장로들의 변질이었다. 세속적 통치자와 야합하여 성소를 변질시켰다. G. Kittle에 의하면 회당은 여왕벌을 중심한 벌들의 집단으로 변질되었다고 진술된 바 있다. 예수님께서 사단의 세력과 싸웠던 곳이 바로 이 변질된 회당에서이다. 요한계시록에서는 변질된 유대인의 무리를 향해서 사단의 회로 언급된 바 있다.

이상에서 구약에서 언급한 시대별, 인물별의 지도력은 예수 그리스도의 지도력의 표상적 의미는 지니고 있다. 특히 왕과 선지자와 제사장의 삼직의 구약적 지도력은 예수 그리스도에 의해 완전히 계시되었다. 예수 그리스도는 하나님의 나라의 왕이였으며, 사람들이 자신을 선지자 반열에 포함시키는 것을 거부하지 않았으며, 십자가 상에서 제물이 되심으로 영원한 속죄를 이루신 대제사장이었기 때문이다.

예수 그리스도는 성육신하셔서 바로 변질된 왕국종교나, 성전종교나 회당종교나 제사종교나, 율법종교나 그들의 종교 지도자들로부터 나와서(Called Out) 전무 후무하고 완전무결한 독특한 지도력을 선포하였다.

예수 그리스도의 지도력의 권위는 그의 본질적 칭호에서부터 가시화되었다. 그 칭호는 "주"와 "그리스도"와 "하나님의 아들"과 "인자"였다. 예수 그리스도의 지도력의 본질은 세속적인 왕으로서의 지배나 정죄나, 종속이나 종교 재판과 같은 세속적 권위적 지도력이 아니라 "바실레이아"와 "에클레시아"를 세우시기 위한 사랑과 용서와 섬김의 영원한 지도력이었다. 이것이 그의 복음이다. 예수 그리스도의 복음의 지도력은 우주적인 지도력으로 인종과 계급과 계층과 민족과 국경과 사상과 종교까지 넘어 어느 누구에게도 기쁜 소식이 되는 복음적 지도력이었다. 예수 그리스도의 놀라운 복음의 지도력은 누구든지 복음을 믿고 경험하고 따르는 자들에게는 새로운 변화를 가져왔기 때문이다.

예수 그리스도는 지도력은 언제나 "바실레이아"에 들어가게 하는 지도력이었다. 그 "바실레이아"에 들어가는 조건으로 예수 그리스도는 회개하고 "복음을 믿으라고" 선포하였다.

뿐만 아니라 예수 그리스도의 지도력은 철저하게 본(本)의 원리로 "나를 따르라"라고 하였으며, 예수 그리스도 자신은 선한 목자임을 선포했다. 사도 바울은 예수 그리스도의 교회를 유기체적인 몸으로 비유하여 교회의 머리되신 예수 그리스도의 지도력을 헤더십(Headership)의 지도력으로 언급한 바 있다.

예수 그리스도의 실제적인 지도자의 양성 원리는 그의 열두 제자를 부르시고 세우시고 보내시고 위임하심에서 볼 수 있다. 예수의 열두 제자들은 사상적으로 환경적으로 도저히 융합될 수 없는 사람들이였으나, 가시적인 "에클레시아"의 원형을 지향하는 이른바 제자 공동체를 만들었다. 이 열두 제자들은 예수 그리스도의 복음의 지도력으로 변화를 받아 한결 같이 예수 그리스도의 "바실레이아"와 "에클레시아"와 "복음"을 위하여 순교한 점은 인류 최대의 지도자를 양성한 지도력으로 보아야 할 것이다.

21세기를 바라보는 오늘의 시점에서 인류와 교회는 여전히 반목과 갈등과 시기와 쟁투와 전쟁과 억압의 양상에서 벗어나지 못하고 있다. 예수 그리스도의 "바실레이아"와 "에클레시아"보다는 왕국화, 세속화, 율법화, 회당화, 성당화, 관광명소화로 그 변질을 가져오고 있다. 성직자 상호간의 모함과 시기, 목사와 장로간의 갈등, 평신도 상호간의 반목은 한 마디로 예수 그리스도의 복음적 리더십의 부재로 보아야 할 것이다. 예수 그리스도의 복음적 리더십의 부재는 수많은 행정학적, 경영학적, 회계학적, 지역사회개발학적인 지도자론의 기법을 절

대시하여 교회에 도입하는 경향이 있으며 이들의 모방과 추종은 "에
클레시아"의 변질을 가져왔으며, 지도자론의 부재를 가져온 것이다. 뿐
만 아니라 예수 그리스도의 복음적 리더십의 부재는 시대에 맞지 않
은 구약 시대의 변질된 성전종교의 제사장이나, 왕국종교의 혼합사상,
그리고 율법주의자들, 사단의 세력과 야합하여 세력화한 회당장의 변
질된 지도력를 모방하는 우를 범하게 된 것이다.

또 사회의 물질 만능에 편성하여 자신의 배만 채우고 양들을 철저
하게 이용하는 이른 바 삯꾼으로 목자상으로 까지 그 변질을 가져왔
다. 주님의 복음적 Leadership은 바로 이와 같은 변질된 교회와 사상
과 지도력에서 Called Out하여 예수 그리스도의 복음인 사랑과 용서
와 섬김의 지도력인 선한 목자로 돌아오도록 간절히 기다리고 계시는
것이다.

그러므로 예수 그리스도의 지도자로 부름을 받은 오늘의 목사와 장
로와 교회 지도자들은 먼저 예수 그리스도의 복음과 그의 "바실레이
아"와 "에클레시아"에 대한 새로운 이해가 선행되어야 하며 이를 위해
부르시고 세우시고 보내심을 받은 직분임을 명심해야 할 것이다.

주님은 오늘도 비(非)복음과 타협하거나 협상하지 않고, 세상의 유
혹에서 과감히 나와서 주님의 말씀 앞에 바로 서서 생명 바쳐 복음을
증거하는 복음적인 예수 그리스도의 지도자를 간절히 요구하고 있다.

"네가 죽도록 충성하라 그리하면 내가 생명의 면류관을 네게 주리
라"(계2:10)

◆ BIBLIOGRAHPY

A. 국내 서적

1. 강저대, 현대 경영 조직론, 박영사, 1994.

2. 국민일보 경제부, 아이디어 비화, 국민일보사, 1993.

3. 기독교 신문 편, 한국 교회의 허와 실1, 서울: 쿰란 출판사, 1993.

4. 기업경영문제연구소, 일류리더가 일류인생을 만든다, 서울: 비즈니스아카데미, 1993.

5. 김규정, 행정학 원론, 법문사, 1995.

6. 김상복, 지도자에게서 배우라, 서울: 도서출판 엠마오, 1992.

7. 김순규, 크리스찬의 리더십, 서울: 성음소리, 1987.

8. 김혜성, 성공 리더십, 서울: 미디어, 1995.

9. 맹용길, 기독교 윤리와 생활 문화, 서울: 쿰란 출판사, 1993.

10. 명성훈, 창조적 리더십, 서울: 서울 서적, 1991.

11. 박기삼, 고정 관념의 벽을 넘어서, 대장간, 1993.

12. 박영률, 리더십과 교회성장, 서울: 성광문화사, 1991.

12. 박형렬, 탁월한 목회 리더십, 서울: 치유, 1993.

14. 손병호, 복음 신학 원론, 서울: 도서출판 그리인, 1992.

15. 신석환, 이런 목사님을 찾습니다, 서울: 요단 출판사, 1995.

16. 신성종, 이런 목회자가 교회를 변화 시킨다, 서울: 도서출판 하나, 1995.

17. 신연식, 훌륭한 어머니가 큰 지도자를 만든다, 서울: 도서출판 학문사, 1994.

18. 이규태, 한국인의 정서구조1, 서울: 신원 문화사, 1994.

19. ――――, 한국인의 정서구조2, 서울: 신원 문화사, 1994.

20. 이연옥, 교회 여성 지도자, 서울: 쿰란 출판사, 1993.

21. ――――, 별세의 지도자, 서울: 쿰란 출판사, 1994.

22. 황보 갑, 에클레시아, 서울: 도서출판 다리, 1996.

23. 황위섭, 크리스찬의 리더십, 서울: 한국로고스 연구원, 1989.

24. 황의영, 교회의 직임과 리더십, 서울: 생명의 발씀사, 1993.

B. 외국 서적

1. Adams, Jay. E., *Shepherding God's Flock*, Grand Rapids:Baker Book House, 1981.

2. Alfred Plummer, *Critical and Exegetical Commentary on the Gospel according tos, Luck*, Edinburgh: T&T. CLARK, 1981.

3. Alvin Toffler, *The Third Wave*, New York, William Marrow, 1980.

4. Aron Pick, *Dictionary of O.T. word*, Kregel Publications, Grand Rapids, Mich, 1982.

5. A. M. Adams, *Effective Leadership for Today's Church*, Philadelphia: The Westminster Press, 1978.

6. Callahan, Kennon L., *Effective Church Leadership : Building on the Twelve Keys*, San Francisco, California : Harper & Row, Publishers, 1990.

7. Damazio, Frank., *The Making of a Leader*, Portland, Oregon

: Bible Temple Publishing, 1988.

8. Cattell, R.B., *The Dimension of Syntality in Small Group*, Human Relations, 1953.

9. Clinton, J. Robert., *Leadership Training Models : A Self-Study Manual For Evaluating Training*, Altadena, California : Barnabas Resources,1984.

10. Clinton, J. Robert., *The Making of a Leader*, Colorado Springs, Colorado : Navpress, 1988.

11. Davis, K. and Newstrom, J.W., *Human Behavior at Work*, McGraw-Hill, 1985.

12. Dimock, M. E and Gladys O. Dimock, *Public Administration, 4th edition*, New York; Holt, Rinehart and Winston, 1969.

13. Dodd,C.H., *The Sacrament of the Lord's Supper in the New Testament, "Christain Worship"*, N. Micklem, 1980.

14. Douglas. J. D., *The New International Dictionary of the Christian Church*, The Paternoster Press, 1977.

15. Engstrom, Ted W., *The Making of a Christin Leader*, Grand Rapids, Michigan : Zondervan, 1976.

16. Ford, Leighton., *Transforming Leadership*, Downers Grove, Illinois : Inter- Varsity Press, 1992.

17. Frank Goble, *The Man at the Top*, Thornwood, N.Y.: Caroline House Publishers, 1972.

18. Gangel, Kenneth O., *Feeding & Leading*, Wheaton, Illinois : Victor Books, 1989.

19. Gangel, Kenneth O., *Building Leaders for Church*

Education, Chicago, Illinios : Moody Press, 1981.

20. George F. Trusell, *Helping Employees Cope with Change*, A
    Manager's Guidebook, Buffalo; PAT Publishers, 1988.

21. Gerhard Kittle, *Theological Dictonary of New Testament
    VoI*, Michigan: Eerdmans Publishing Company, 1971.

22. Goodwin II E.. Beennie, *The Effective Leader*, I.V.P.Downers
    Grove, 1981.

23. Harold Koontz and Cyril O'Donnell, *Principles of Management;
    An Analysis of Management Unctions, 5th, New york,*
    McGraw-Hill Book Company, 1972.

24. Henri Fayol, *General and Industrial Administration*, New
    York; pitman Publishing Company, 1949.

25. Hocking, David L., *Be a Leader Peaple Follow*, Glendale,
    California :Regal Books (Gospel Light), 1979.

26. Holland, F. O., *Leadership Dynamics* : a Practical Guide to
    Effection Relationship, New York : The Free Press, 1978.

27. Hollander, E..P., *Leadership Dynamics*, Free Press, 1978.

28. Howard Hendricks, *Teaching to Change Lives*, Portland;
    Multnomah, 1987.

29. Hwang Bo, Kab, *A Study of the Nature of the Ecclesia*, Yuin
    University, 1995.

30. H.H. Rowley, *Worship in Ancient Israel*, London, 1962.

31. Jago, A.G., *Leadership ; Perspectives in Theory and
    Research*, Management Science, 1982.

32. James MacGregor burns, *leadership*, New York: Harper and

Row, 1978.

33. Joachim Jeremias, *New Testament Theology*, London: SCM Press Ltd, 1971.

34. John Piper, *Love Your Enemies*, London: Cambridge University

35. Jonathan E. Smith, Kenneth P. Carson, and Ralph A. Alexander, "Leadership; It Can Make a Difference."*Academy of Management Journal* December, 1984.

36. Julius Gould and William L. Kolb, *A Dictionary of the Social Sciences*, UNESCO; Free Press of Glencoe, 1964.

37. Keith Davis, *Human Relation at Work, 4th ed*, McGraw-Hill, 1972.

38. Kimball Young, *Handbook of Social Psychology*, New York; Appleton Century Croffts, 1951.

39. Larry A. Mitchel, *A Student's Vocabulary for Biblical Hebrew and Aramaic*, California: A Zondervan Publication. 1989.

40. Lawrence O. Richards., *A Theology of Church Leadership*, Zondervan, Grand Rapid, Mich, 1981.

41. Leonard Sanderson & Ron Johnson, *Evangelism for All God's People*, Nashville: Broadman Press, 1980.

42. Leonwood, *A Survey of Isreal's History*, Grand Rapids: Zondrvan, 1970.

43. Lindsay. T.M., *A History of the Reformation*, charles Scribner's Sons, 1987.

44. Lloyd Perry, *Getting the Church on Target*, Chicago; Moody, 1977.

45. Luthans, F., *Organizational Behavior*, McGraw-Hill, 1981.

46. Lutzer, Erwin, *Managing Your Emotions*, Wheaton, Illinois
    : Victor Books, 1988.

47. Macarthur Jr., John, *Exposing False Spiritual Leader*, Chicago
    : Moody Press, 1986.

48. Means, James E., *Leadership in Christian Ministry*, Grand
    Rapid : Bakre, 1989.

49. Michael Green, *Evangelism New & Then*, Cambridge Shire:
    Cambridge, 1973.

50. Michael Haran, *Temple and Temple Service in Ancient
    Israel*, London: Oxford University, 1978.

51. Moule. C.F.D., *The Origin of Christology*, London:
    Cambridge University Press,1977.

52. Paul Hersey and Kenneth H. Blanchard., *Management of
    Organizational Behavior: Utilizing Human Resources, 3rd
    edition*, Englewood Cliffs, N. J:Prentice-Hall, 1977.

53. Paul Piger, *Leadership or Domination*, London; Whittlessey
    House, 1935.

54. Paul Pigors, *Leadership of domination*, Boston; Houghton-
    Mifflin Co.1953.

55. Raines, Robert A., *New Life in the Church.*, New York :
    Haper and Row, 1961.

56. Rensis Likertm,"Foreward"*in Daniel Katz, nathan Maccoby,
    and Nancy C. Morse, Productivity, Superuision and Morale
    in An Office Situation,*

university of michigan Survey Research Center, 1950.

57. Richard Wolff, *Man at the Top*, Wheaton,III: Tyndale, 1969.

58. Robert P. Kerr, *Presbyterianism for the People*, Philadelphia, 1926.

59. Ross, Murray G. & Hendry, Charles E., *New Understandings of Leadership*, New York : Association Press, 1957.

60. R.Newton Flew, *Jesus and His Church*, London, 1938.

61. Sanders, J. Oswald., *Spiritual Leadership*, Chicago : Moody Press, 1979.

　　　　　　　　　　————.,*Paul The Leader*, Chicago : Moody Press, 1984.

62. Stogdill, R.M. and Coons, A.E., *Leader Behavior : Its Description and Measurement*, Research Monograph, No.88, Ohio State University, Bureau of Business Research, 1957.

63. Stogdill, R.M., *Handbook of Leadership*; A Survey of Theory and Research, New York; The Free Press, 1974.

64. Swindoll C.R., *Hand Me Another Brick*, Tran, Jonathan M. Kwon, Voice, Seoul, 1982.

65. Szilagyi, A.D. and Wallace, M.J., *Organization Behavior and Performance*, Scott, Foresman, 1983.

66. Tead, Ordway., *The Art of Leadership*, New York : Whittlesey House, 1935.

67. Theimer, W., *An Encyclopedia of Modern World Politics*, 1950.

68. *The Oxford English Dictionary*, London: Oxford Press, 1970.

69. Tidwell. Charles, A., *Church Administration Effective*

Leadership for Ministry, Nashvill, Tennessee : Broadman Press, 1985.

70. Victor Paul Furnish, *The Love Command in the New Testament*, London: SCM Press, 1973.

71. White, John., *Excellence in Leadership*, Downers Grove. III. I.V.F. 1986.

72. Wiersbe, Warren. W. & Wiersbe, David., *Making Sense of the Ministry*, Chicago : Moody Press, 1983.

73. Warren G. Bennis, *Leadership Theory and Administrative Behavior : The Problem of Authority*, Administrative Science Quartery, Vol. 4, 1959.

74. Youssef, Michael., *The Leadership Style of Jesus*, Wheaton III, 1986.

C. 번역 서적

1. 고노다 다이조, 신라원 편집부 역, 노자에게서 배우는 리더가 되는 처세학, 서울: 신라원, 1995.

2. 구니도미 쓰요시, 황병수 역, 앞서가는 리더의 행동학, 서울: 한국 산업훈련 연구소, 1994.

3. 노엘M. 티키, 박영종 역, 개혁을 추구하는 리더십, 서울: 21세기 북스, 1994.

4. 데이비드 호킹, 김영국 역, 사람이 따르는 지도자, 서울: 생명의 말씀 사, 1984.

5. 라이스 엔더슨. 잭 헤리포드. 벤 페터슨, 정태욱 역, 능력있는 지도
   자, 서울: 은성, 1995.

6. 란 베이미, 허광일 역, 21세기의 지도자, 서울: 예수 전도난, 1993.

7. 로렌스O. 리쳐즈, 클라이드 홀드키, 남철수 역, 교회 지도자 신학,
   정경사, 1991.

8. 로버트E. 켈리, 장동현 역, 폴로어십과 리더십, 서울: 고려원, 1994.

9. 로버트 슬레터 Robert Slater, 이진주 역, 잭 웰치의 31가지 리더십
   비밀, 명진 출판, 1994.

10. 리오이 아임스, 네비케이토 역, 당신도 영적 지도자가 될 수 있다,
    네비케이토, 1982.

11. 리차드 본디, 하해룡 역, 목회와 지도력, 서울: 한국 장로교 출판사,
    1993.

12. 리턴포드, 김기찬 역, 변화를 일으키는 리더십, 서울: 생명의 말씀사,
    1994.

13. 마르틴 부버, 표재명 역, 나와 너, 서울: 문예 출판사, 1977.

14. 마이클 뉴셉, 고봉한 역, 예수님의 리더십, 요나 출판사, 1994.

15. 마이클 뉴셉, 예수님의 지도 방법을 배웁시다, 서울: 나침판사,
    1990.

16. 브루스 존스, 주상지 역, 목회 리더십과 경영, 서울: 생명의 말씀사,
    1994.

17. 빅터H. 브룸, 아서G.제이고, 김남현 역, 뉴 리더십, 매일경제 신문사,
    1994.

18. 오까베 히로시, 정상곤 역, 전략 행동형 리더십, 서울: 삶과 꿈,
    1995.

19. 올란 헨드릭스, 차종율 역, 크리스천 지도자들을 위한 경영 관리,

기독교문서 선교회, 1991.

20. 워런W. 위어스비H.F. 서드든, 조천영 역, 목회자 지침서, 서울: 나침판, 1983.

21. 윈안 박사, 이윤호 역, 나도 교회성장을 진단할 수 있다, 베다니 출판사, 1994.

22. 윌리엄 코헨, 김창원 역, 당신도 리더가 될 수 있다, 서울: 동아 출판사, 1993.

23. 이나게 노리코, 이용구 역, 리더하는 여성 러더 당하는 여성, 서울: 도서출판 글사랑, 1994.

24. 제임스 모이스, 이건일 역, 느헤미야의 지도력 연구, 서울: 생명의 말씀사, 1994.

25. 제임스 민스, 주상지 역, 그리스도인 사역의 지도력, 생명의 말씀사, 1991.

26. 조 셉 플레쳐, 이희숙 역, 상황 윤리, 서울: 종로서적, 1994.

27. 존 E 하가이, 권명달 역, 지도자가 되라!, 서울: 보이스사, 1991.

28. 존 화이트, 이석철 역, 탁월한 지도력, 서울: 한국 기독 학생회 출판부, 1991.

29. 죤맥스웰, 오연희 역, 열매 맺는 지도자, 서울: 도서출판 두란노, 1991.

30. 챨스 스윈돌, 김영봉 역, 함께 일하는 지도자, 서울: 생명의 말씀사, 1988.

31. 추아 위 히안, 권영석 역, 오늘을 위한 성경적 리더십, 서울: 한국 기독학생회 출판부, 1990.

32. 카마다 마사루, 강영진 역, 리더십의 포인트, 서울: 갑진 출판사, 1994.

33. 칼죠 오지, 밥로건, 송용조 역, 리더십과 교회성장, 서울: 서울성
    경학교 출판부, 1990.

34. 케네스O. 겐젤, 권명달 역, 교회 교육의 리더십, 서울: 보이스사,
    1991.

35. 탐 마샬, 이상리 역, 지도력이란 무엇인가?, 서울: 예수 전도단,
    1993.

36. 톰 피터즈, 낸시 오스틴, 조영호 역, 엑설런트 리더십, 서울: 21세
    기북스, 1993.

37. D.J.chwartz, 한국 능역 협회 역, 리더의 자기 암시법, 서울: 한국
    능률협회, 1989.

38. DeVille J., 홍대식 역, 리더십의 인간 심리, 서울: 성화사, 1992.

39. Harry Wendt, 바종구 역, 크로스웨이 성경연구, 서울: 신망애
    출판사, 1985.

40. J. Bright, A History of Israel, 김윤주 역, 이스라엘 역사, 서울:
    1979.

41. J. Oswald Sanders, *Men From God's School*. 김용호 역, 서울:
    종합선교나침판사, 1985.

42. J. 스튜어트 아베리, 김태복 역, 느헤미야를 통해 본 참 지도자론,
    서울: 기독교 문화사, 1991.

43. J.E. Adams, 정상지 역, 성공적인 목회지도, 서울: 예수 문서선교회,
    1981.

44. J.K 클라멘즈, D.F.메이어, 차배국 역, 서구 고전을 통해 본 리더
    십, 대구: 보문사, 1994.

45. K.블랜차드, P.지가미, D.지가미, 안상기 역, 1분 리더십, 서울: 청
    림출판, 1994.

46. V. 하워드, 최윤영 역, 리더십, 리더십, 서울: 신서 출판사, 1988.

D. 논문

1. 정근호「목사의 인격과 지도력에 관한 연구」감리교 신학대학 신학대
   학원 실천신학 전공 1985. 8
2. 정종호「크리스챤 리이더쉽에 관한 연구」장신대학 신학대학원 신학
   과 실천신학 전공, 1984. 11. 30
3. 차수일「현대 한국 교회에서의 바람직한 리더십 연구」장로회 신학
   대학신학대학원, 1992. 12
4. 허 락「크리스챤 리더십에 관한 연구」 장로회 신학대학 신학대학원,
   1992. 12.

E. 월간지

1. 김삼환「오직 주님 오직 말씀」목회와 신학, 1994. 7 통권 61호
2. 김선도「목회자의 지도력이 교회성장에 미치는 영향」목회와 신학,
   1992. 5. 통권 35호
3. 박광철「영적 지도자의 지도력」목회와 신학, 1993. 1 통권 43호
4. 박용규「교회사에 나타난 지도자의 유형별 분석」목회와 신학,
5. 박인용「목회자들이 본 차세대 목회 지도자상」목회와 신학, 1994.
   7. 통권 61호
6. 송용조「목회 지도력과 갈등 대처」목회와 신학, 1993. 7 통권 49호

7. 양창삼「사회 심리학적 측면에서 본 한국 목회자의 지도유형 분석」
목회와 신학, 1994. 7 통권 61호

8. 유영기「왜 목회 지도력의 변화가 요청되는가」목회와 신학, 1994. 7.
통권 61호

9. 이용원「어떤 지도력이 차세대에 적합할 것인가」목회와 신학, 1994. 7.
통권 61호

10. 이원설「다원화 사회의 영적 지도력」목회와 신학, 1992. 5. 통권 35호

11. 잭 볼스윅 .윌터 라이트「새시대가 요구하는 목회 지도력」목회와
신학, 1993. 6월호

12. 정웅섭「리더십 이론의 어제와 오늘」기독교 사상, 1984. 7. 통권
213권.

13. 존 맥스웰「차세대를 위한 지도력 변혁의 원리와 전략」목회와 신학,
1994. 7. 통권 61호

14. 패트릭 밀러「리더십 신학을 향하여 : 선지자들로부터 얻은 몇가지
실마리」목회와 신학, 1993. 8 통권 50호

정말 지도자입니까?

2012년 07월 10일 초판 발행

지 은 이 · 서 임 중
발 행 인 · 김 수 곤
발 행 처 · 선교횃불
등 록 일 · 1999년 9월 21일 제54호
등록주소 · 서울시 송파구 삼전동 103번지
전　　화 · 02-2203-2739
팩　　스 · 02-2203-2738
E-mail · ccm2you@gmail.com
Homepage · www.ccm2u.com